White Tern Photo Diaries by Cora Young

Photography by Cora Young

In loving memory of my uncles, Charles and Nelson, avid photographers

With thanks to Shiro, Skye, Sunny and their parents

First edition

ISBN: 978-1-7330623-5-0

By the author of the Gecko Tales Trilogy: *Goldy's Gecko Family, Goldy's Gecko Friends* and *Goldy's Gecko Tales*

In the book, *White Tern Photo Diaries,* the author, an amateur photographer living in Honolulu, Hawaii, followed three white terns from the time that they were spotted as babies in neighborhood trees until the time that they fully fledged. The book includes 122 color photographs for your enjoyment.

Introduction

When I learned that my uncle had passed away in May 2021, I felt compelled to take a walk around my neighborhood in Oahu, Hawaii. Looking up at the sky, I saw the comforting sight of graceful white birds with black eyes and bills and notched tail feathers. They were flying high, seemingly without a care in the world. Some were flying solo, in pairs or as a trio (most likely as a family unit). They landed on tree branches, sometimes after hovering. I discovered that they are called white, angel or fairy terns or manu-o-Kū in the Hawaiian language. The white tern is the official bird of the City of Honolulu. Surprisingly, the parents do not build a nest; instead, a single egg is laid in a depression on a tree branch. The parents take turns incubating the egg, protecting it from strong winds and predators. About a month later, a baby bird hatches and hangs on to the breeding branch with webbed feet. It will wait for its parents to bring meals of small fish and other seafood. As the baby grows, it loses its down and feathers appear. About a month later, the baby will wander from the breeding branch and balance on nearby branches. Soon, it will fly to nearby trees. After about 45 days, the fledgling may not return to the breeding branch. To keep better track of the birds while taking photos and videos, I gave them gender-neutral names as males and females look alike. Through the camera lens, faith and trust is captured whenever a baby looks to the sky for its parents to return and whenever parents patiently wait with fish for their fledging to return. The parents' dedication to raising their young reminds me of the devotion to family that I admired so much in my uncle. Although he is not physically here, he is still guiding me: life goes on; don't be alone in grief; open your eyes; just look and you will find joy again.

Table of Contents

CHAPTER ONE

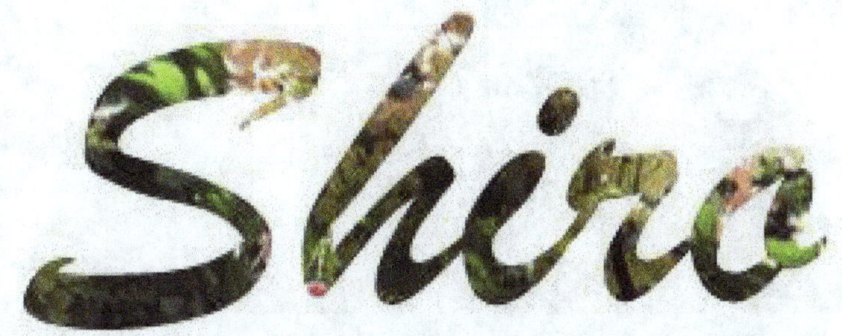

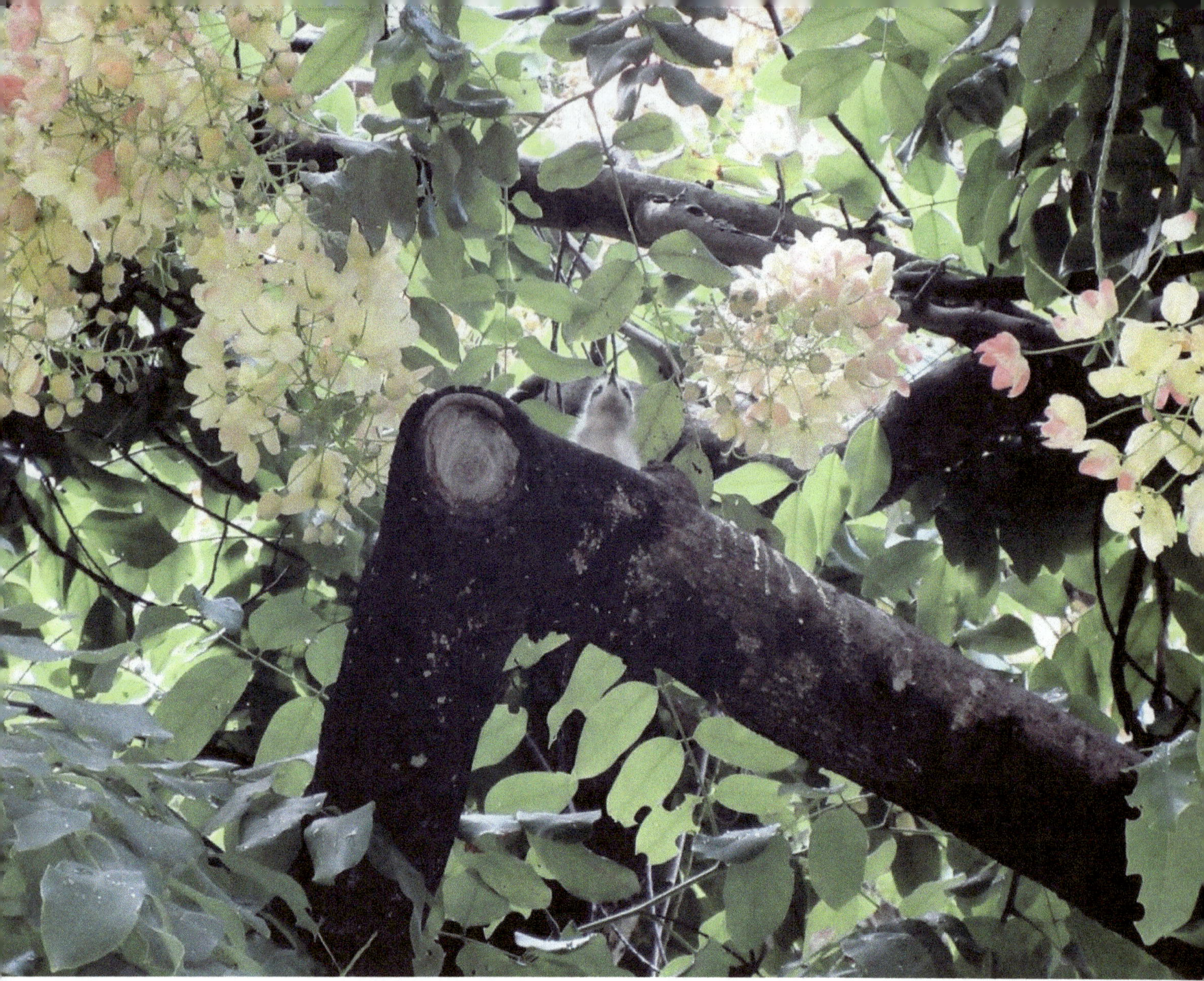

Shiro was born in a rainbow shower tree.

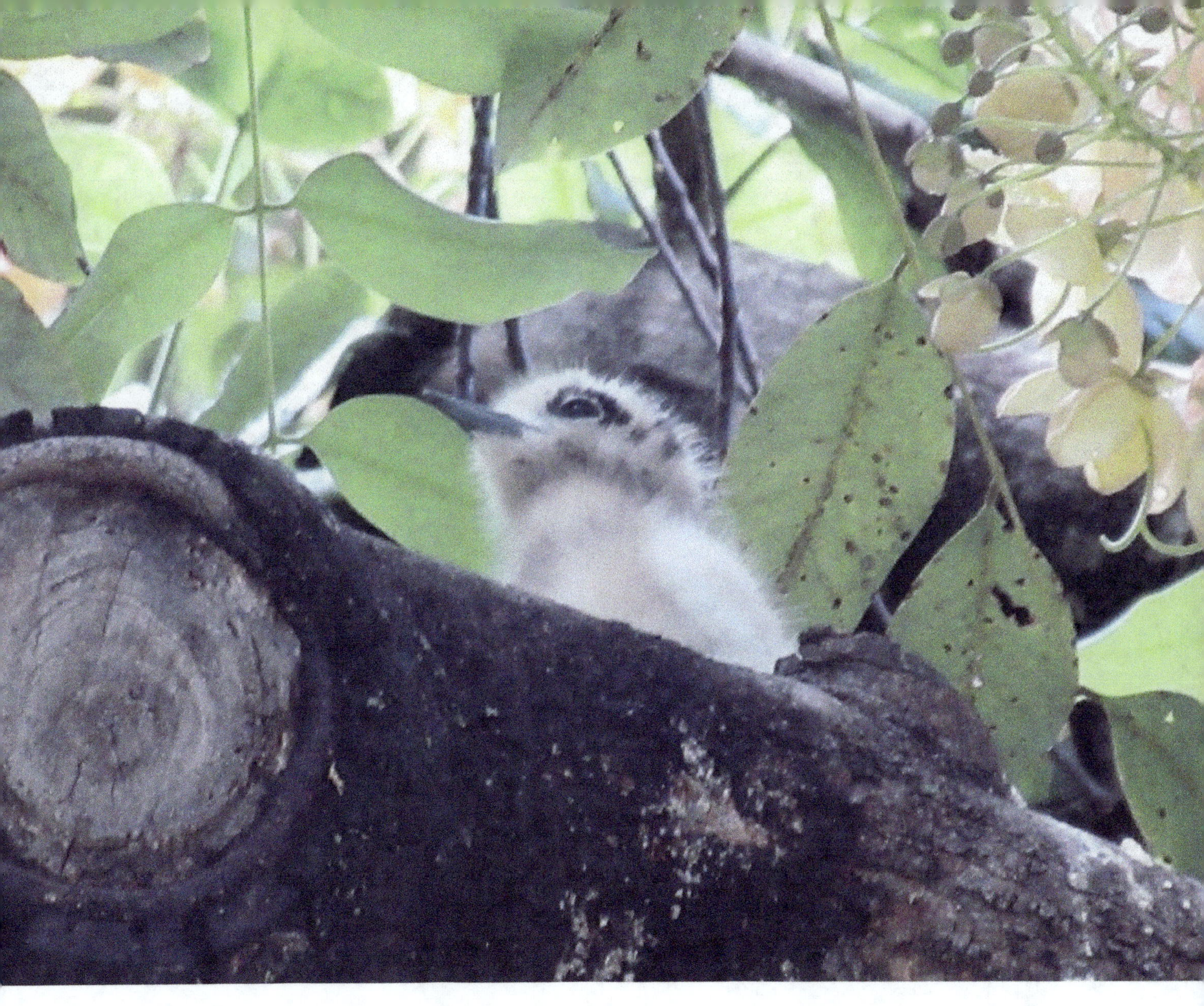

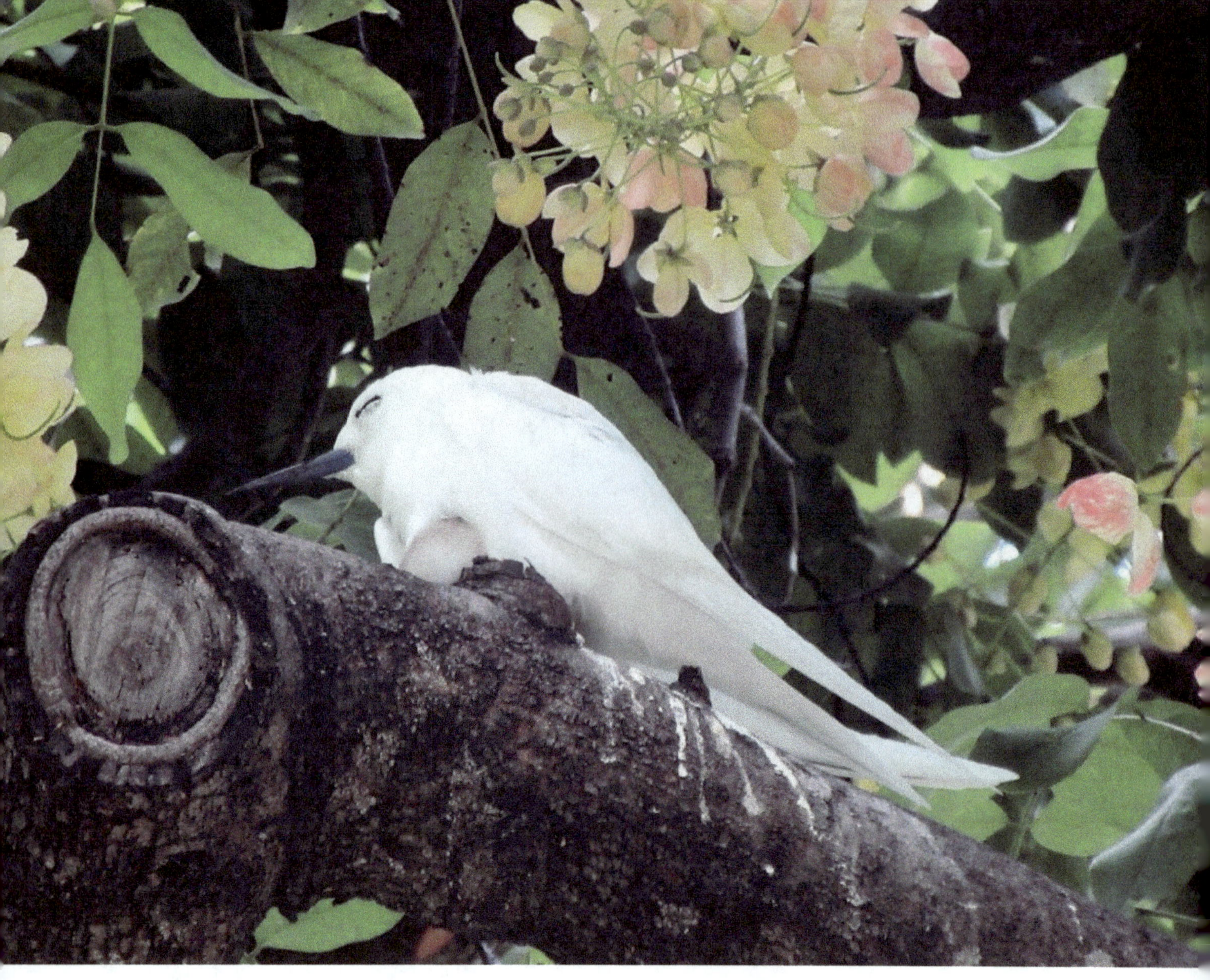

4 days later: A parent is spotted, but where is Shiro?

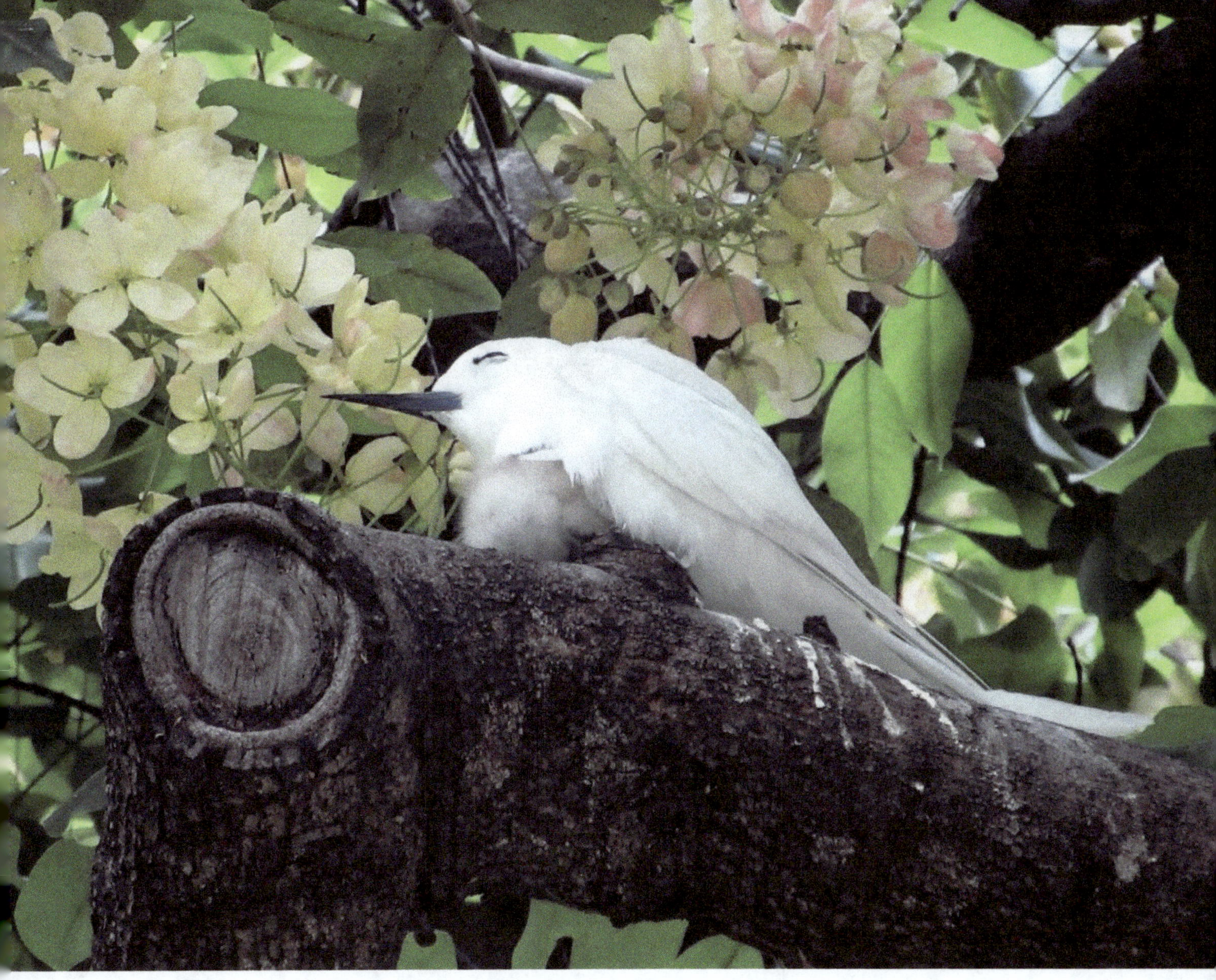

Shiro was hiding underneath its parent!

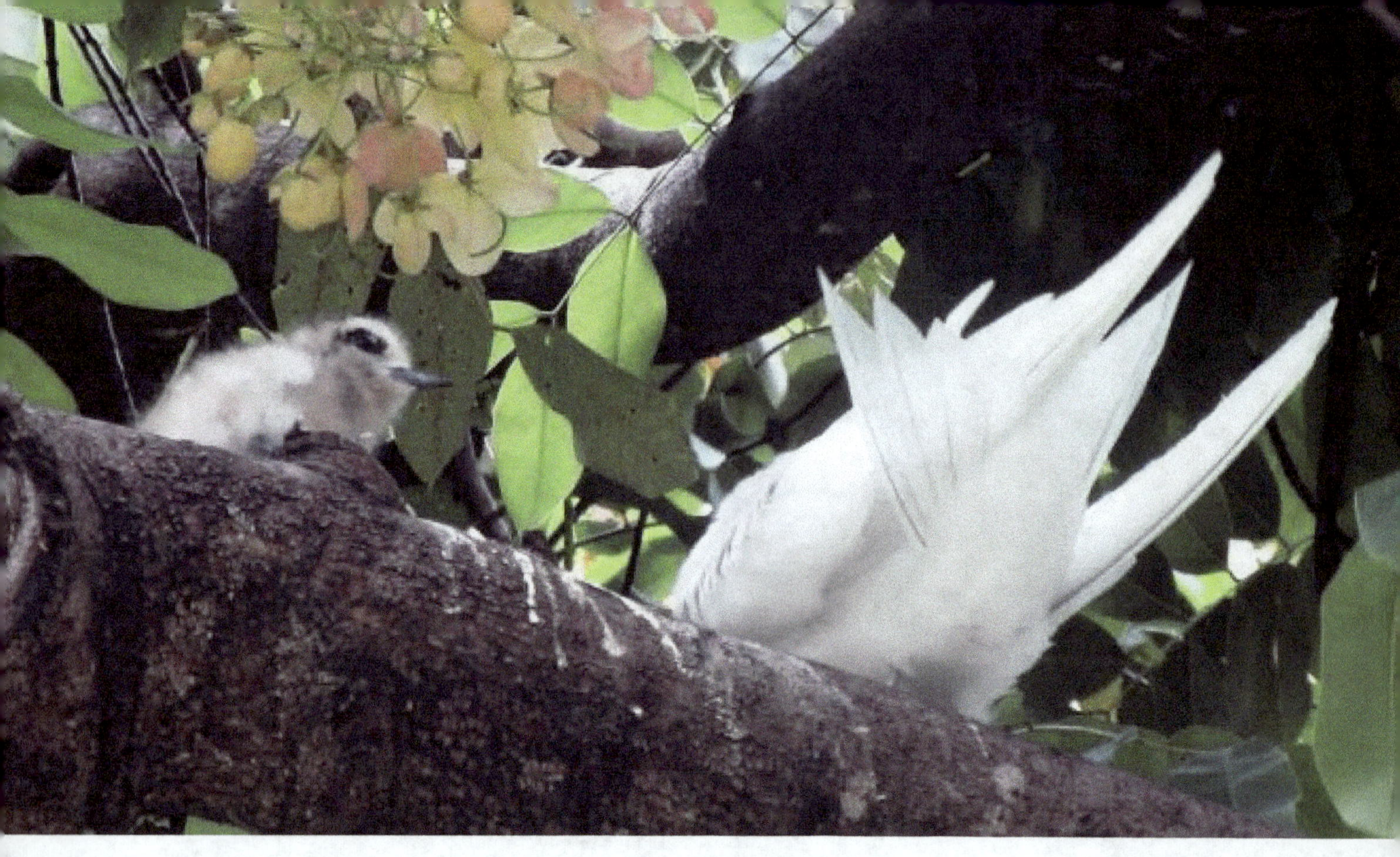

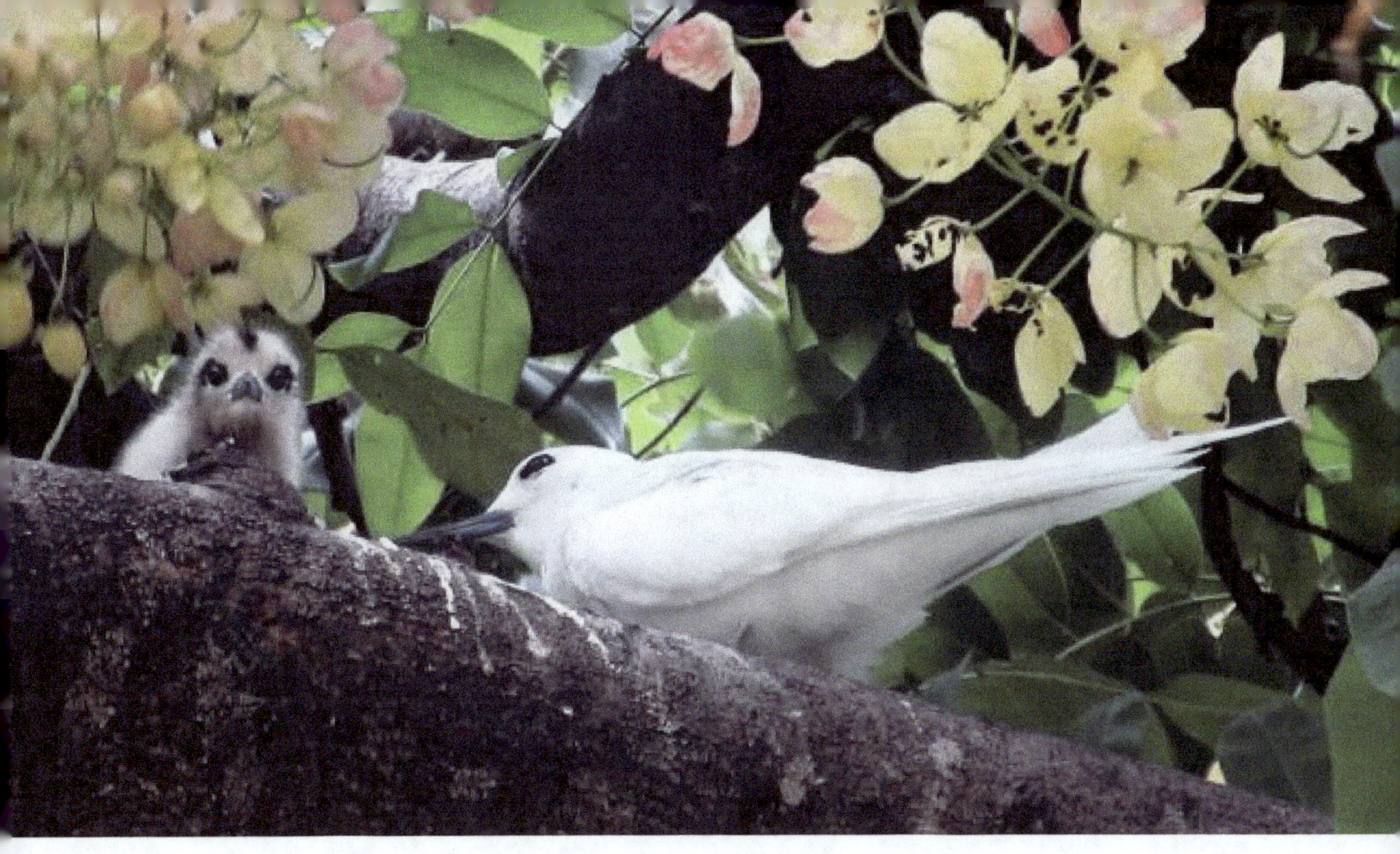

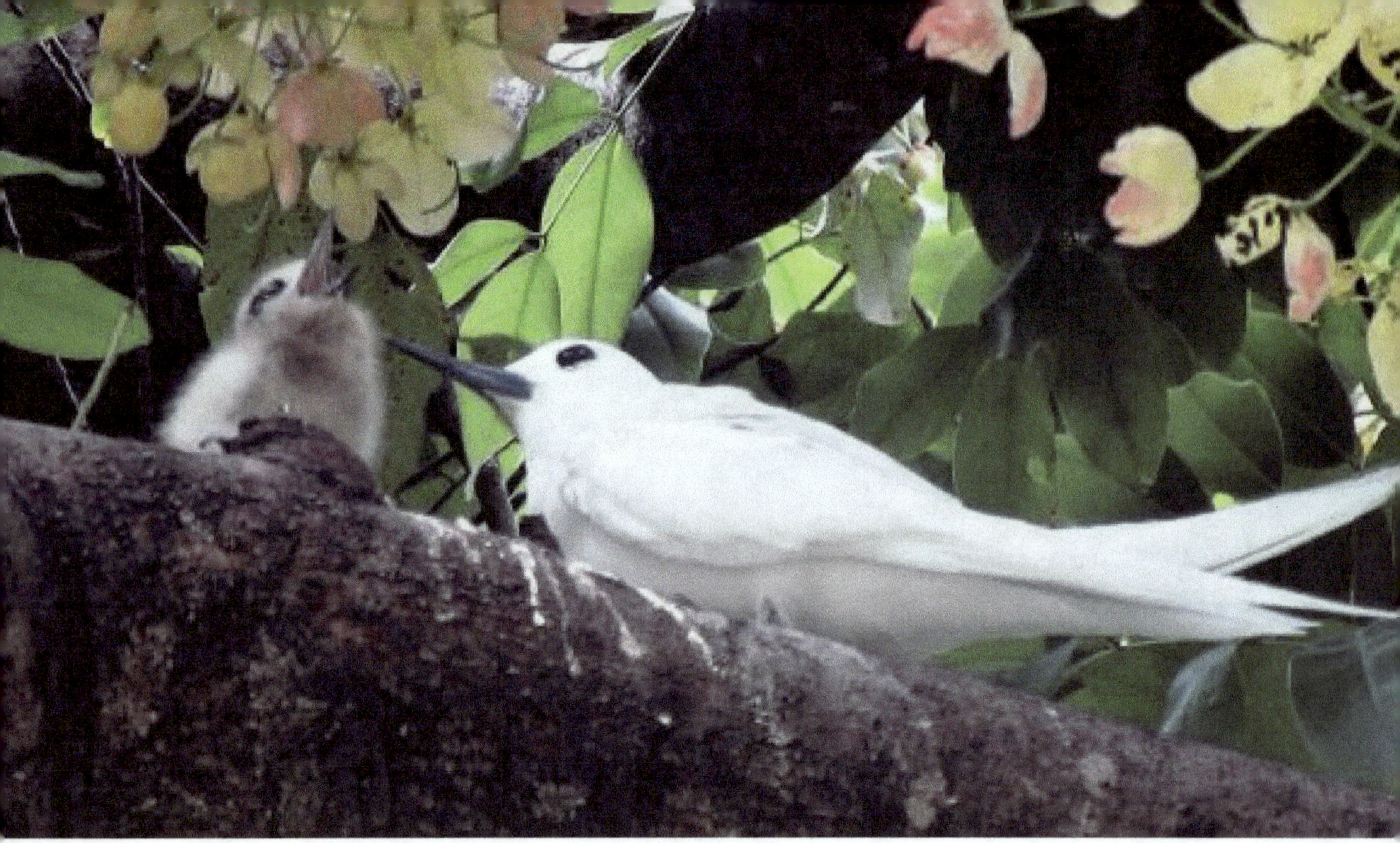

The parent preens Shiro.

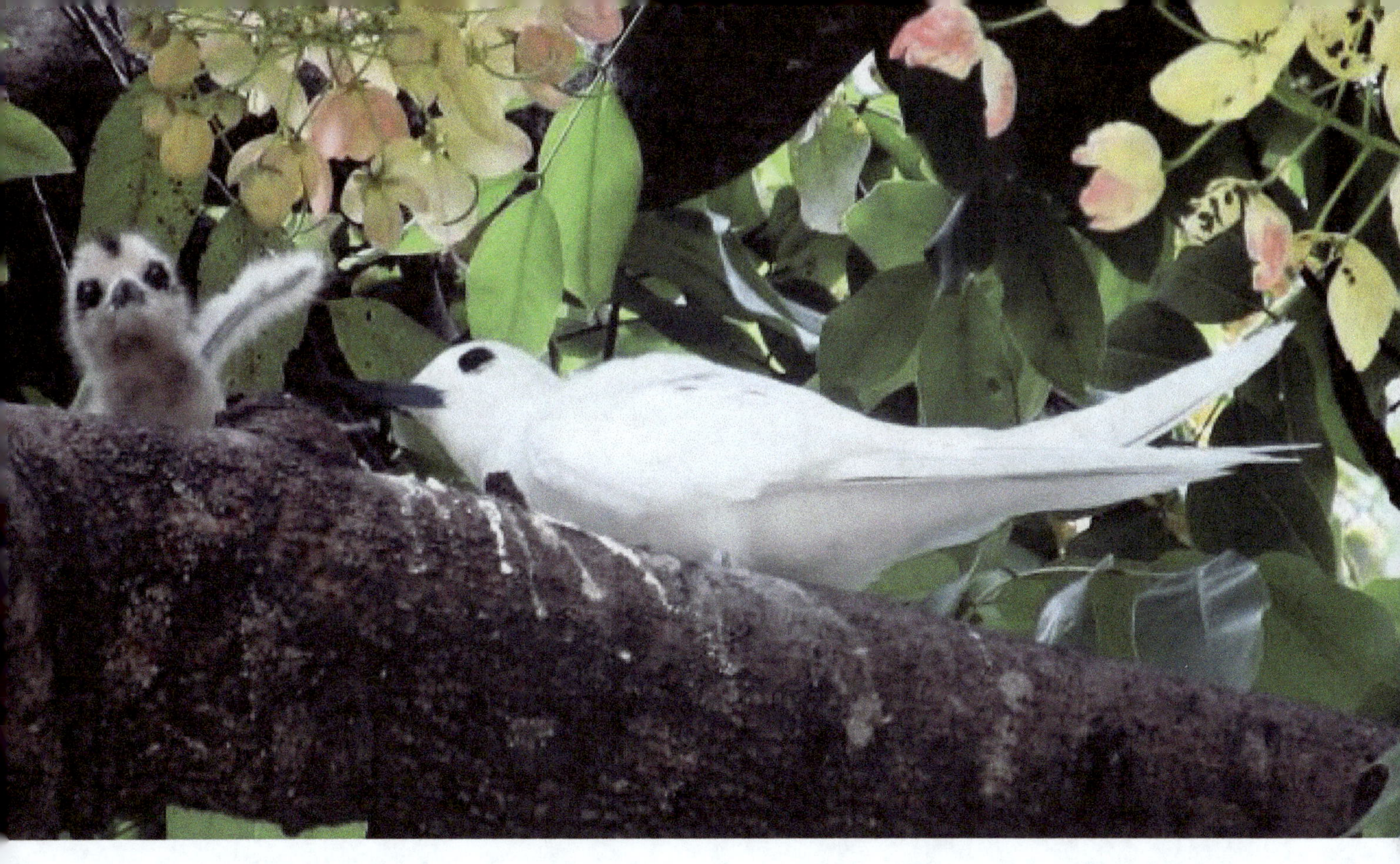

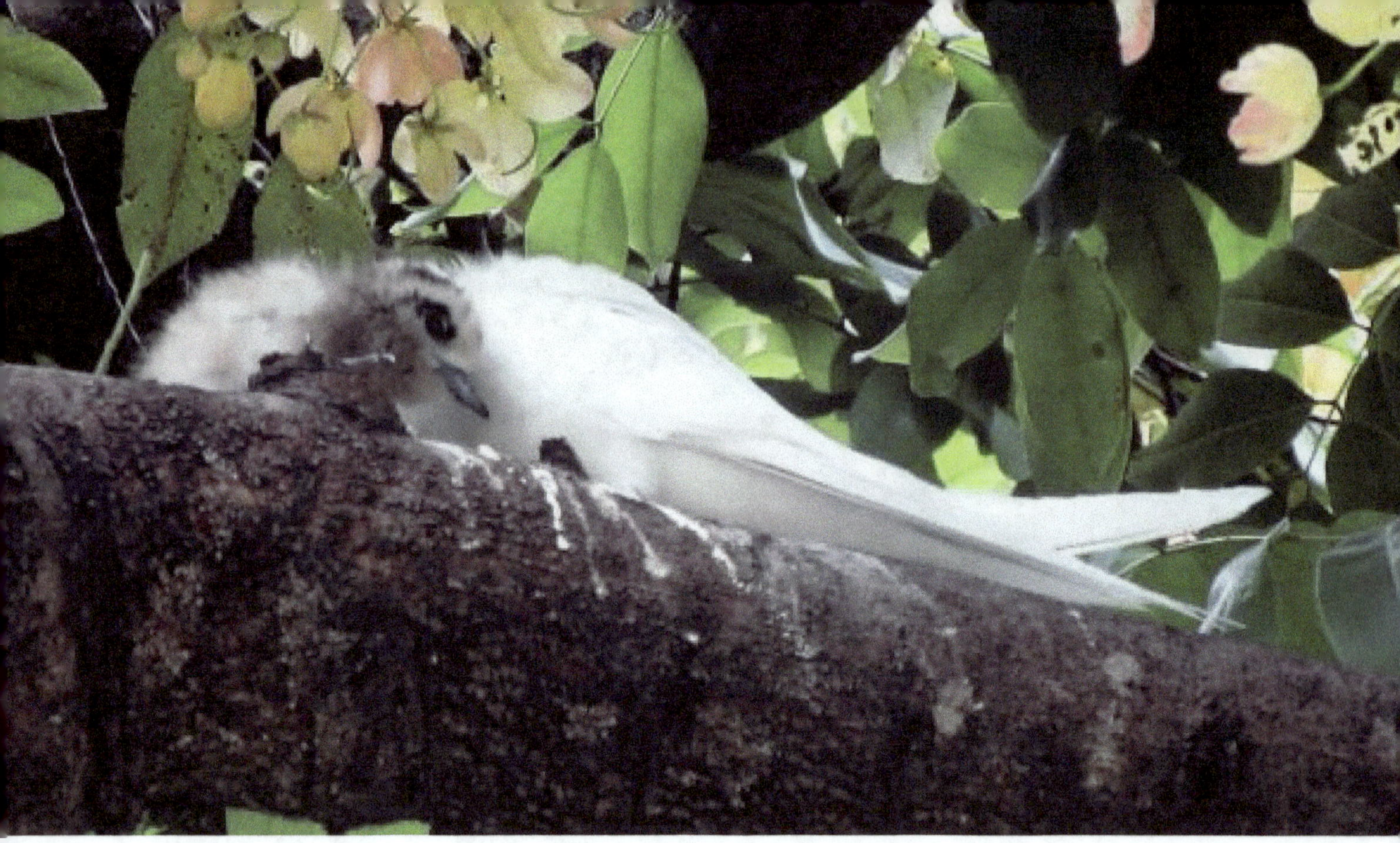

Preening is over. It’s time to nestle again.

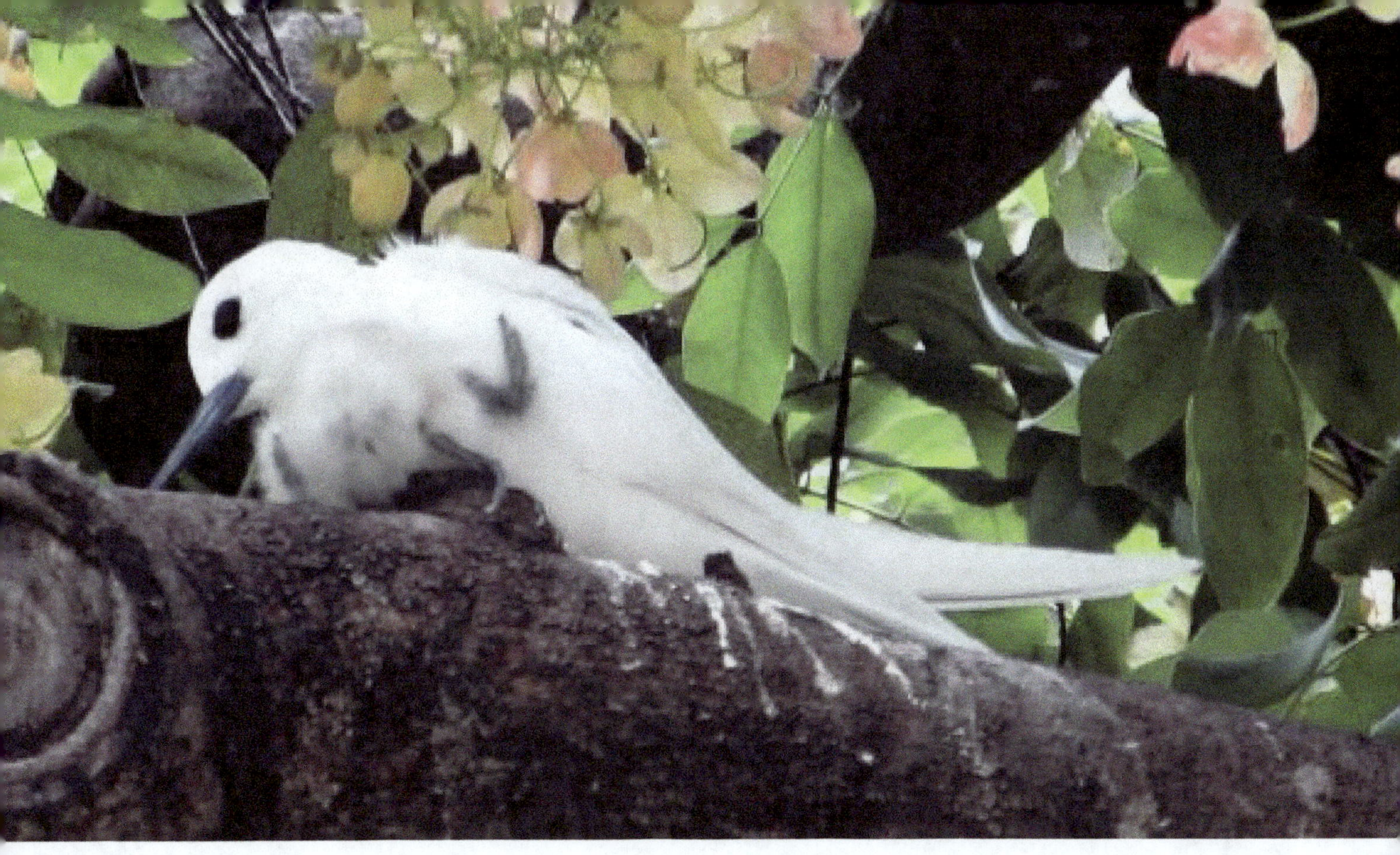

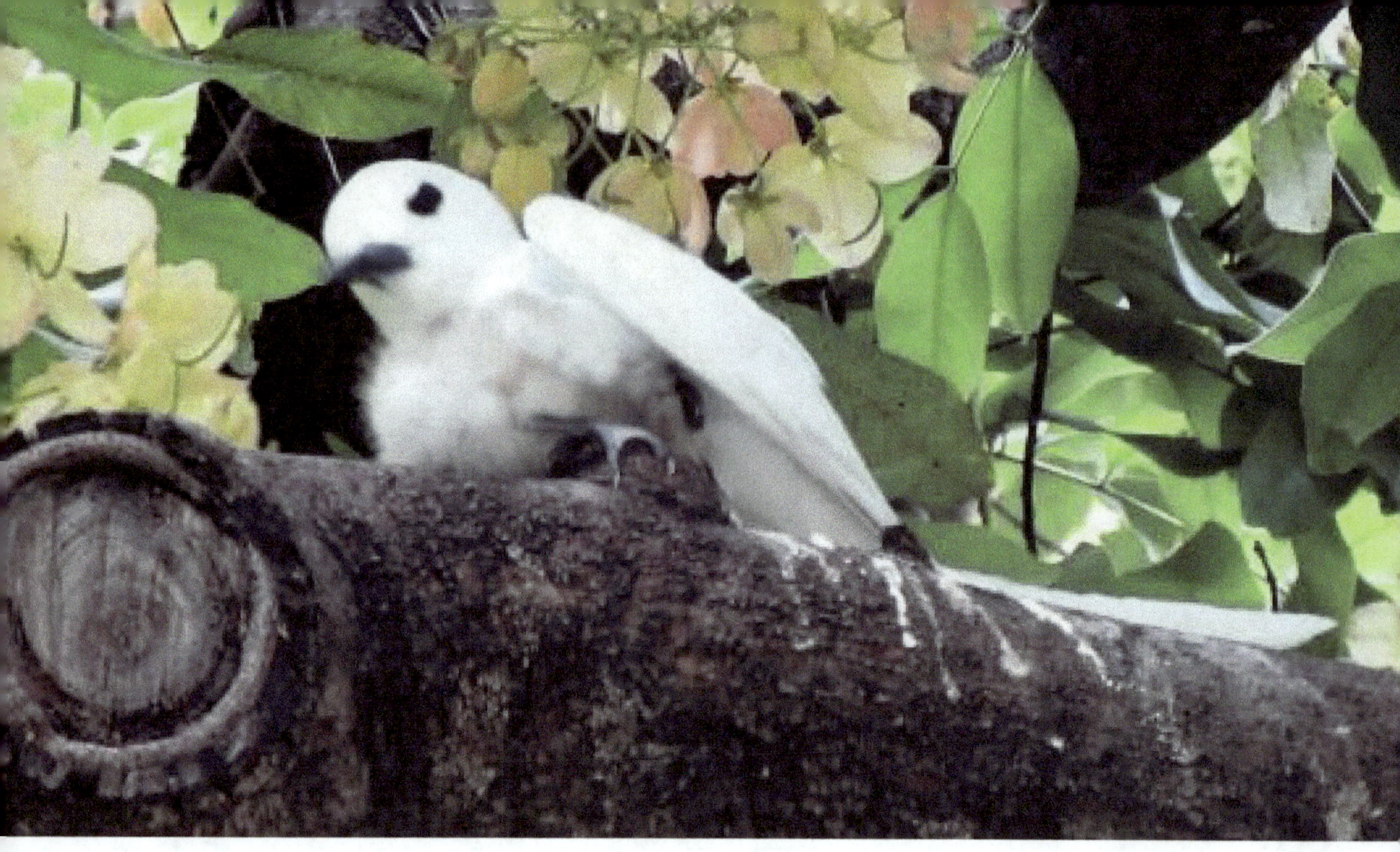

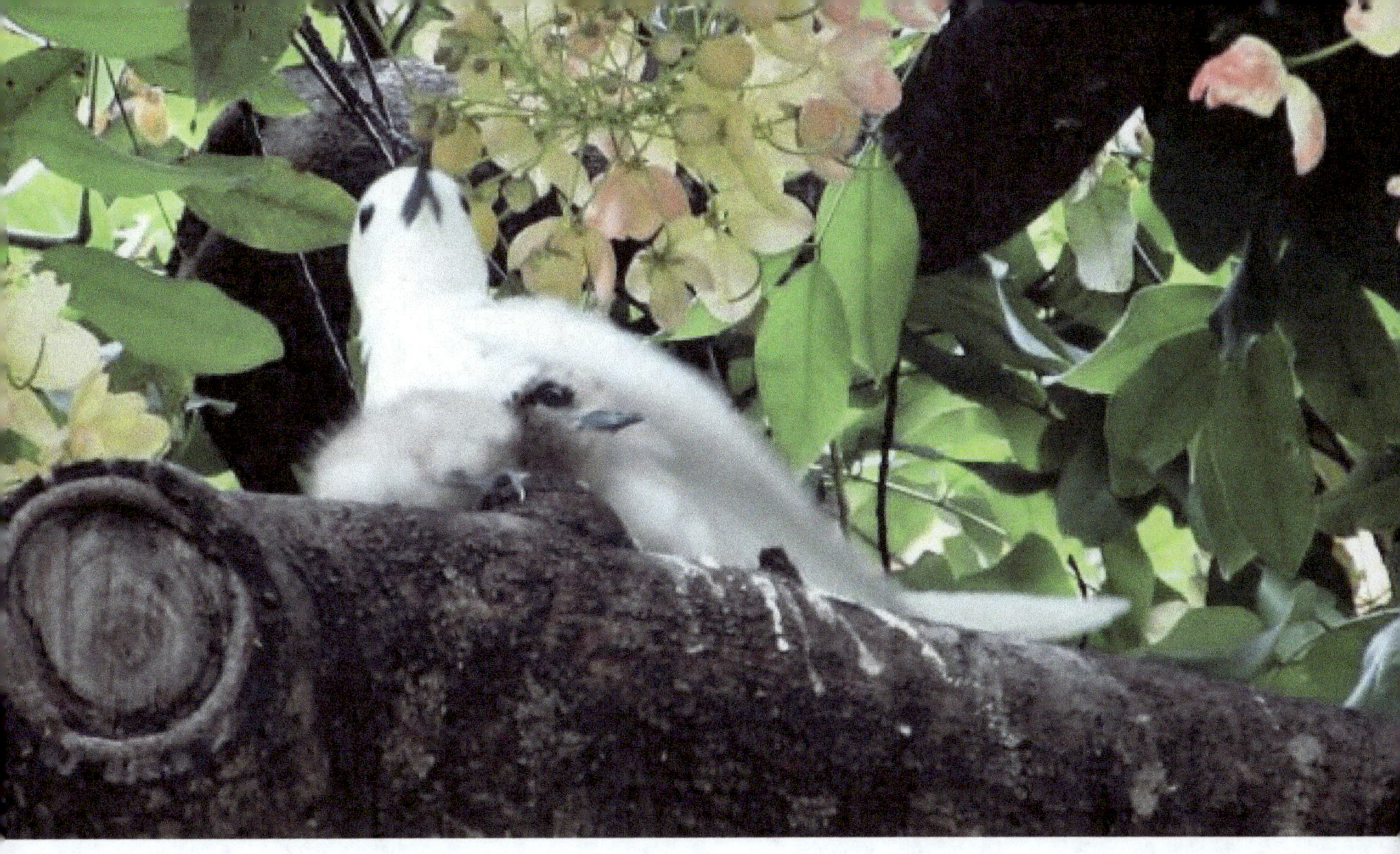

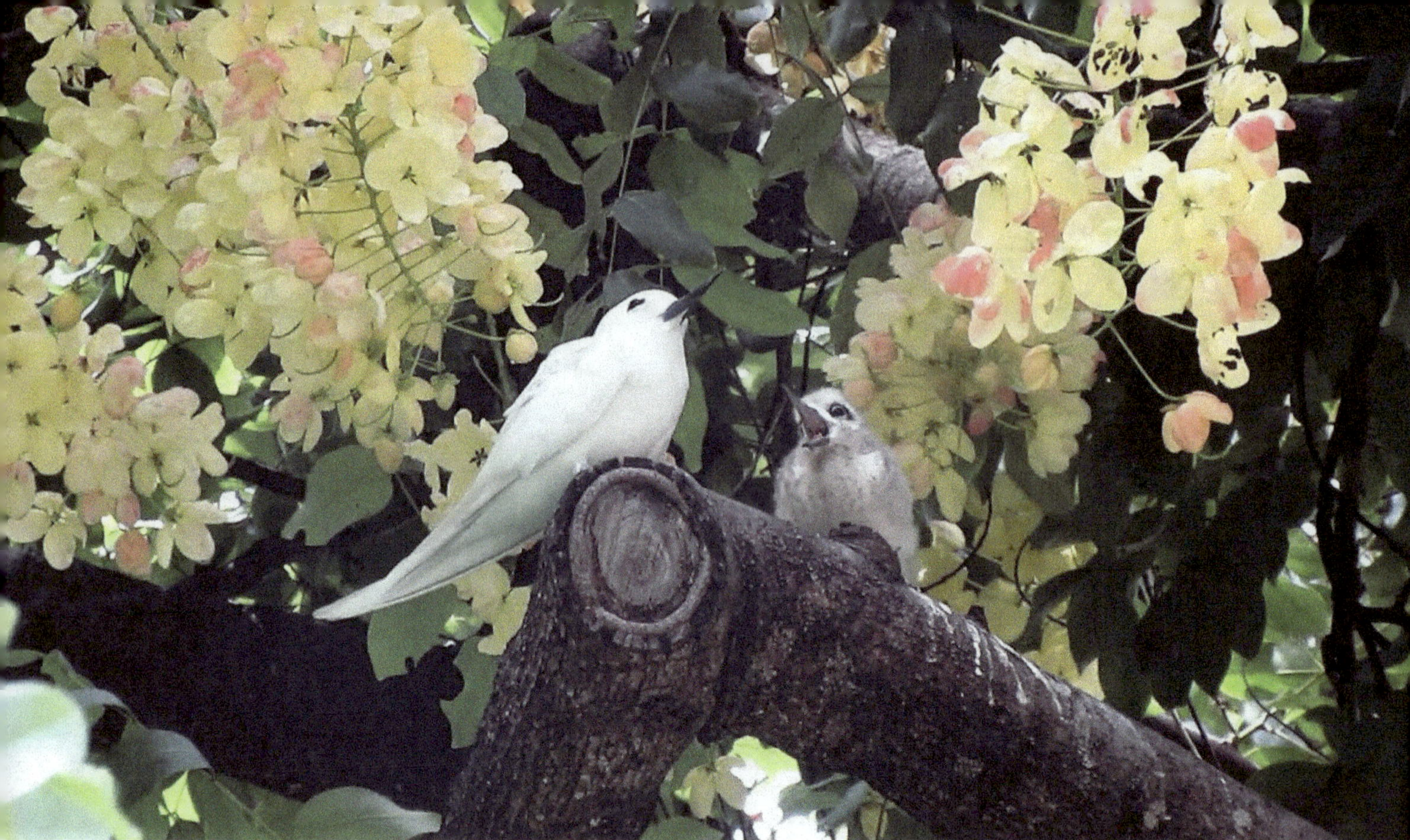

16 days after sighting

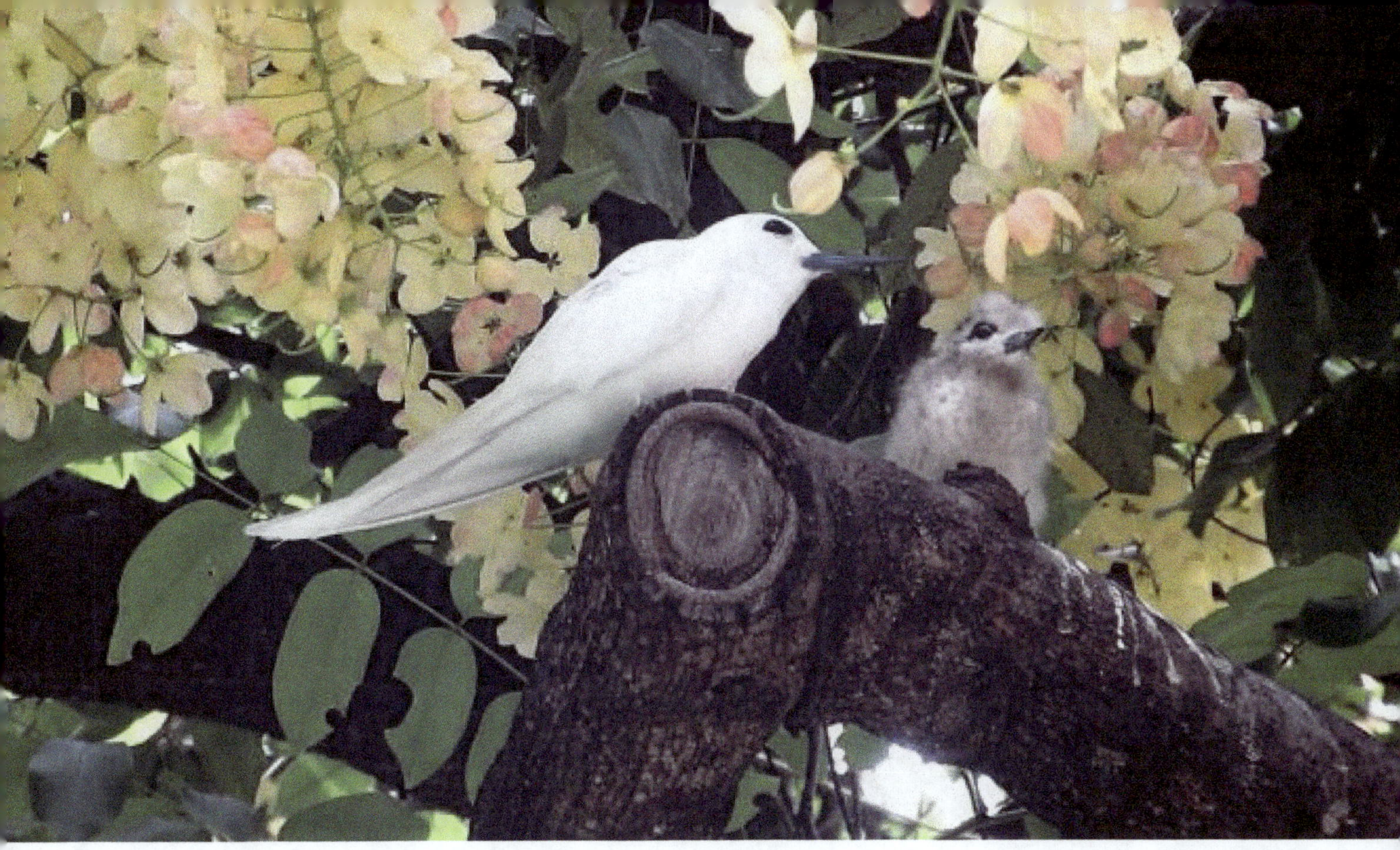

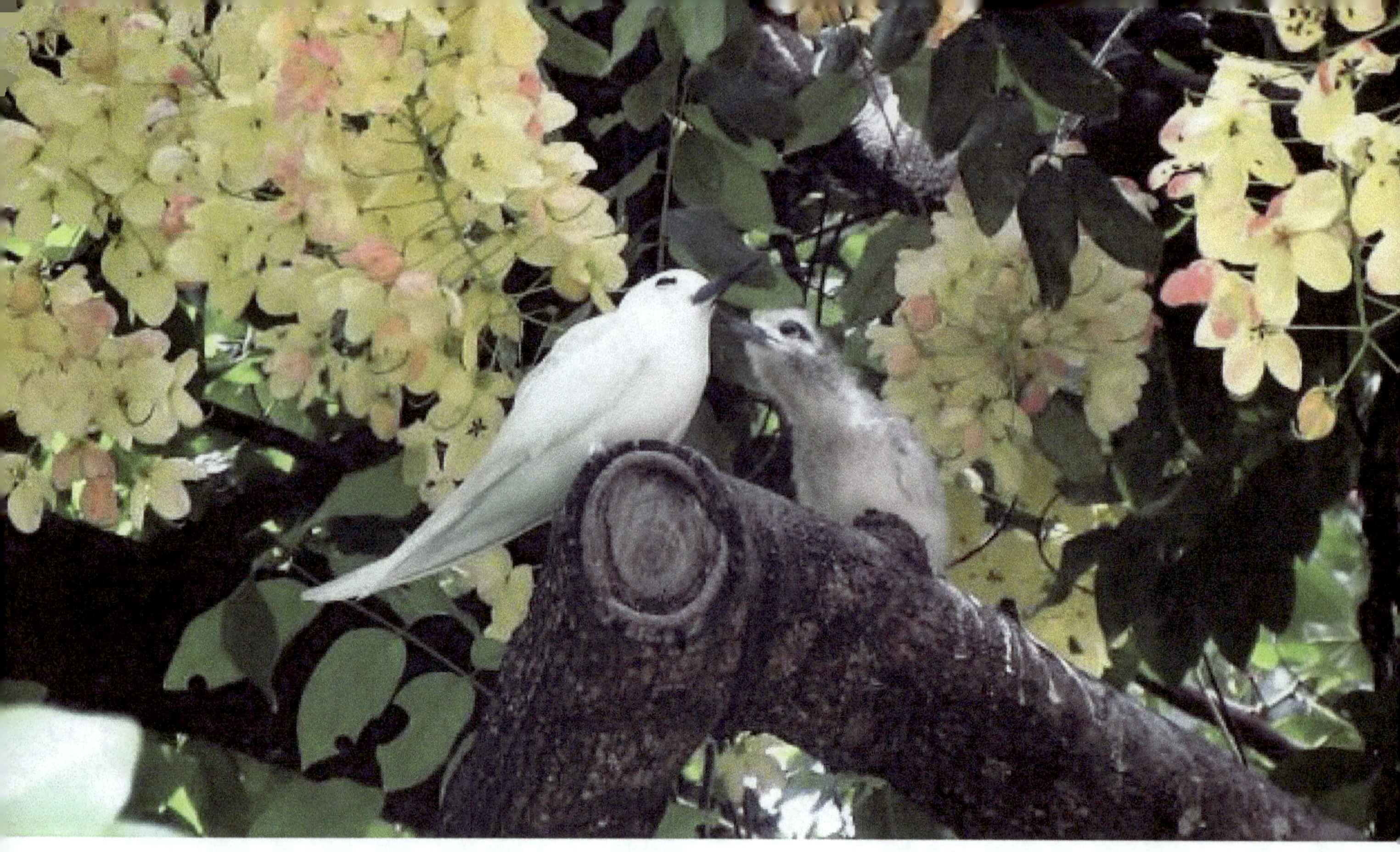

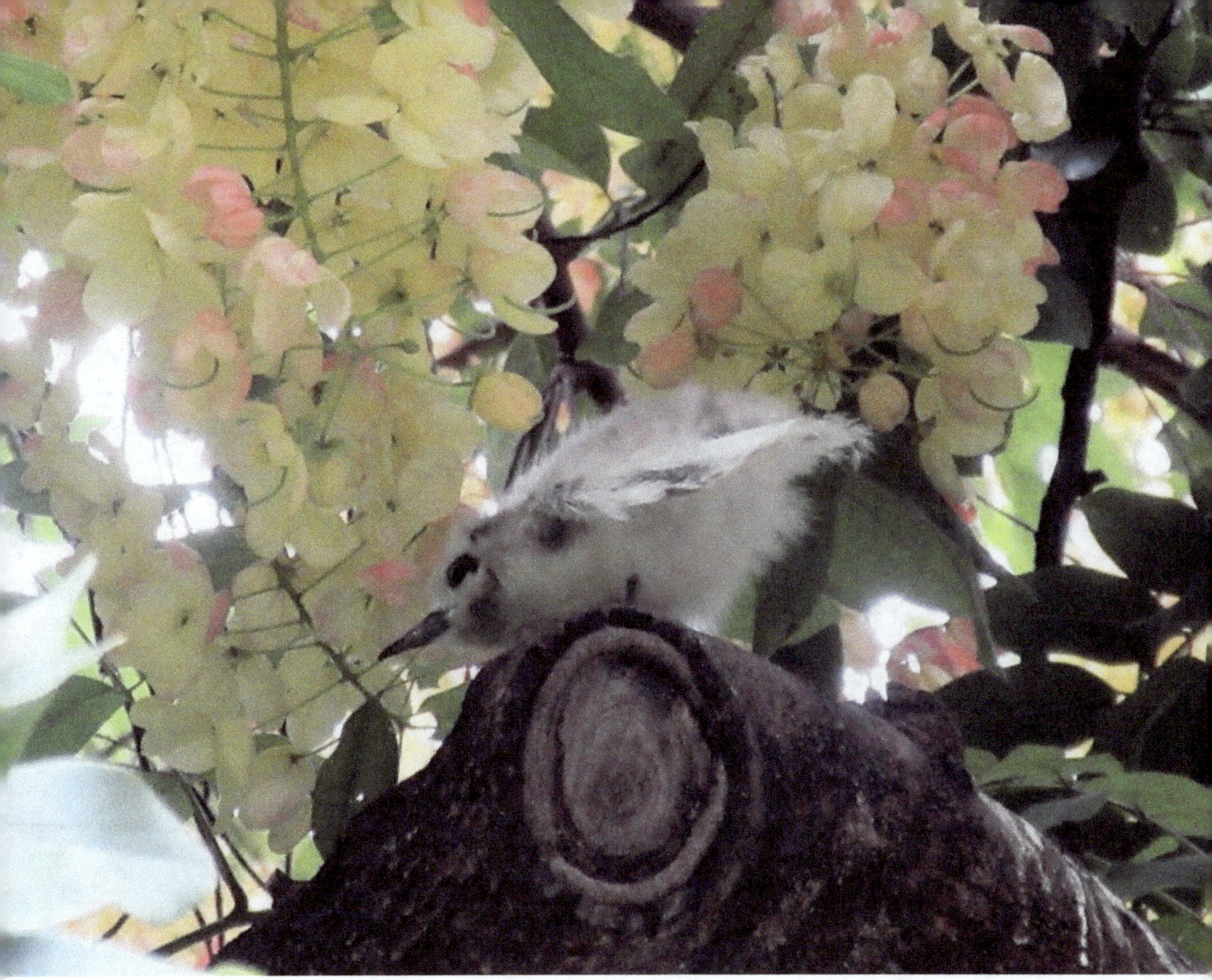

17 days after sighting

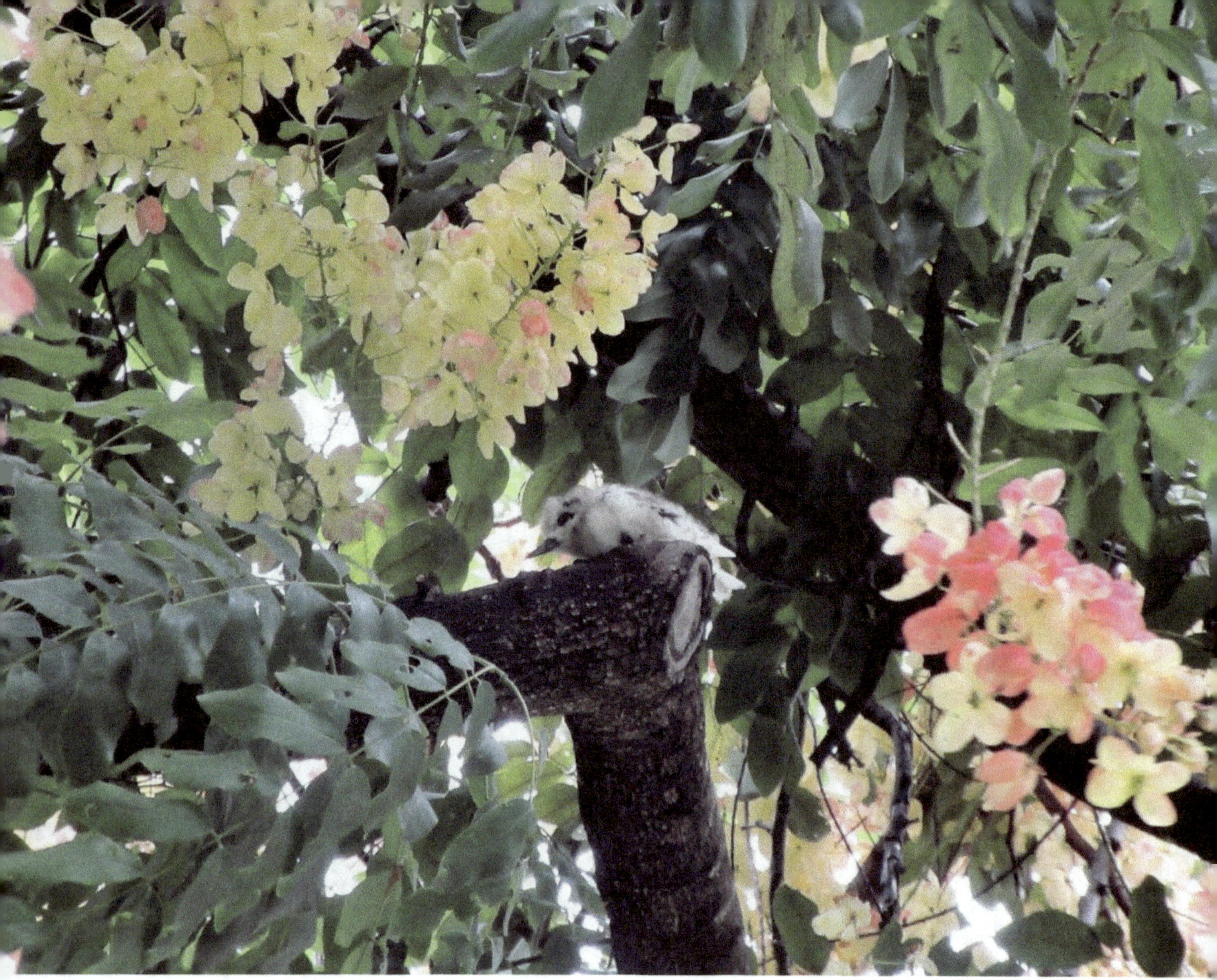

22 days after sighting

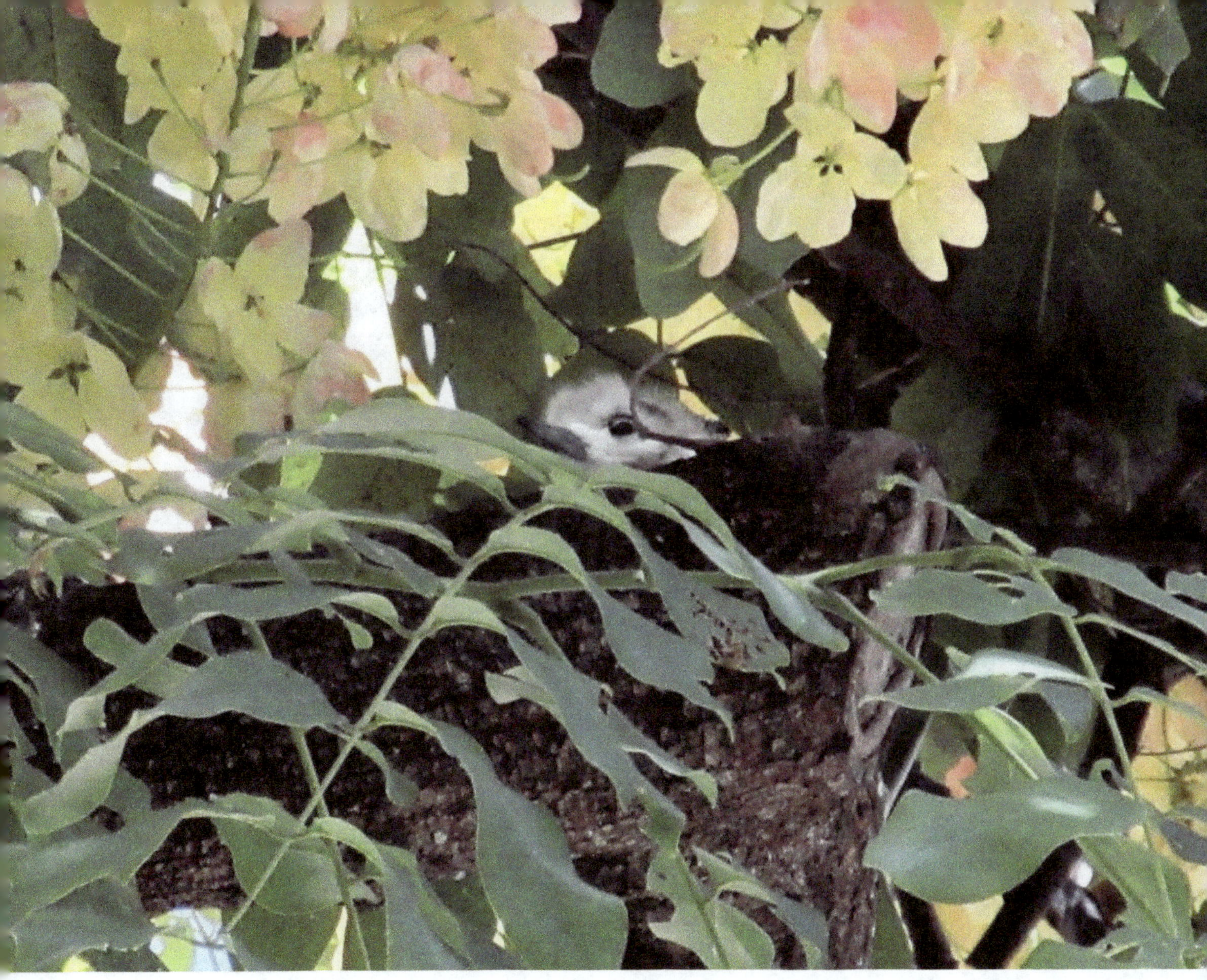

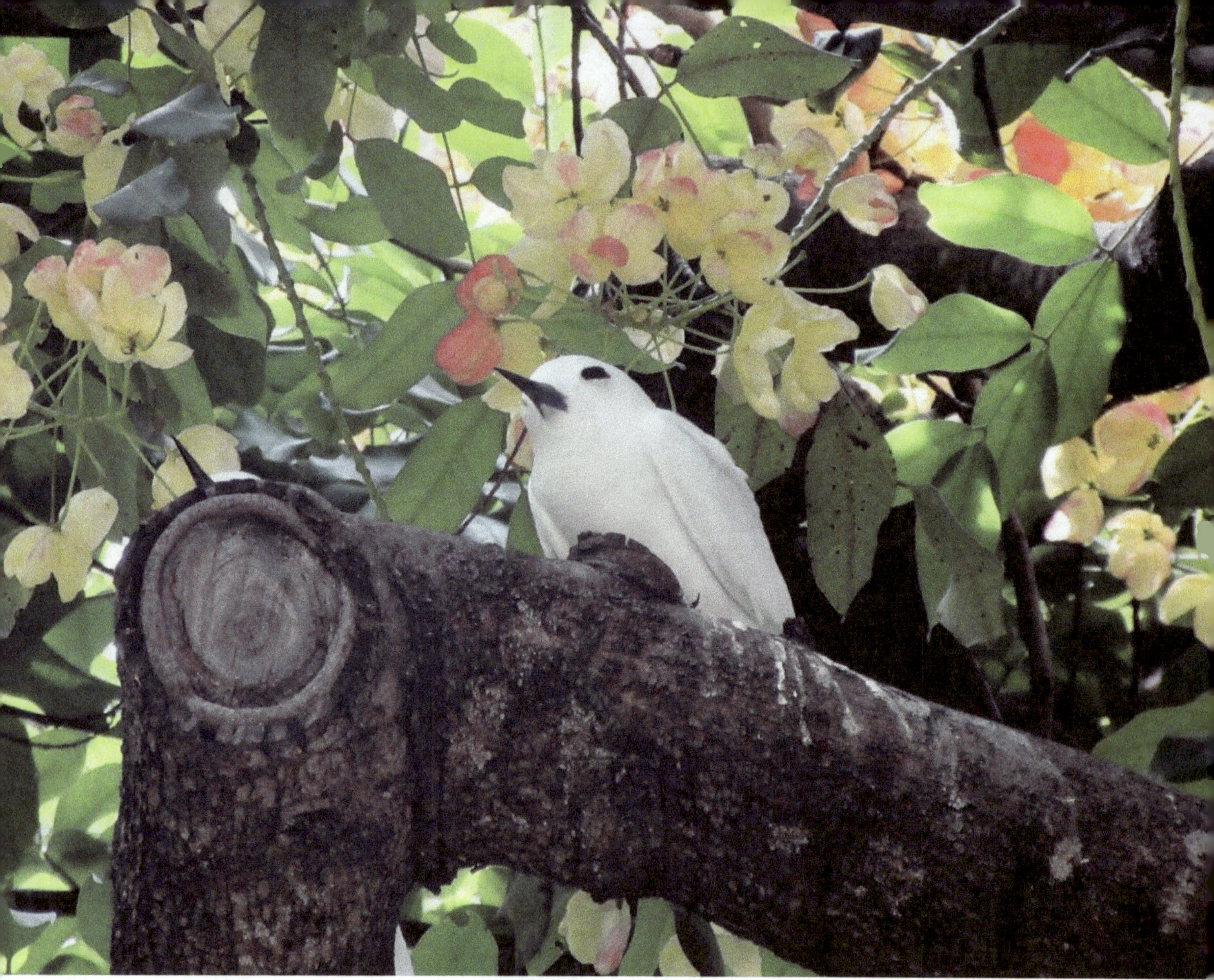

About a month after sighting, Shiro has feathers. Do you see a parent?

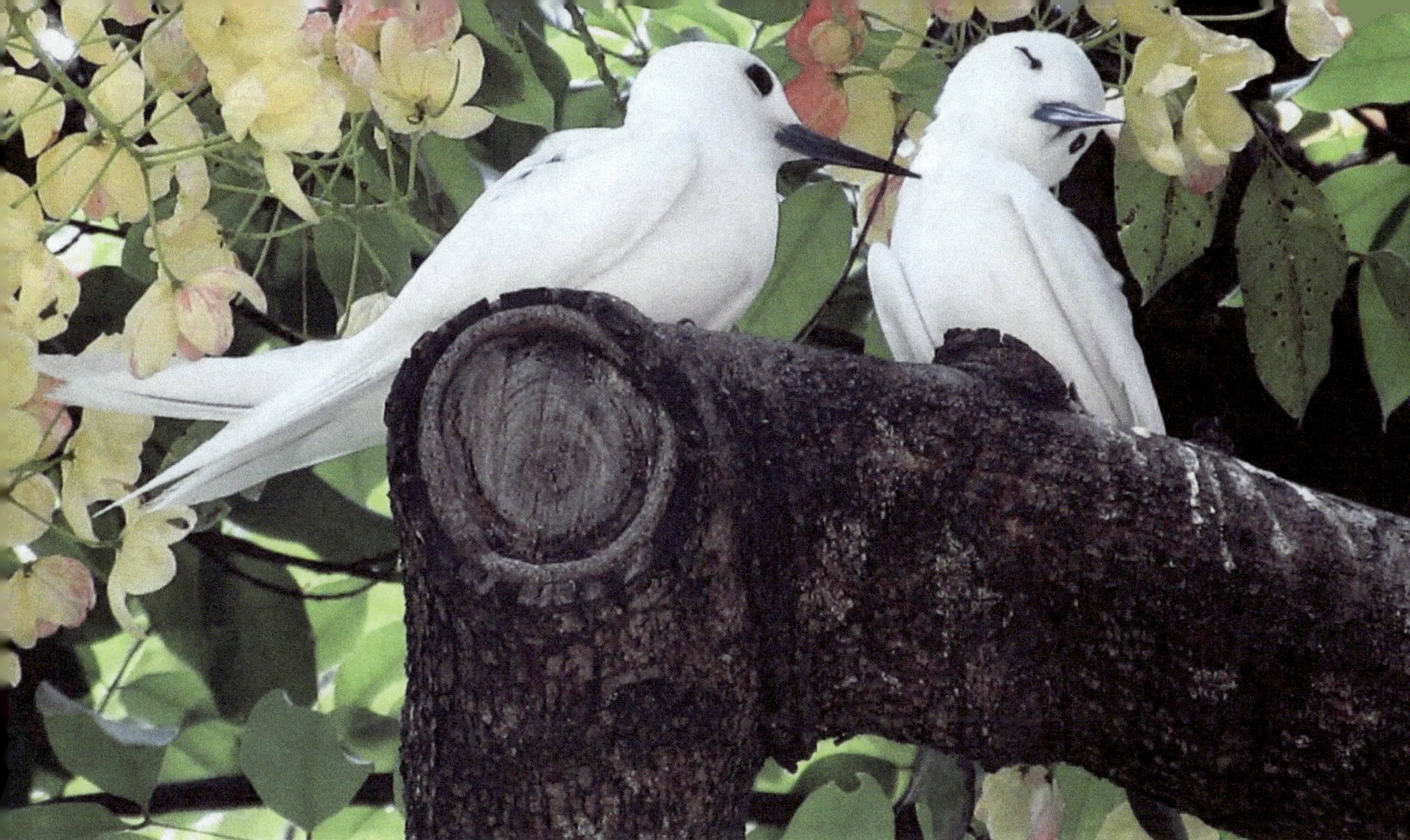

A parent preens Shiro.

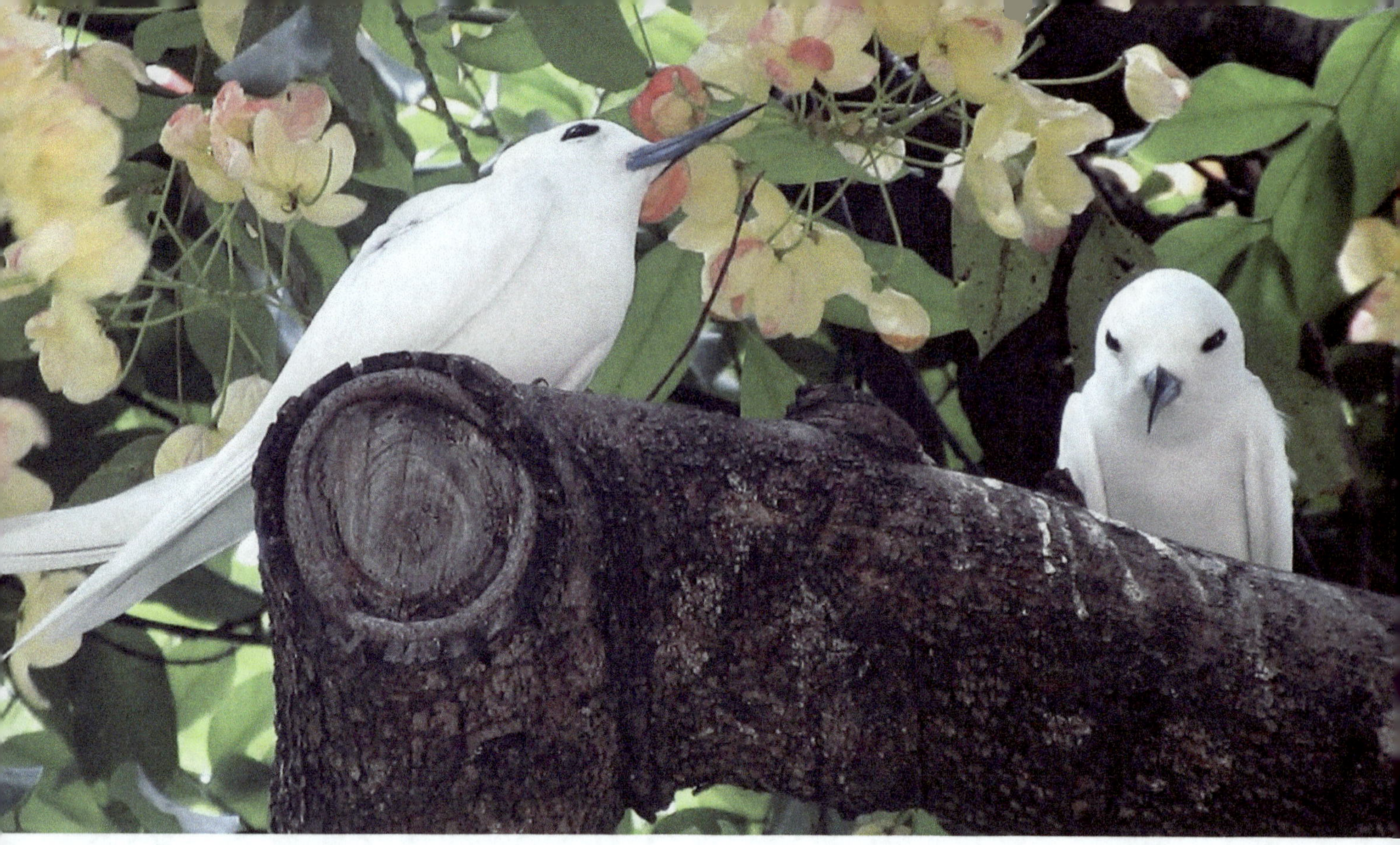

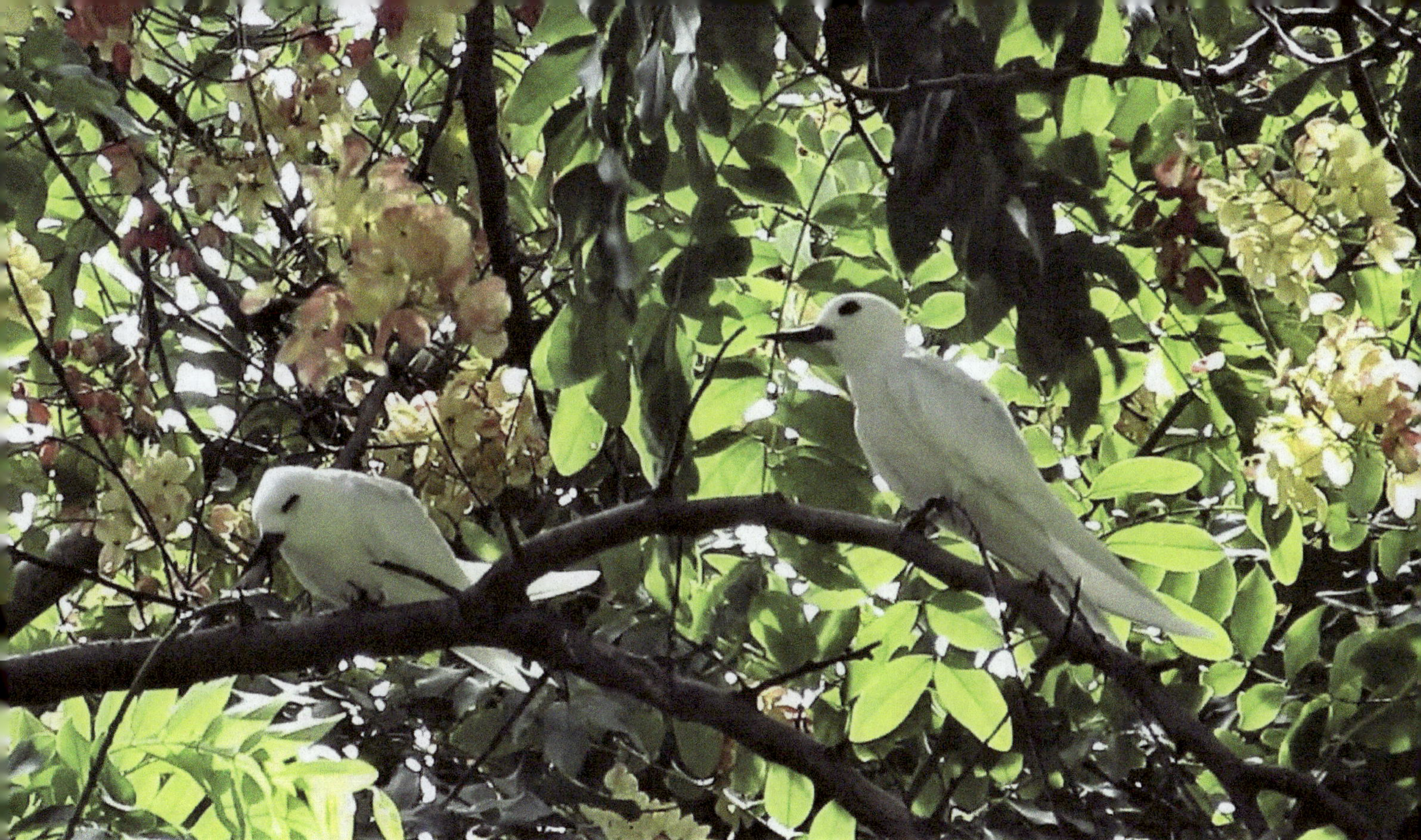

A day later, Shiro and a parent move to another branch in the tree.

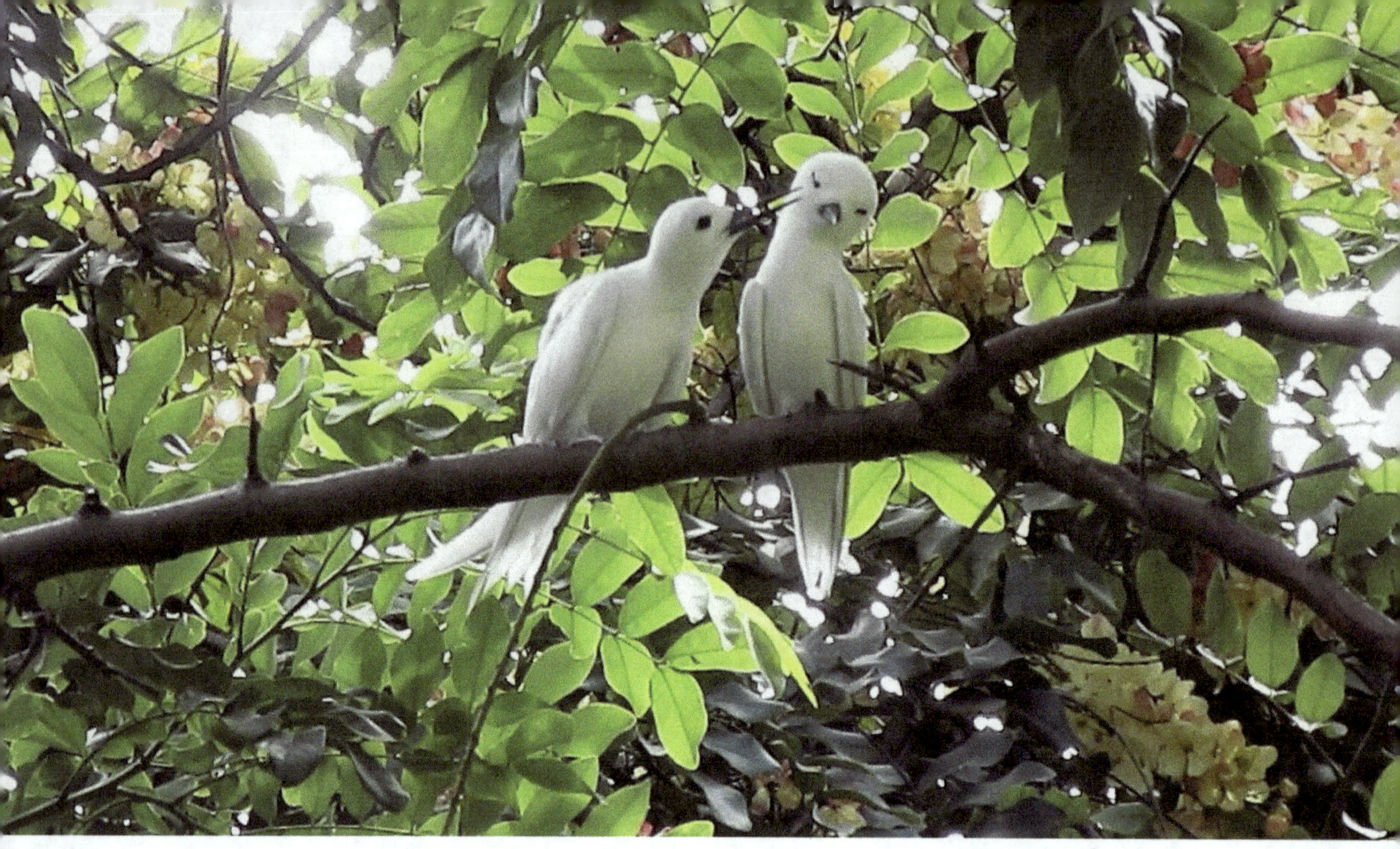

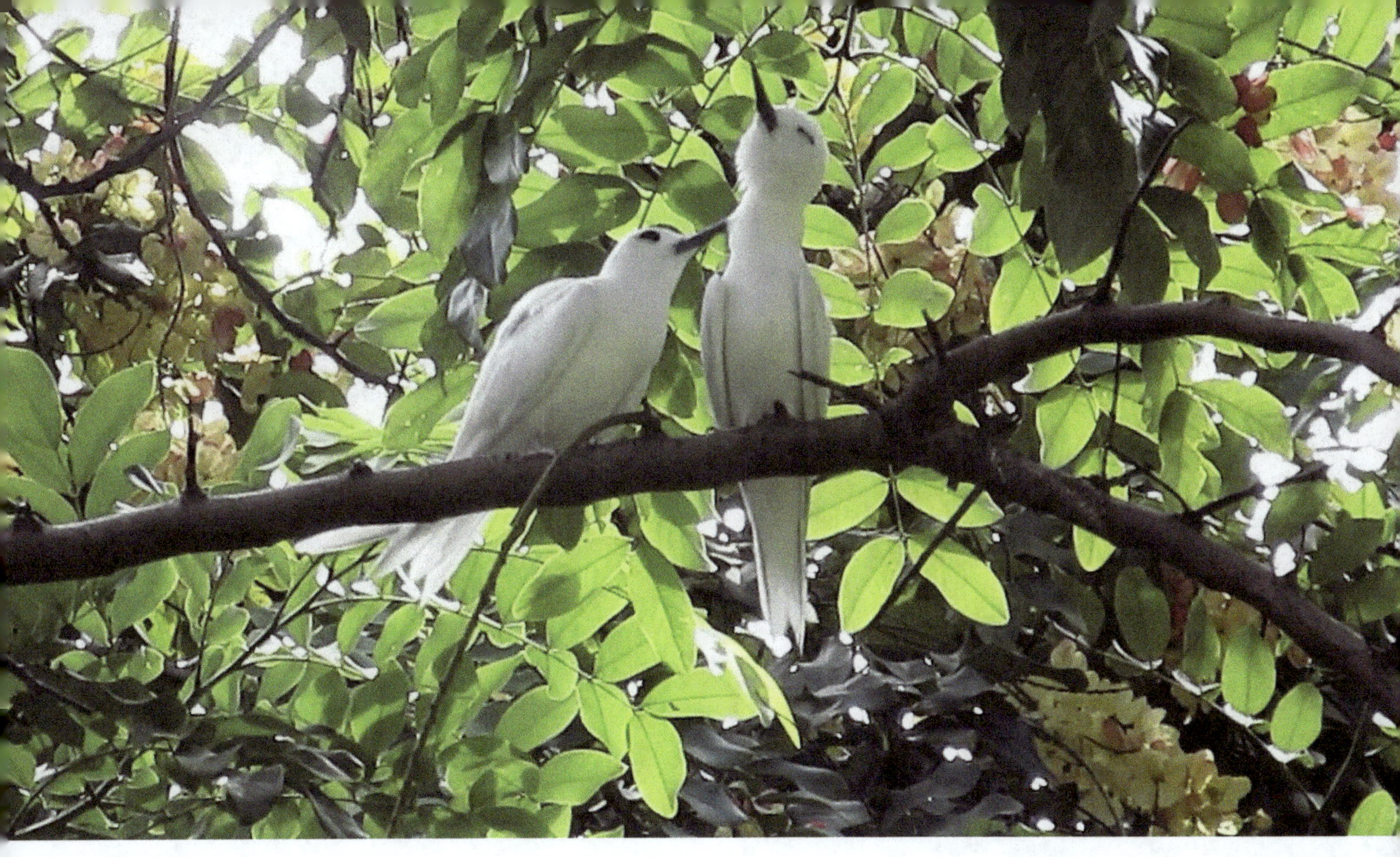

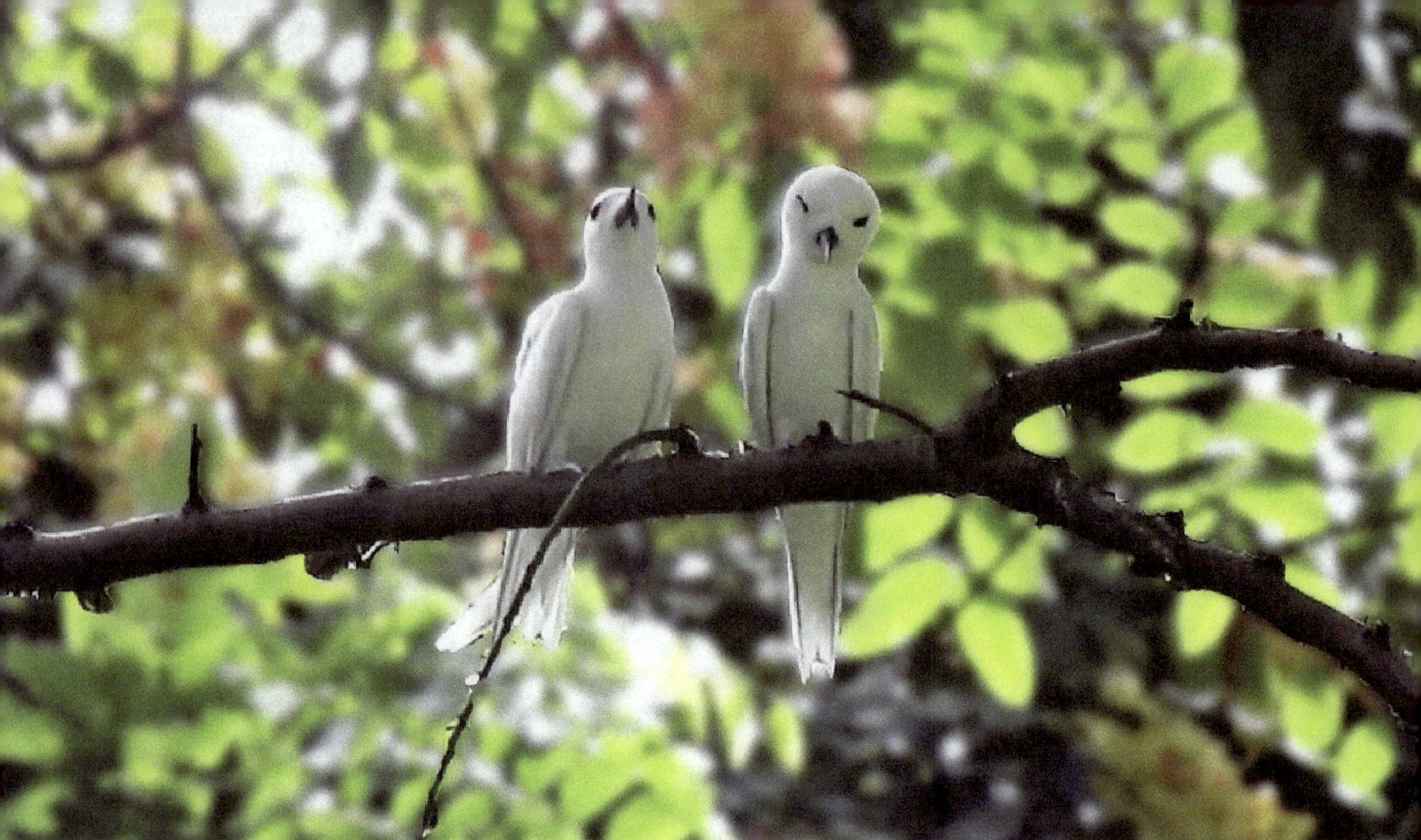

A last look at a parent with Shiro

CHAPTER TWO

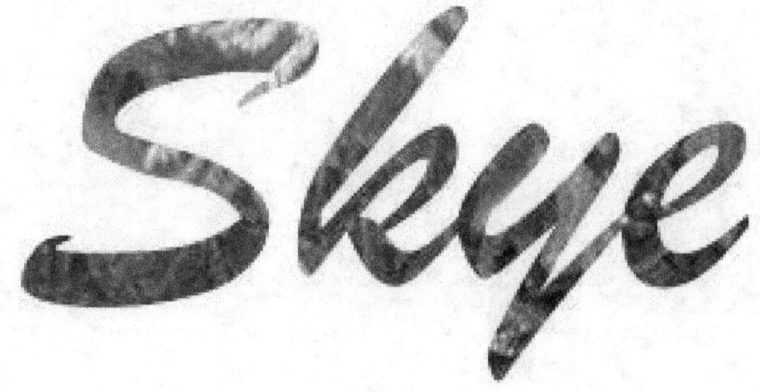

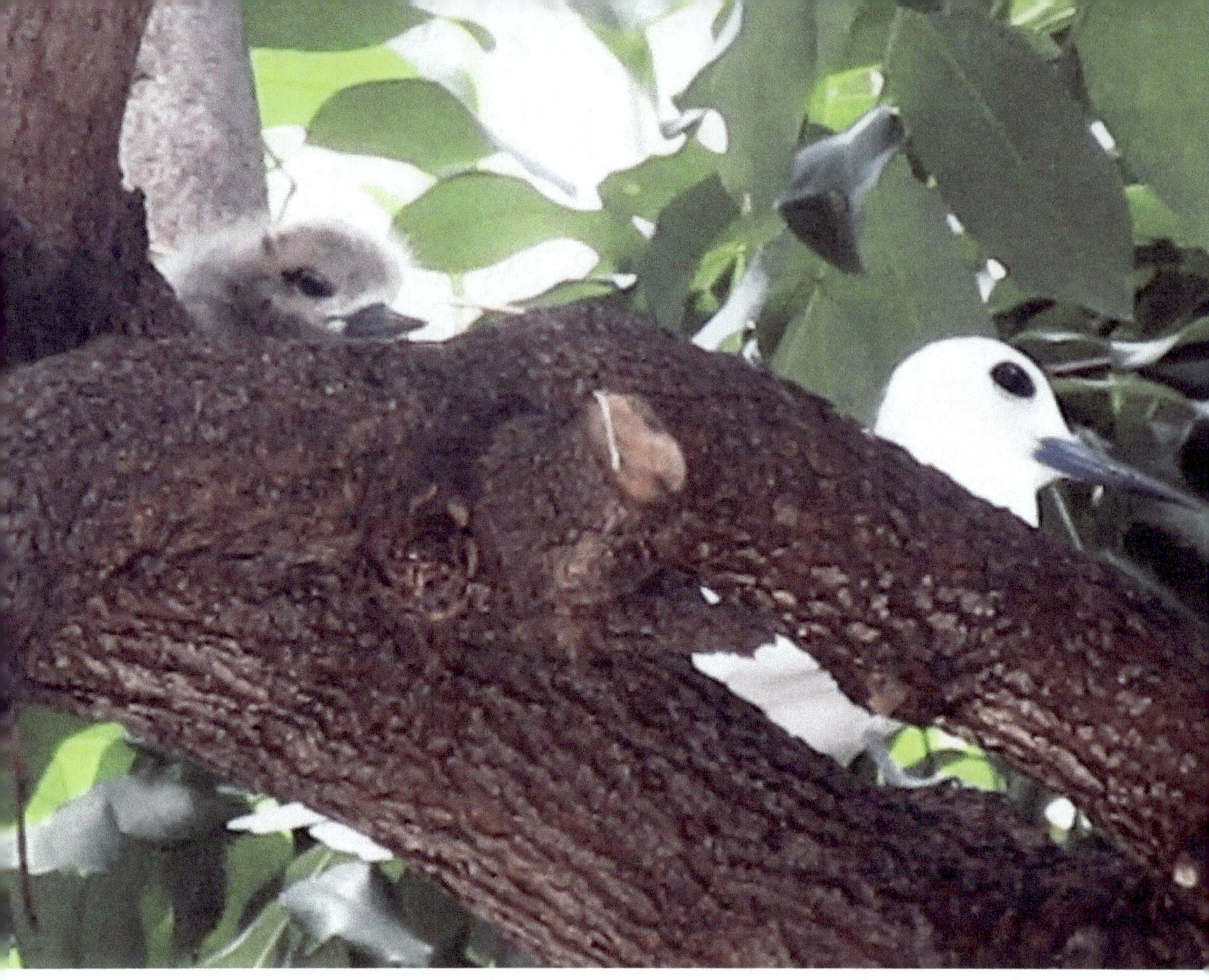

Skye was first spotted with a parent.

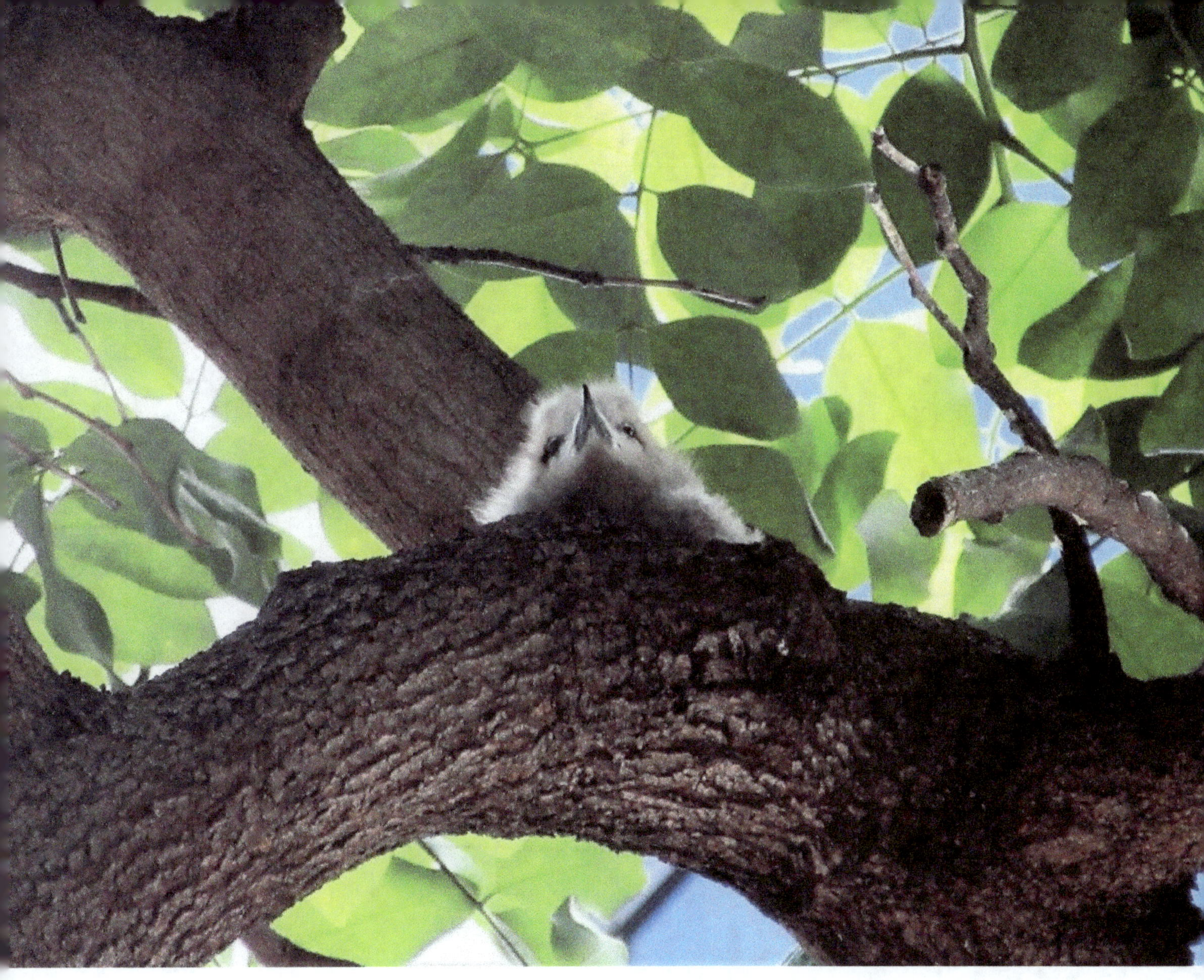

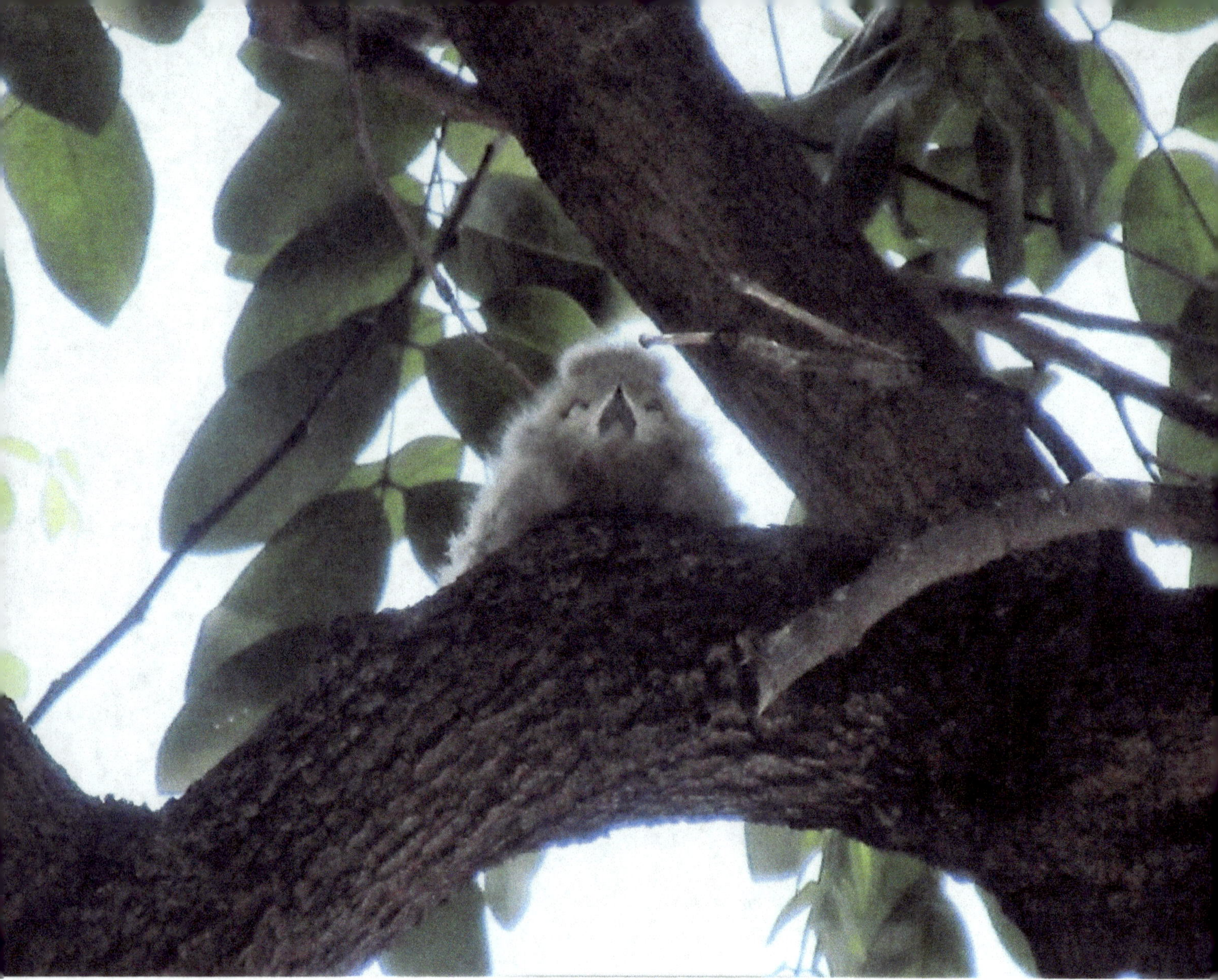

Day 4 after sighting

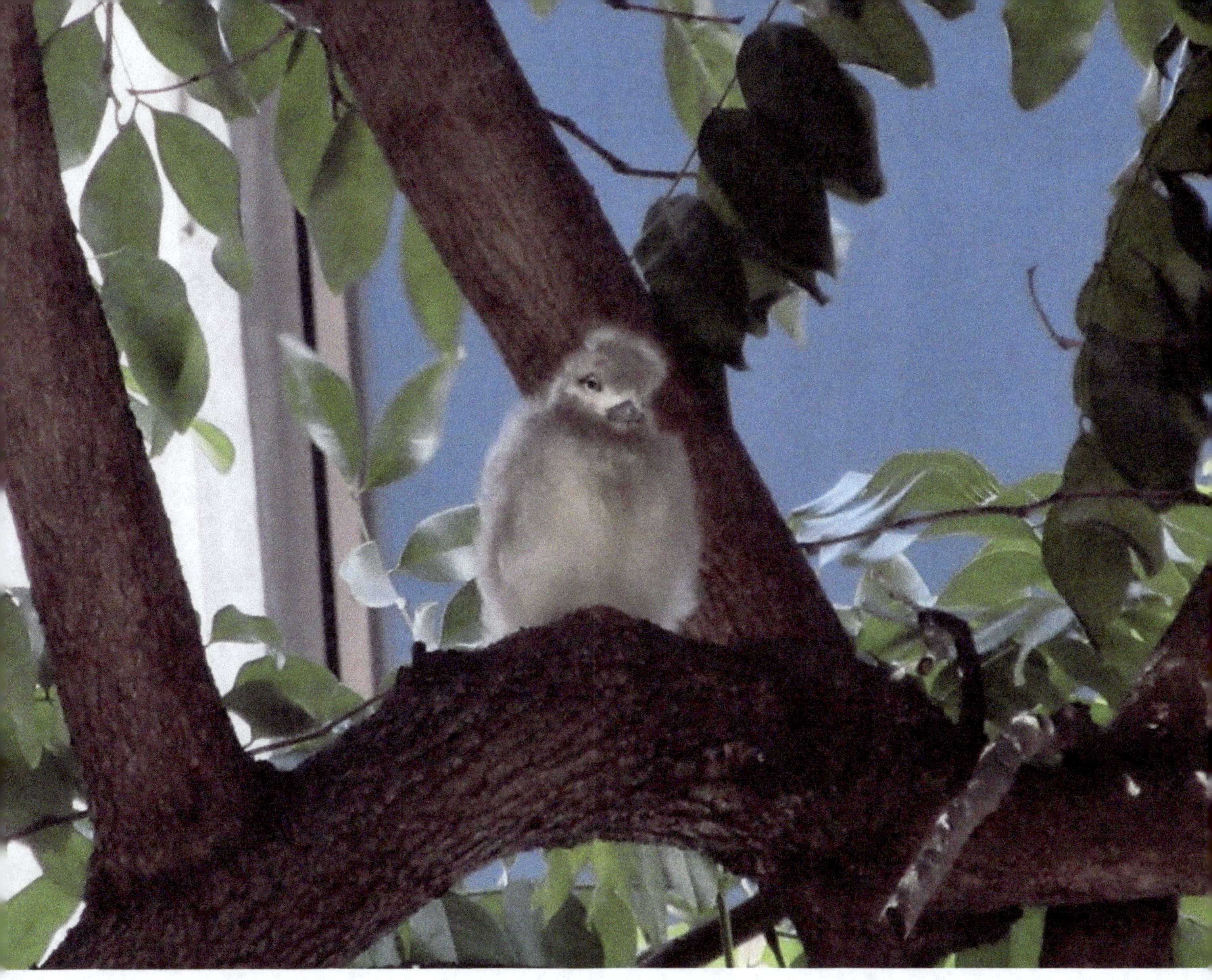

Day 6 after sighting

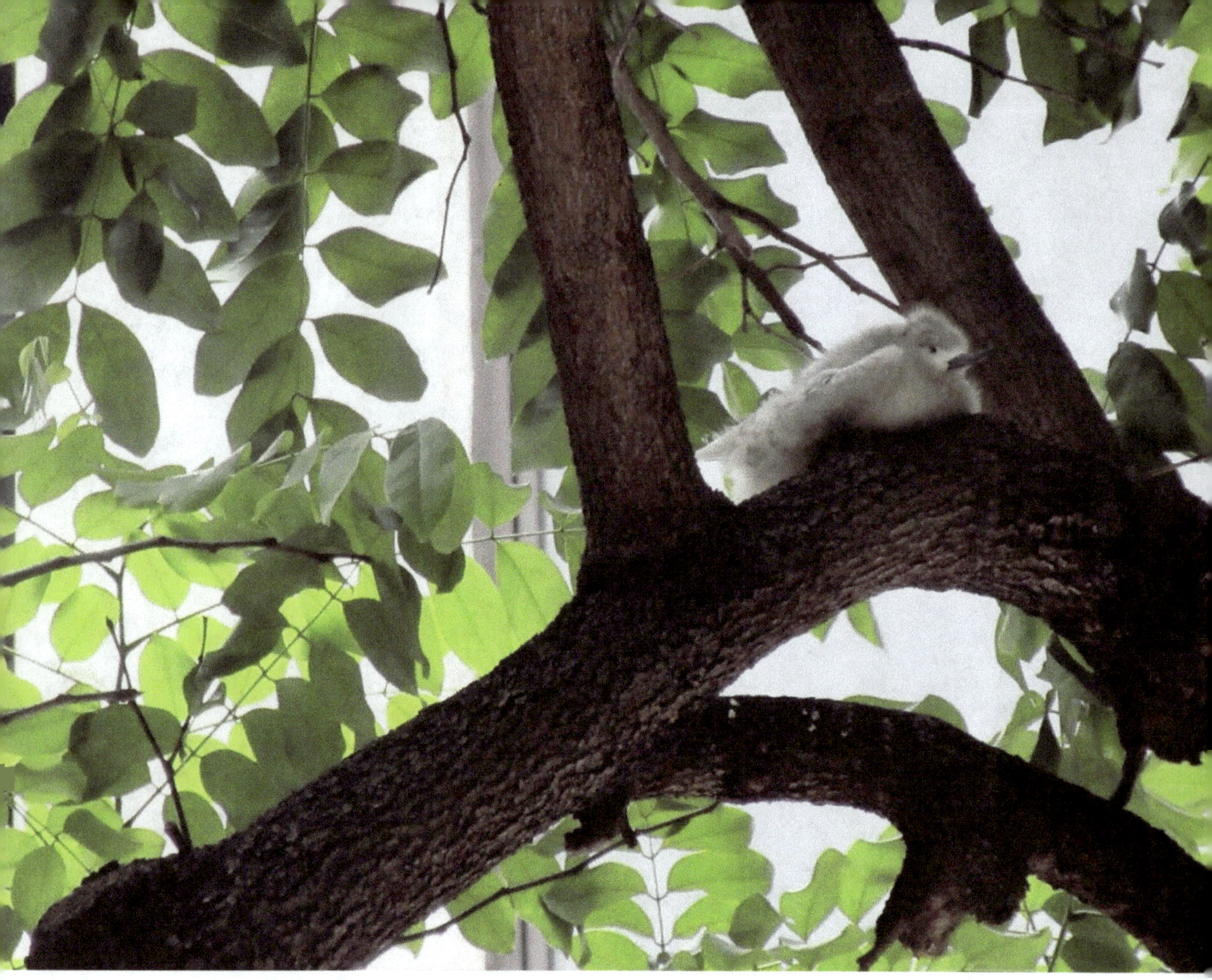

Day 12 after sighting

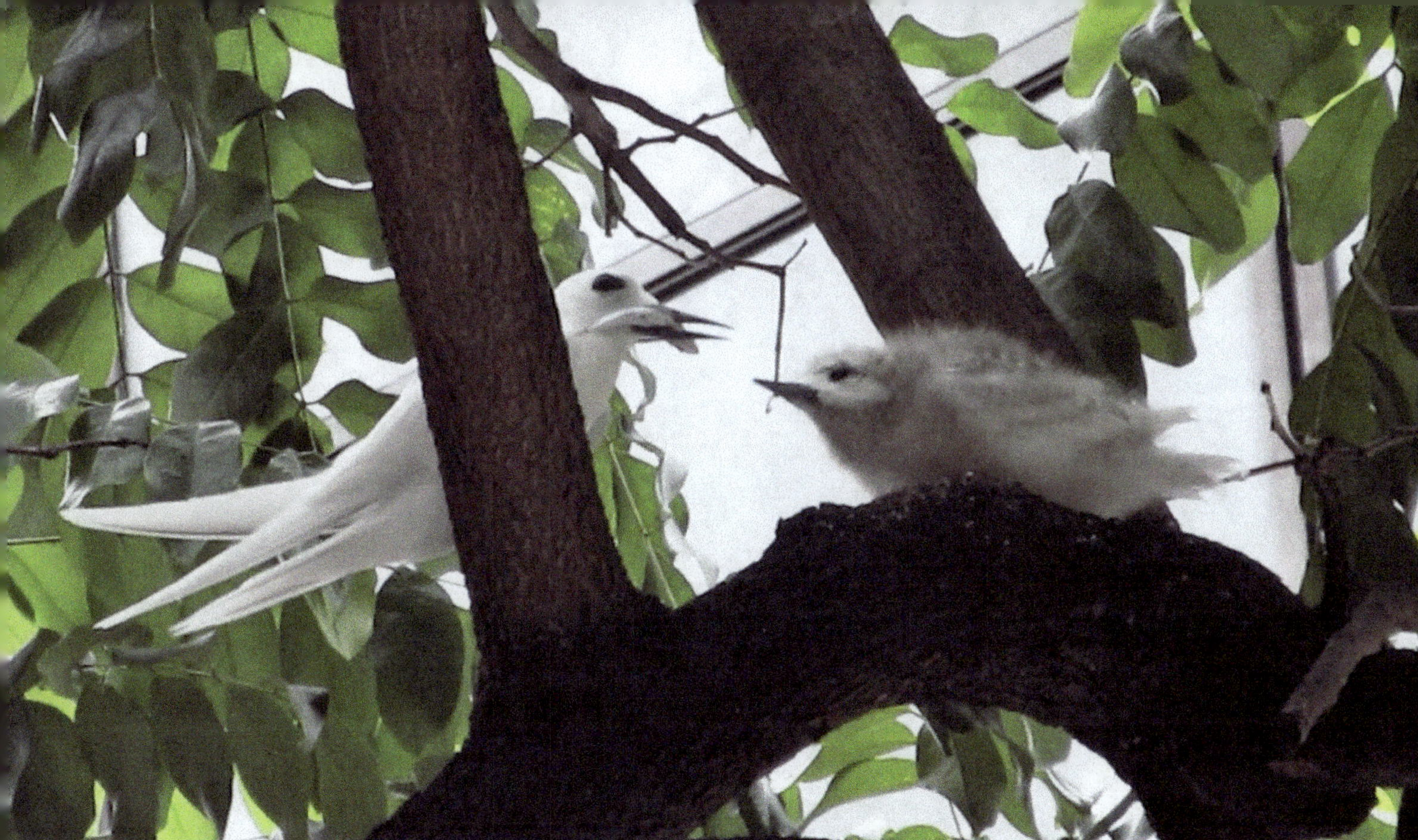

Day 17 after sighting: A parent brings a meal of fish for Skye.

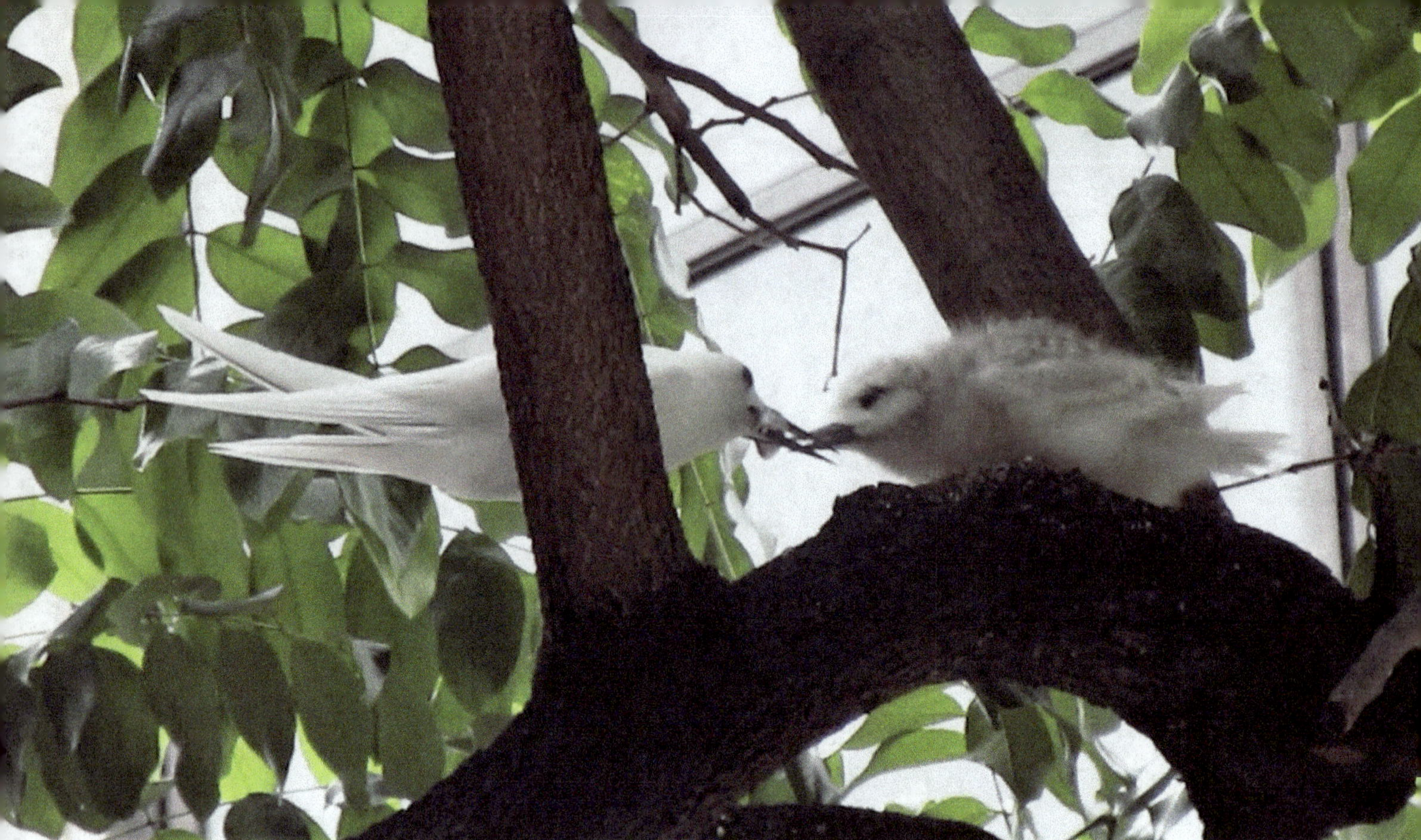

A careful transfer takes place.

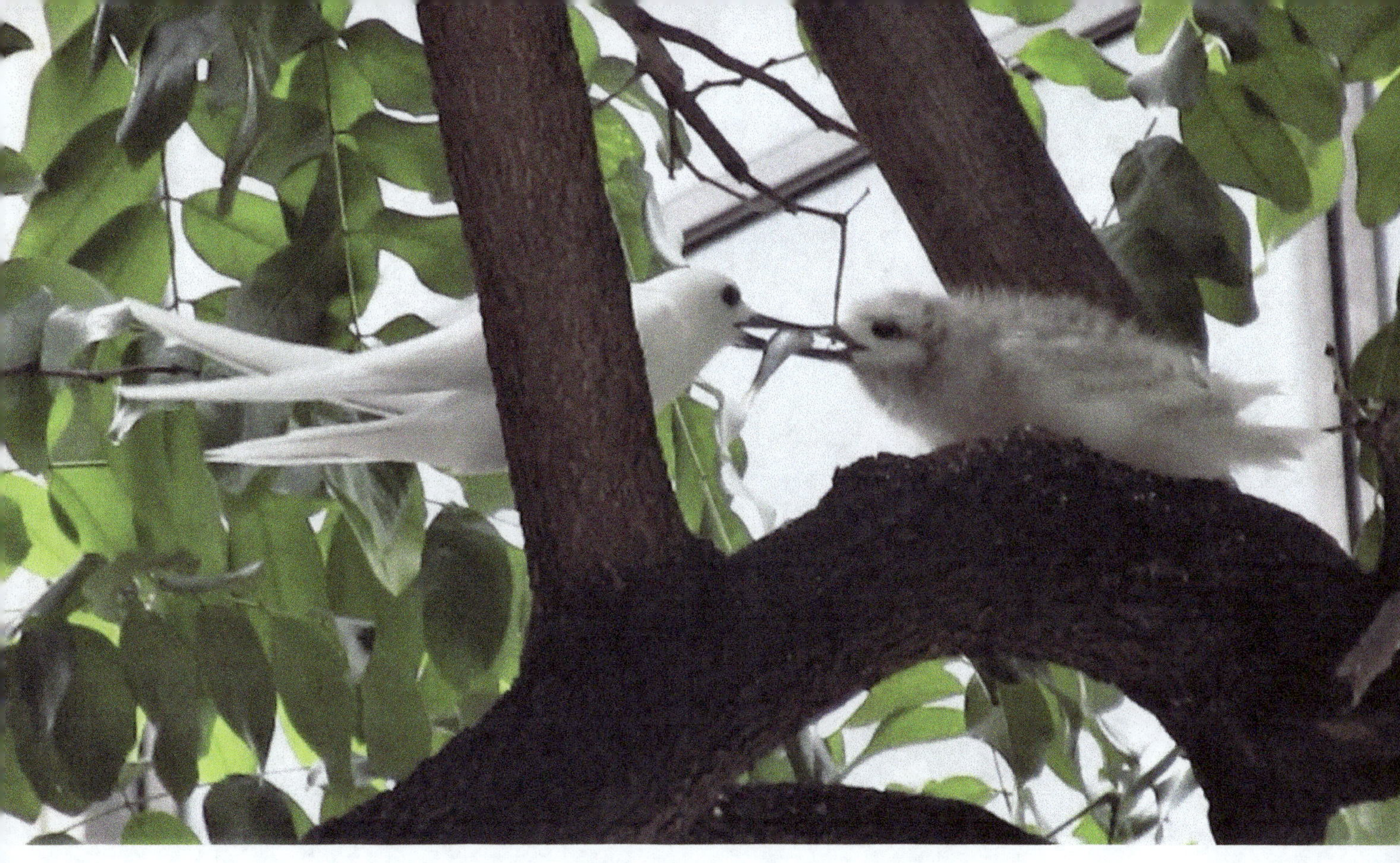

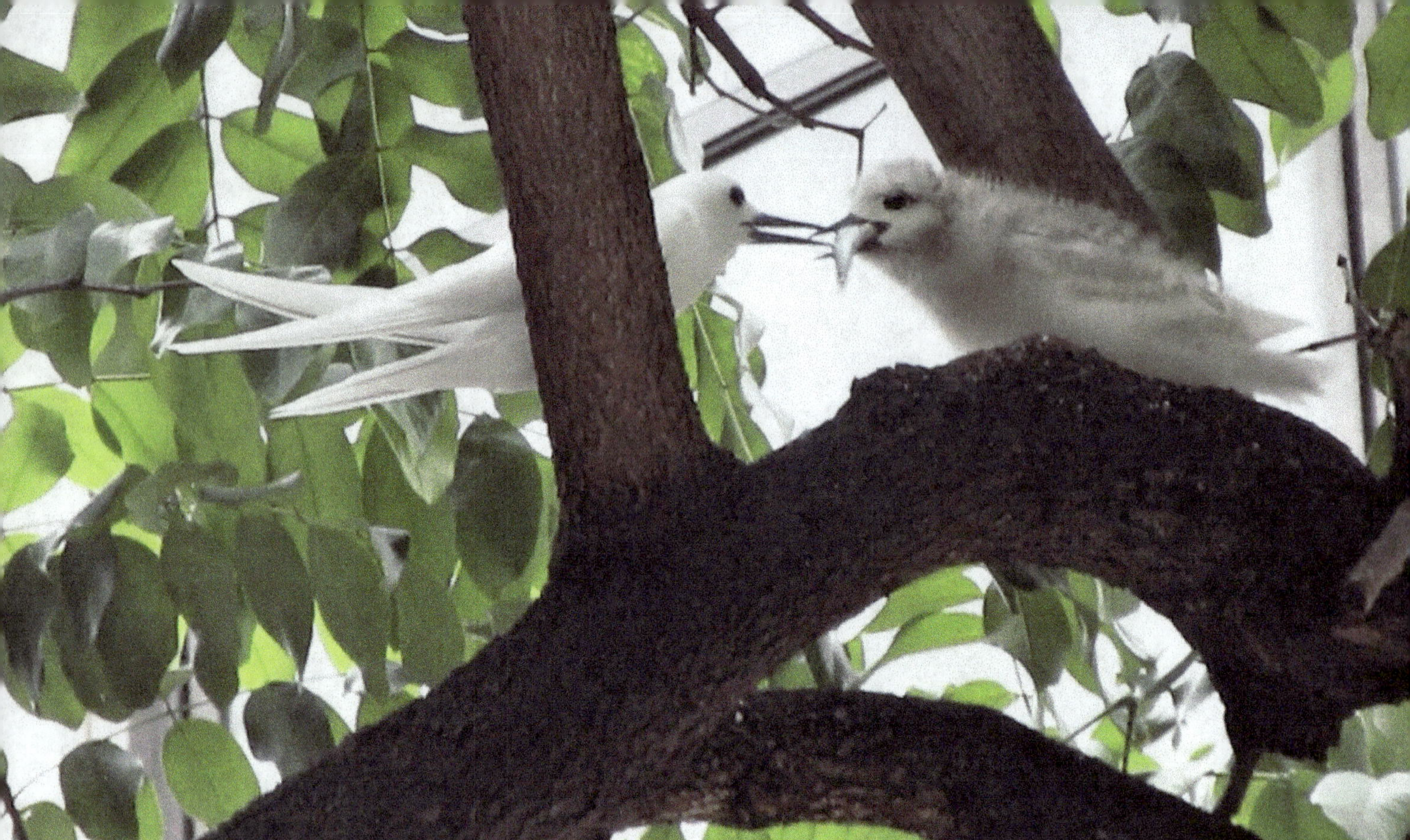

Skye eats the fish, head first.

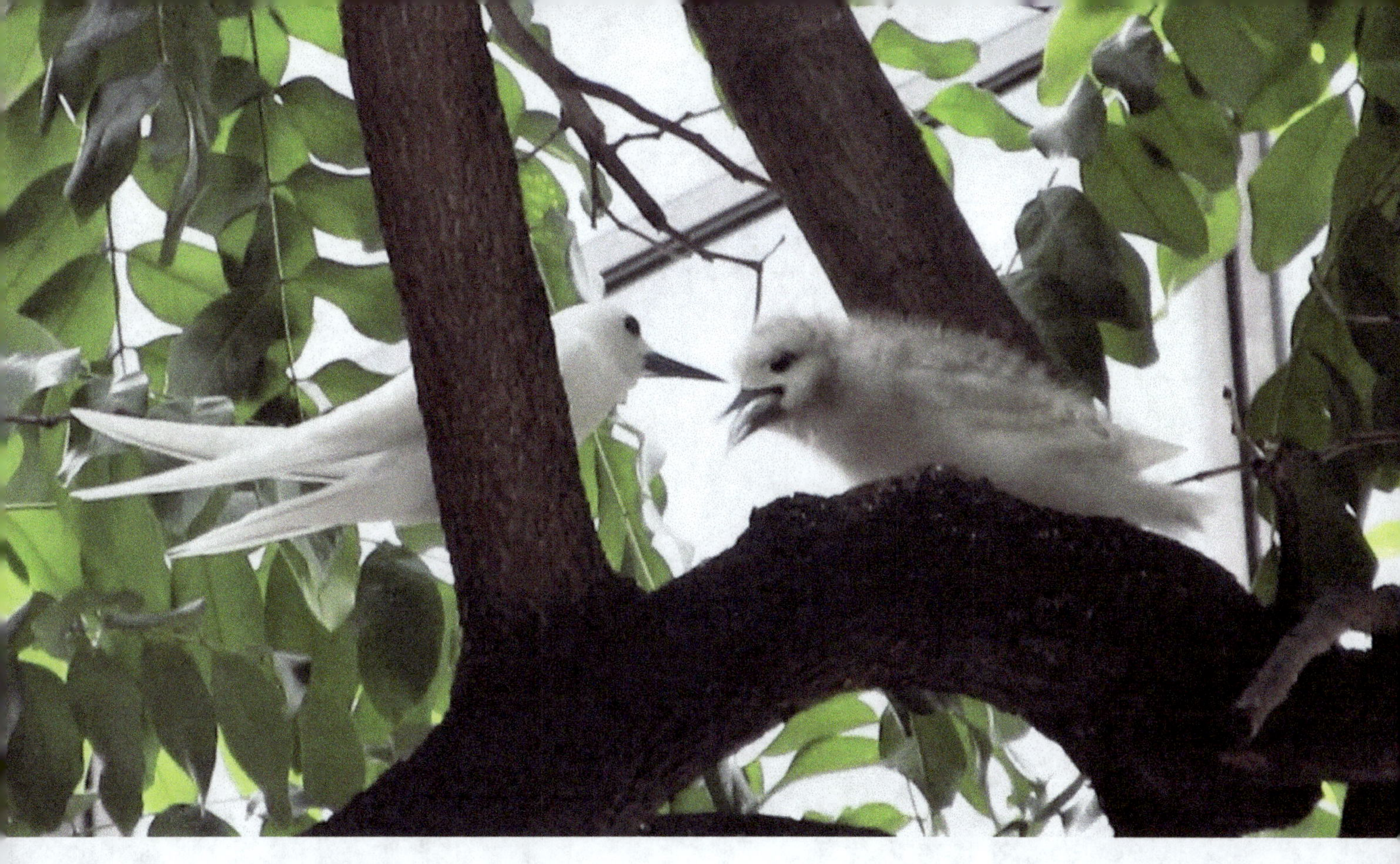

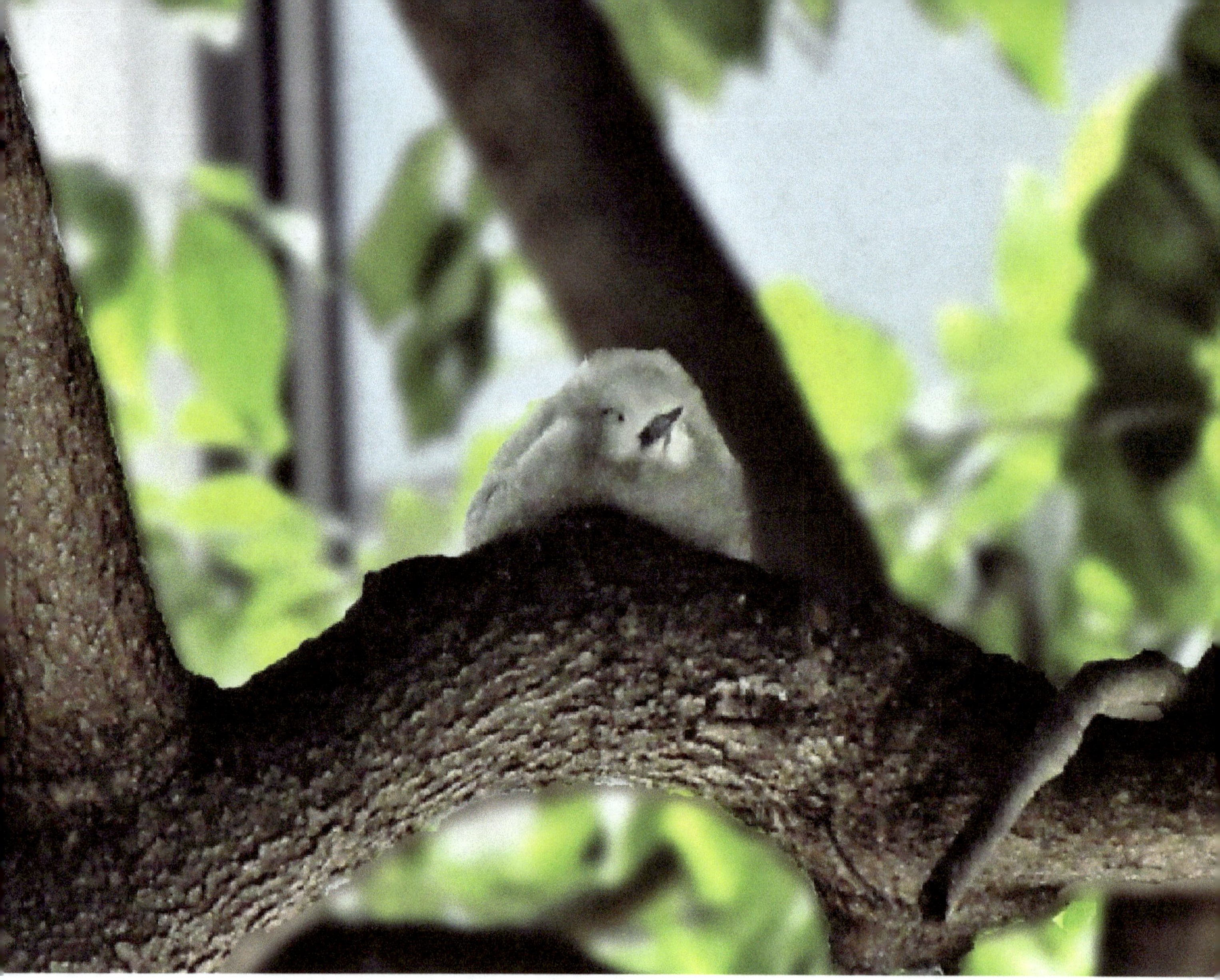

Day 18 after sighting: Skye sleeping

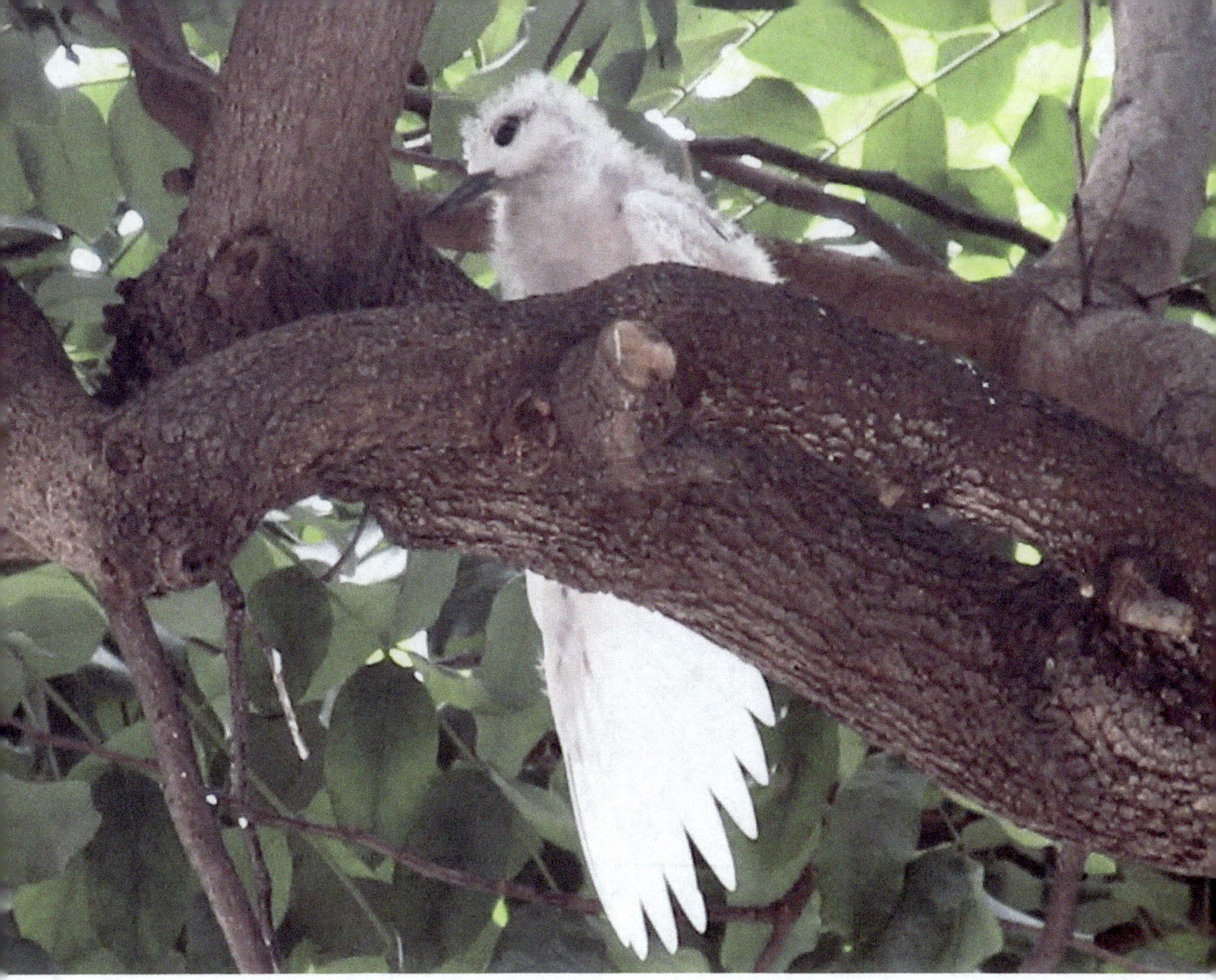

Day 21 after sighting

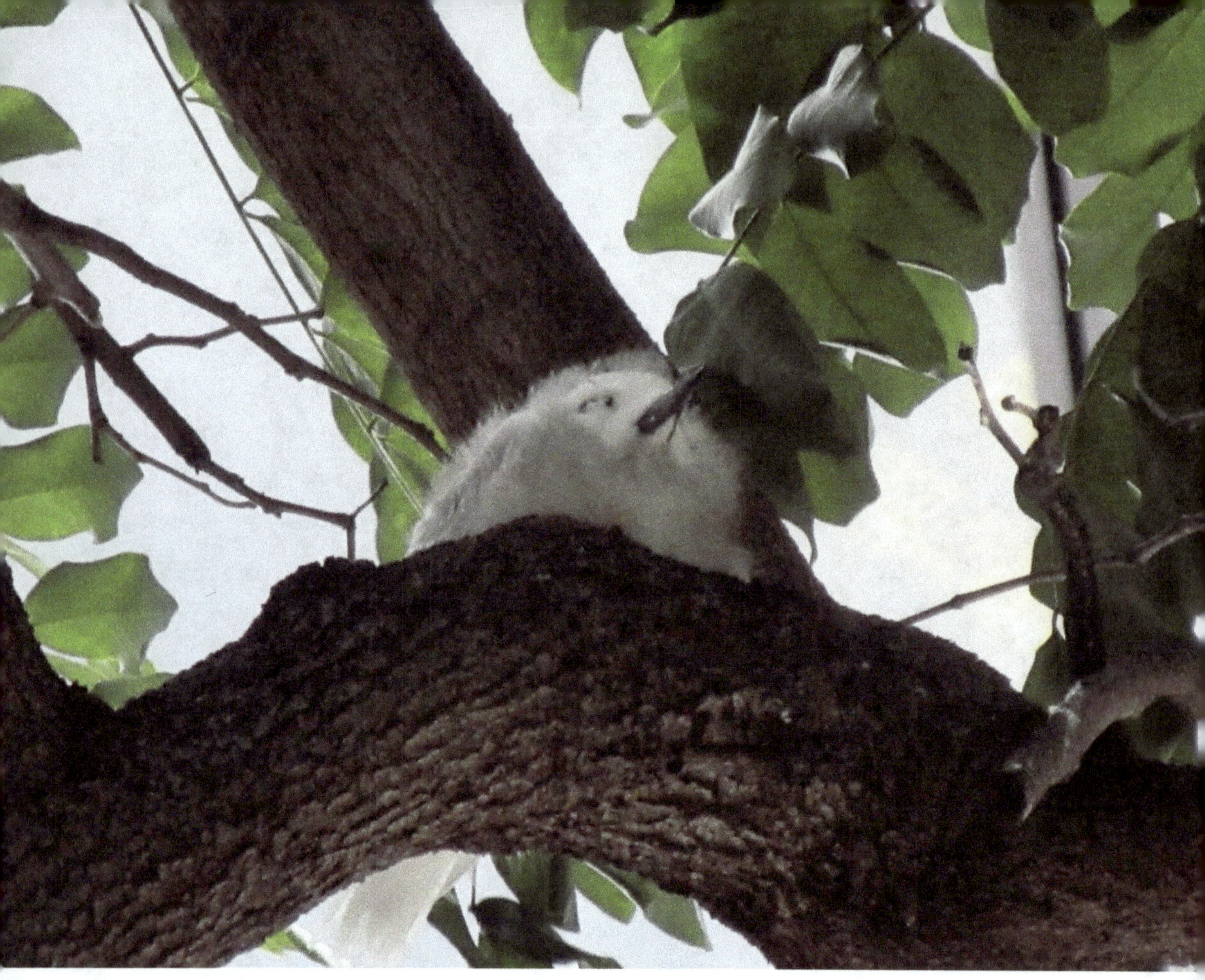

Day 24 after sighting

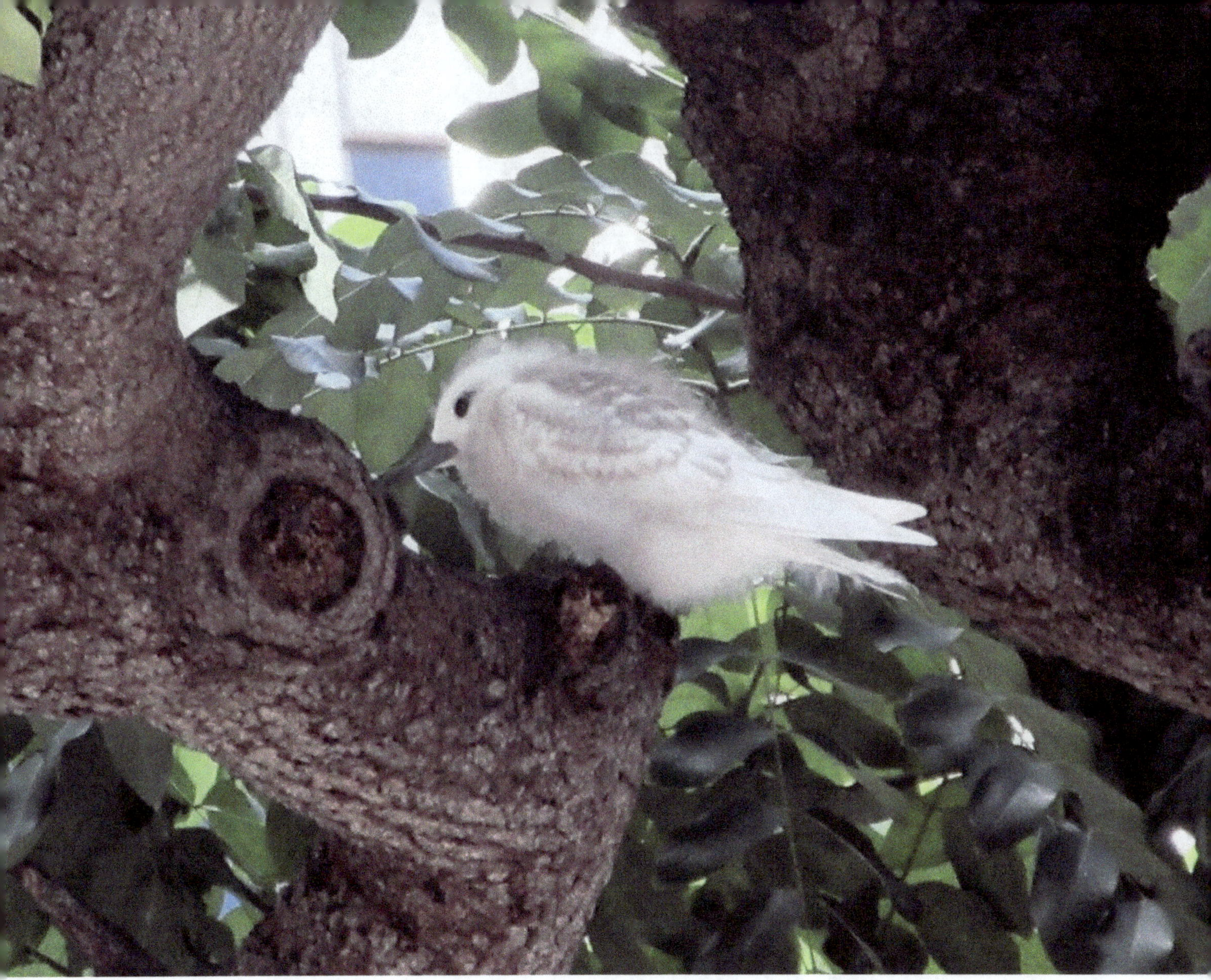

Day 26 after sighting

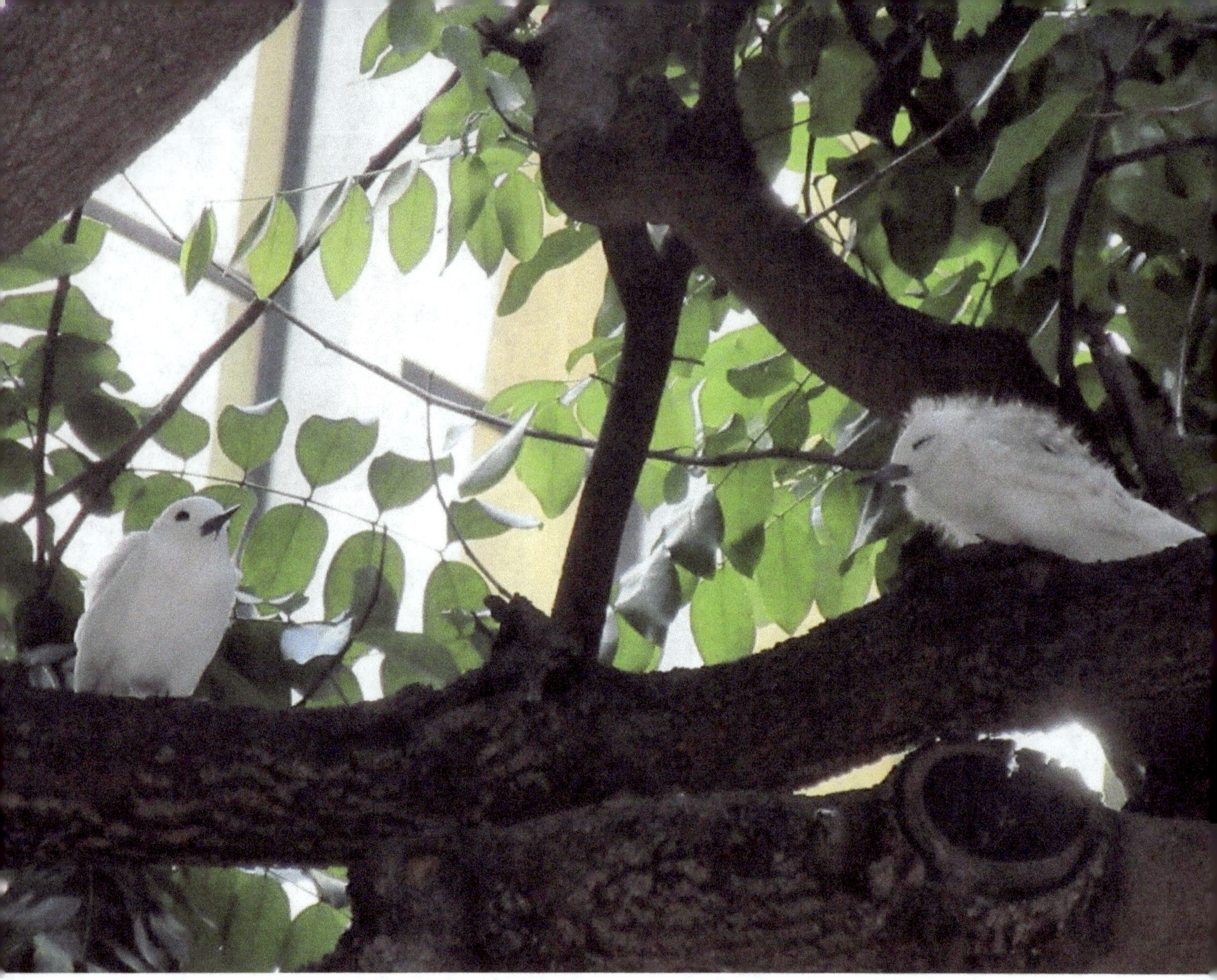

A parent with Skye one month after sighting

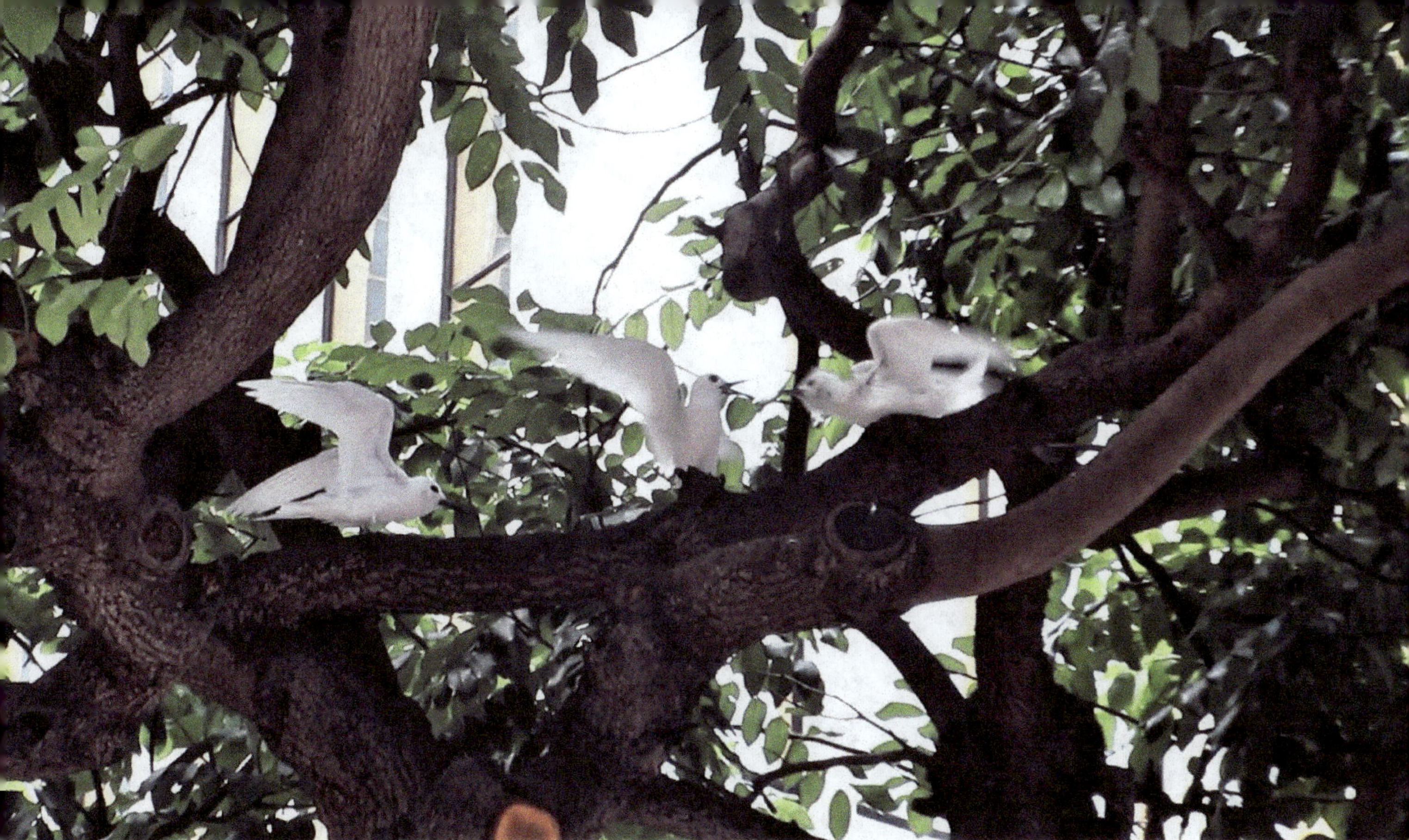

The next day, the parents communicate with Skye before leaving.

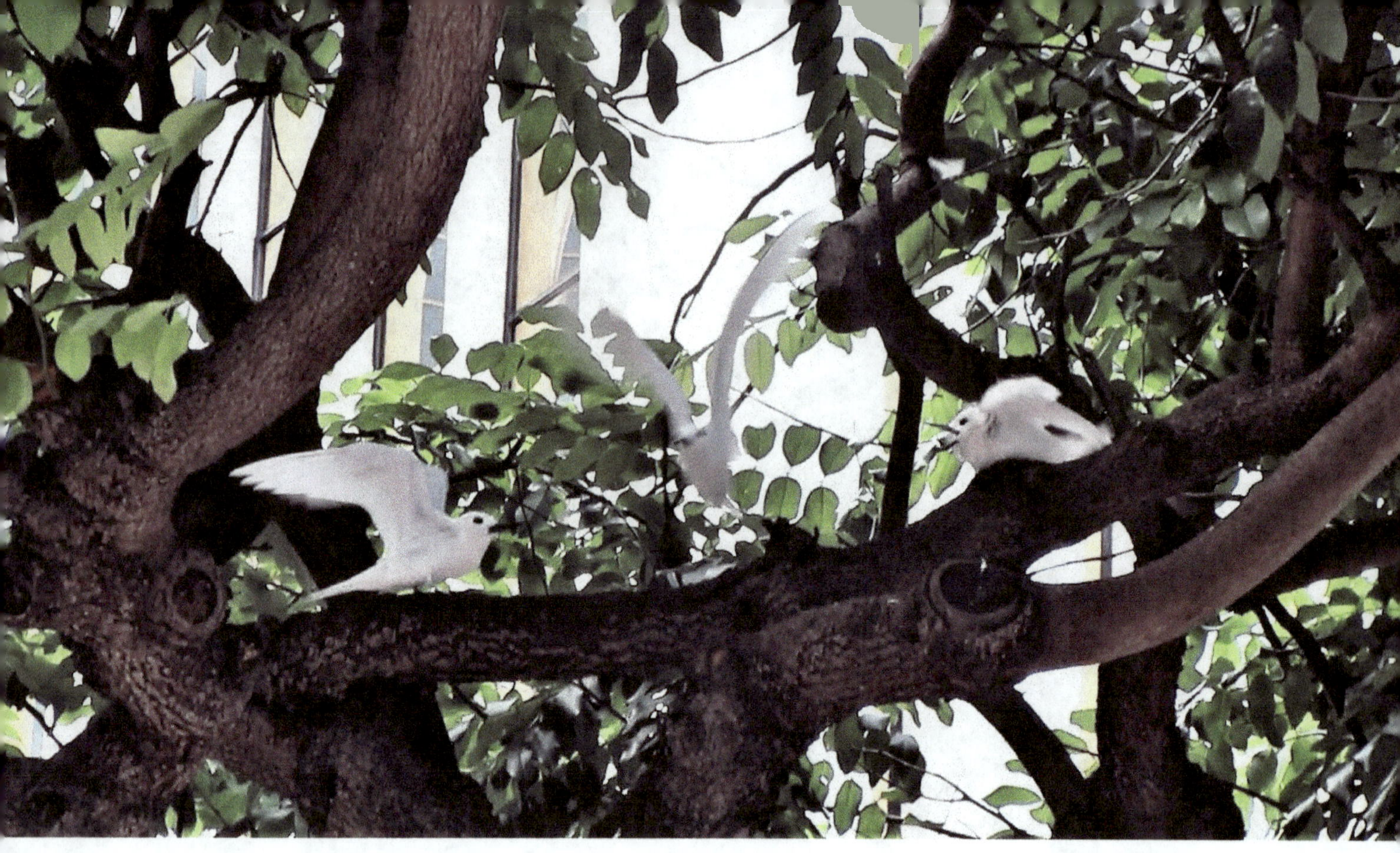

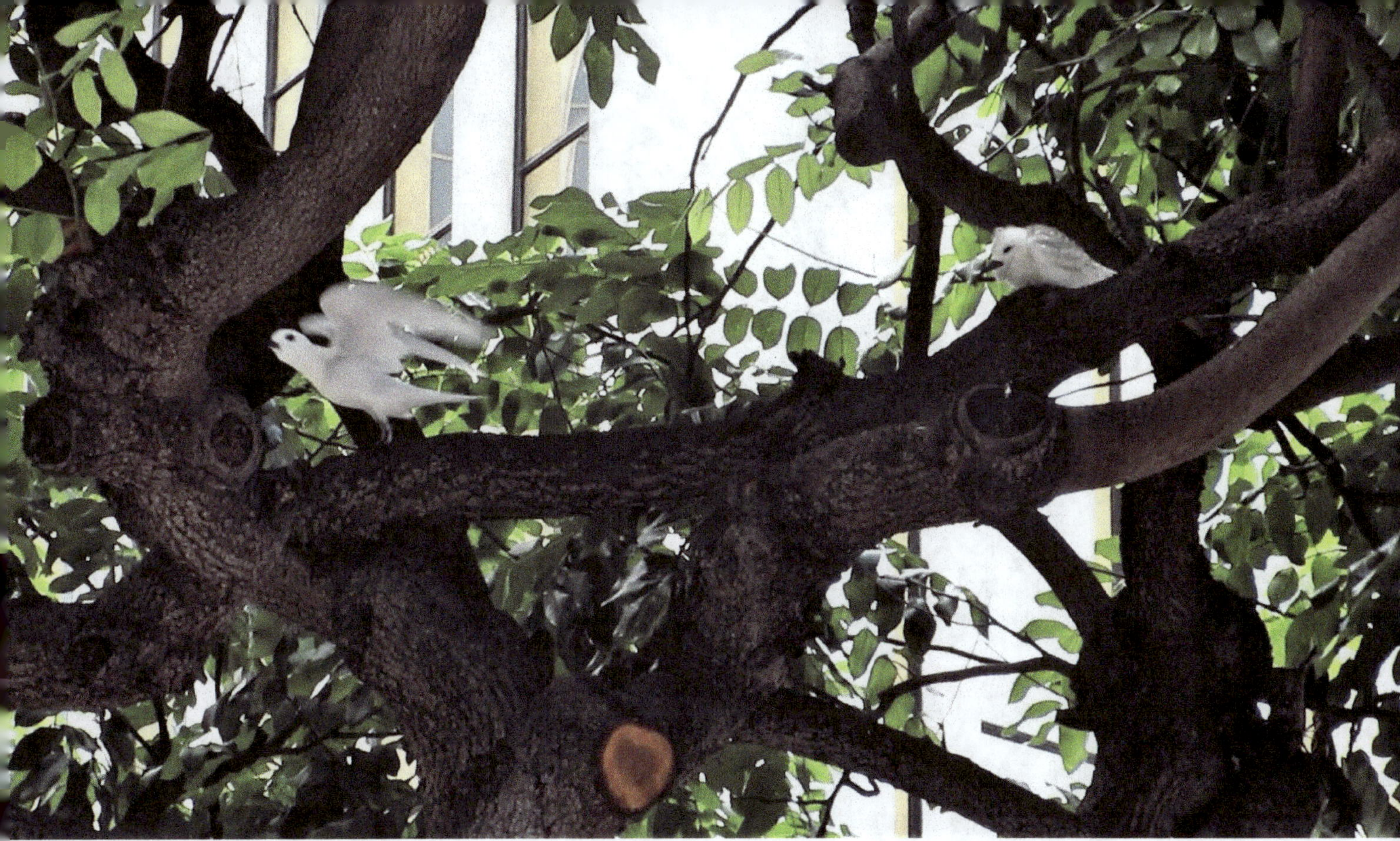

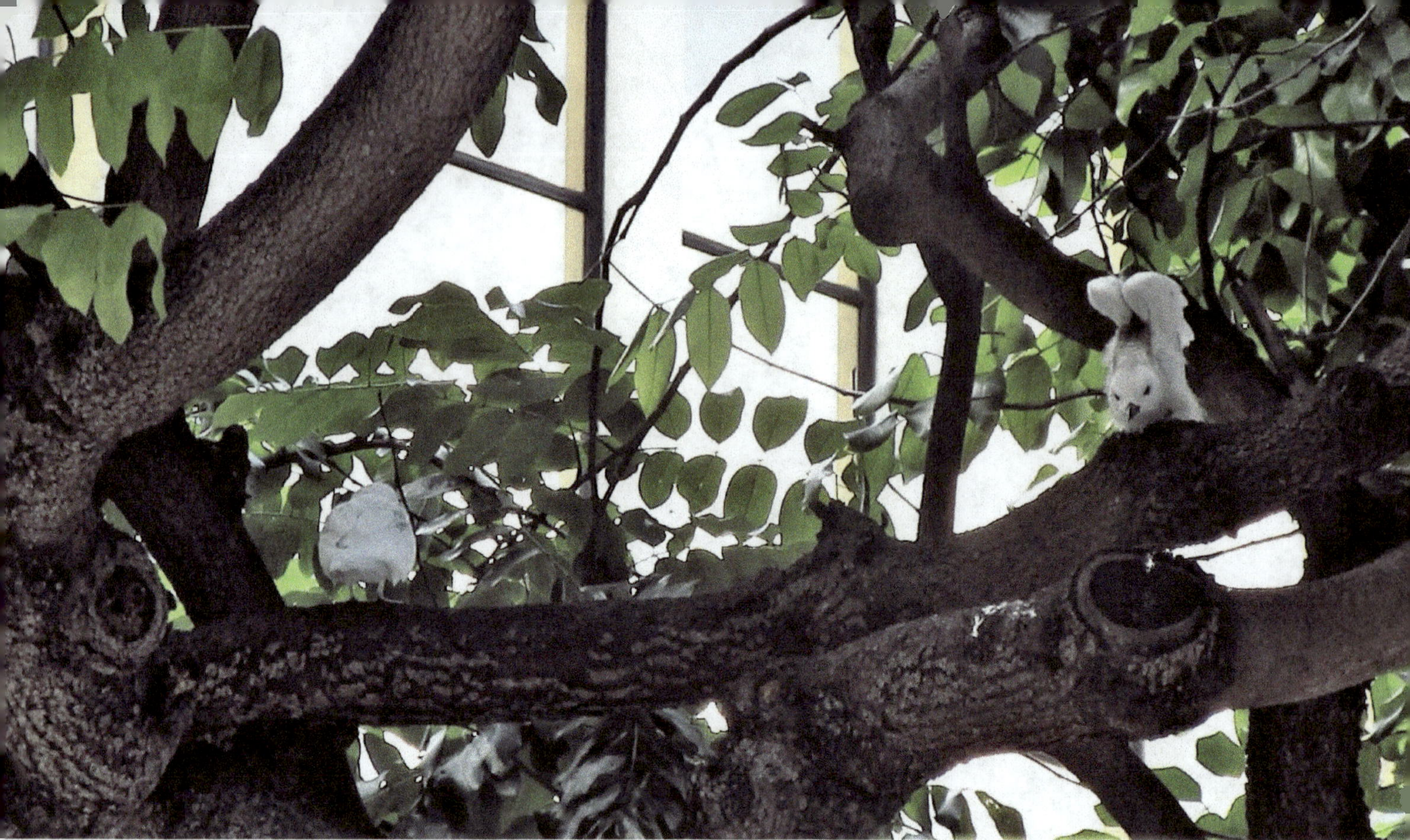

Day 33 after sighting: Skye stretches and balances on a branch to walk over to a parent.

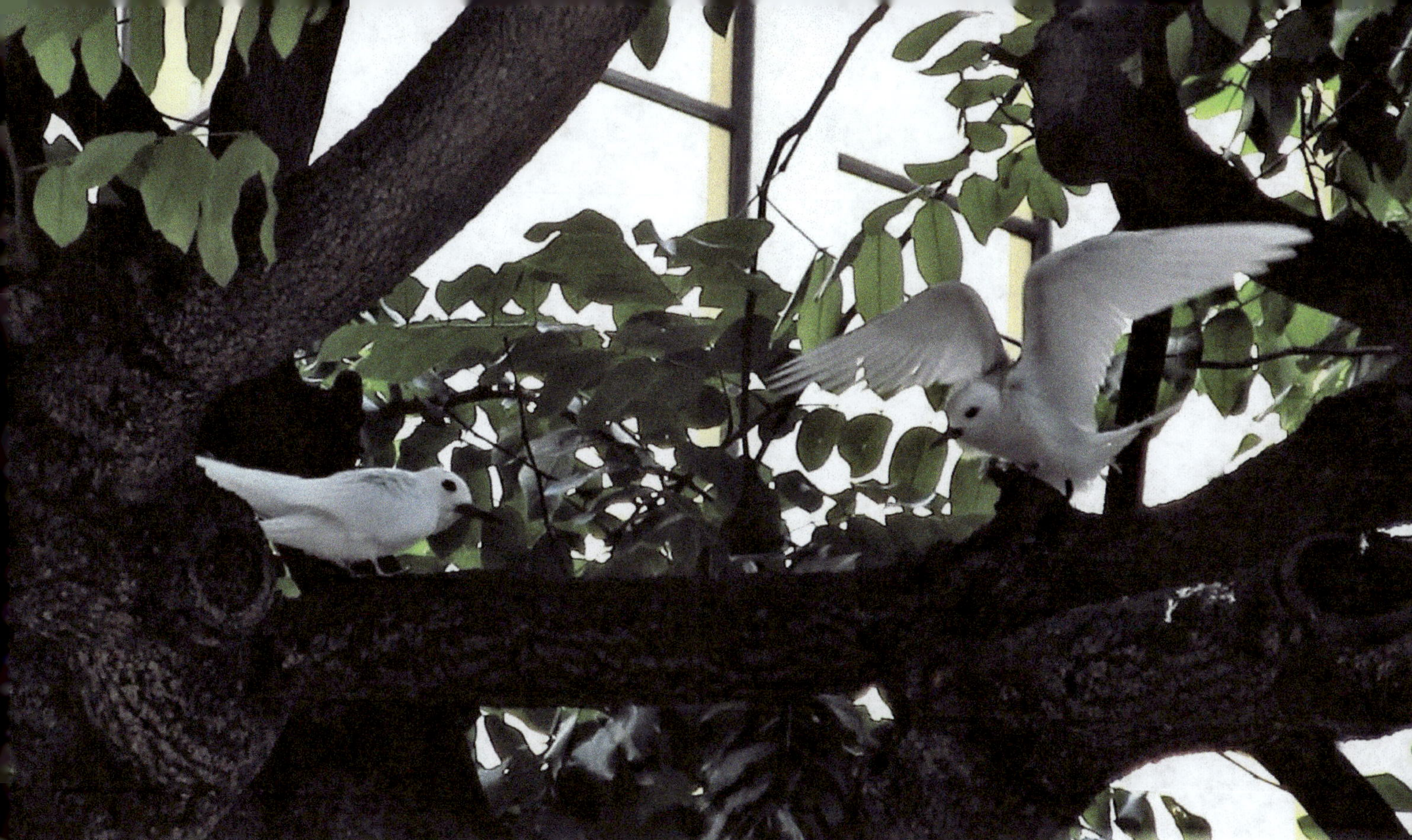

The parent observes Skye's progress.

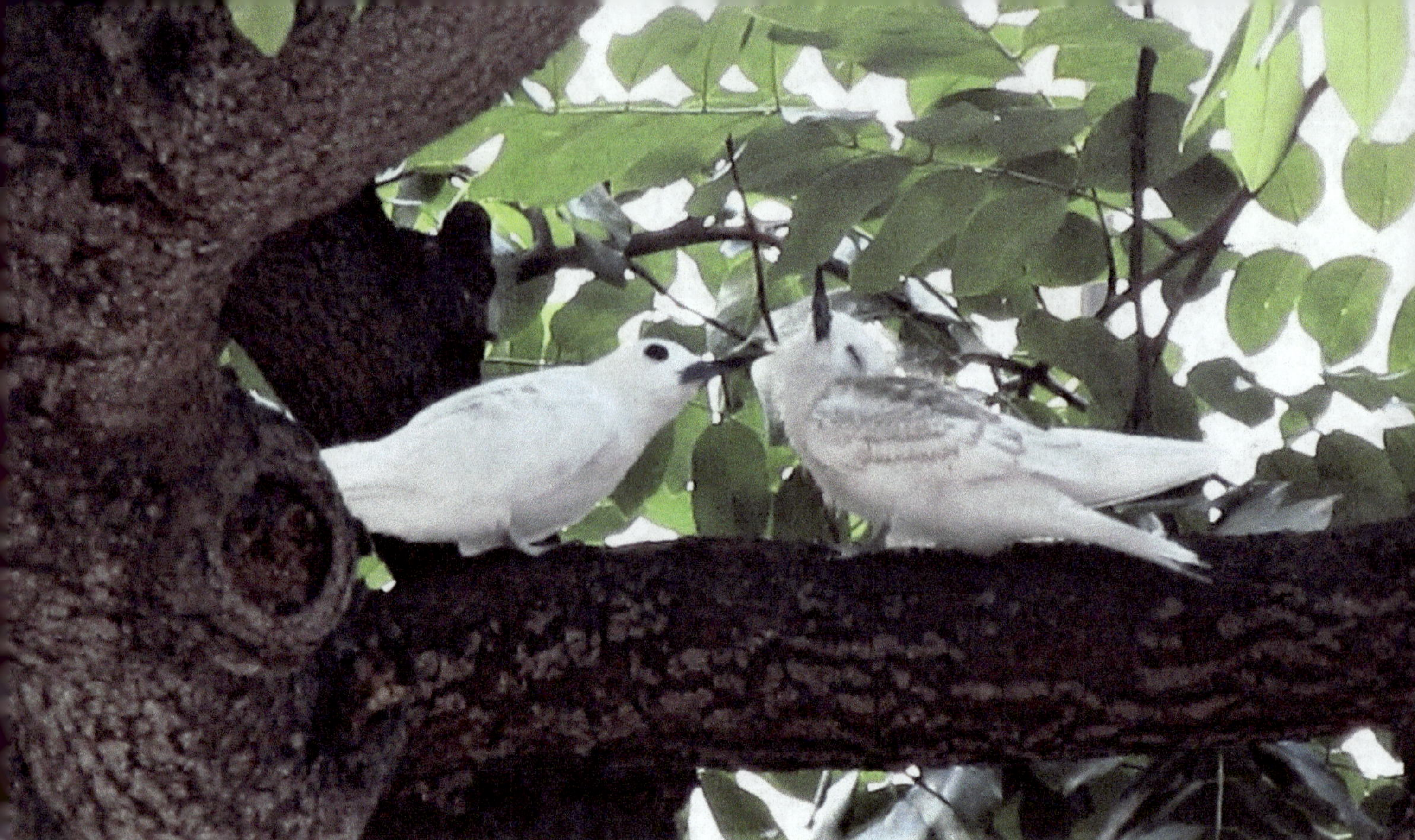

Skye is rewarded with some preening for making it all the way.

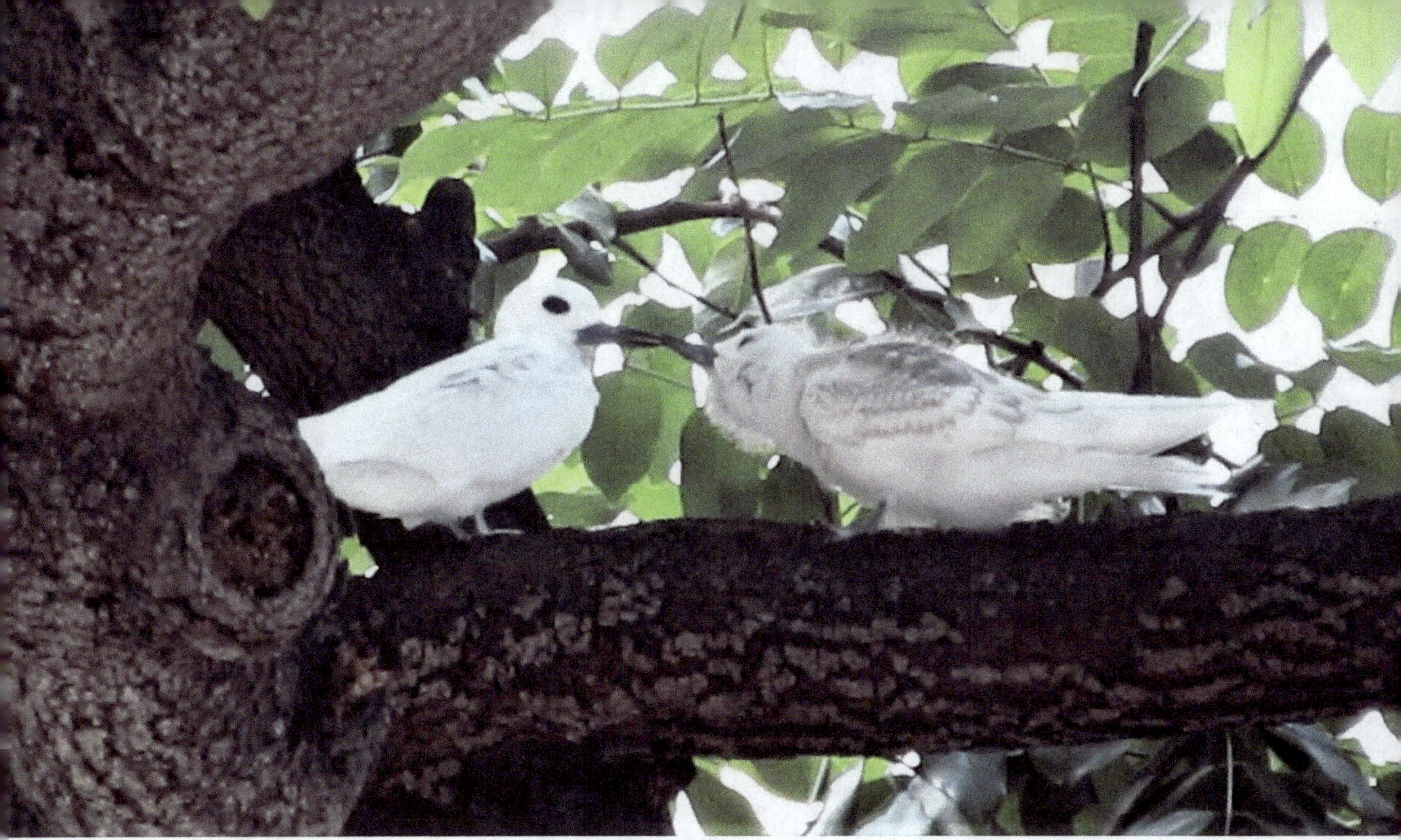

Skye returns the favor.

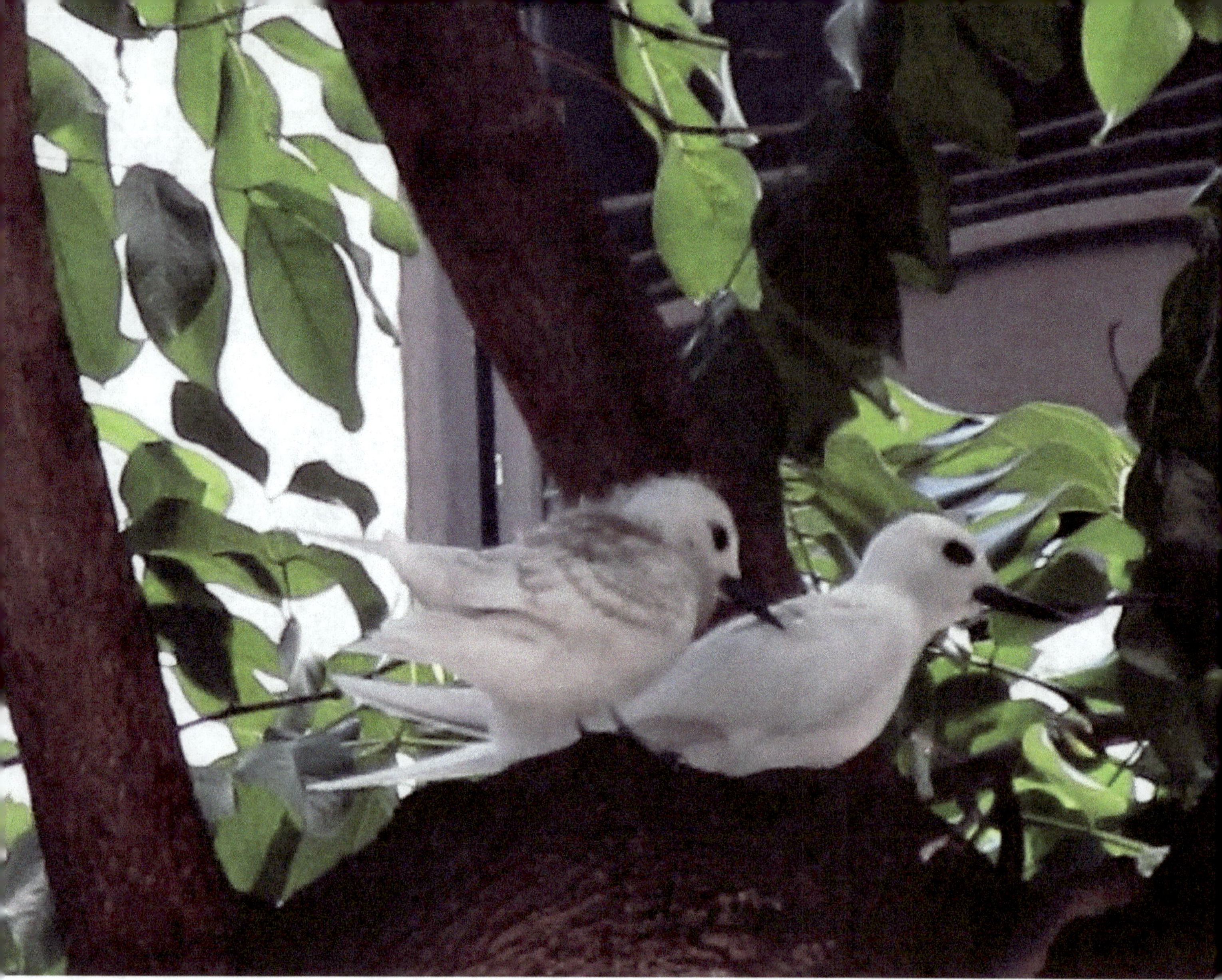

Skye scratches a parent's back.

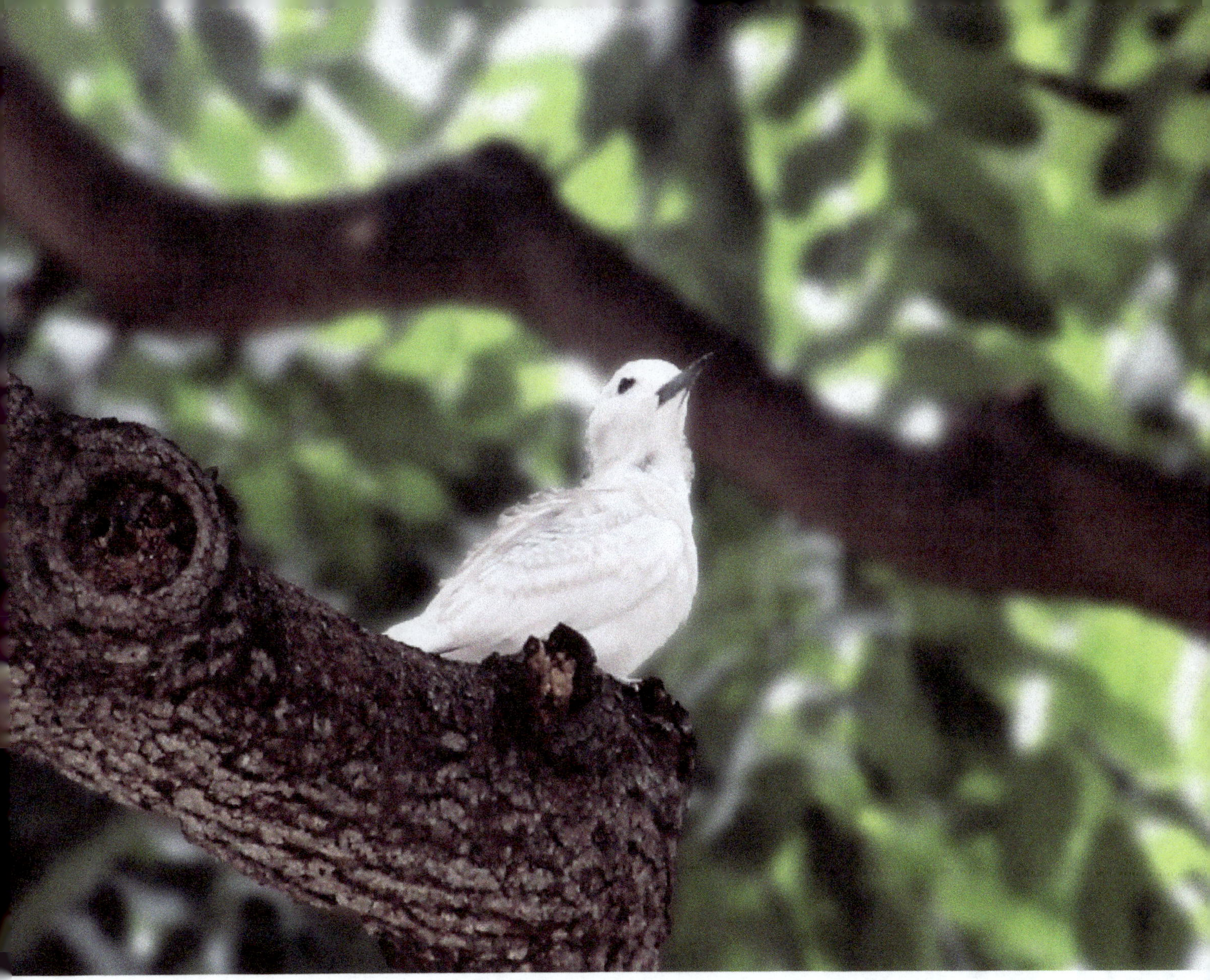

Day 35 after sighting

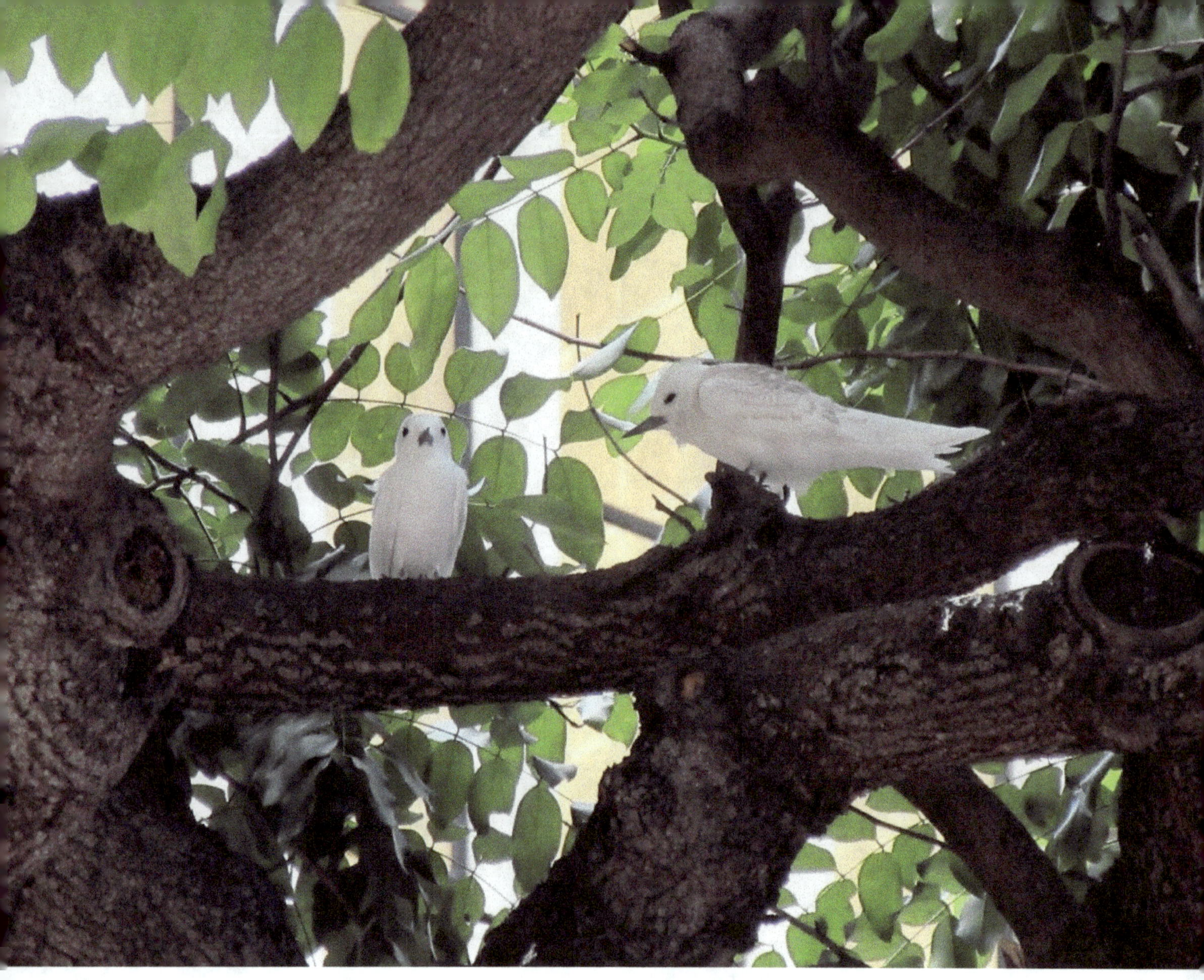

Day 38 after sighting: A parent with Skye

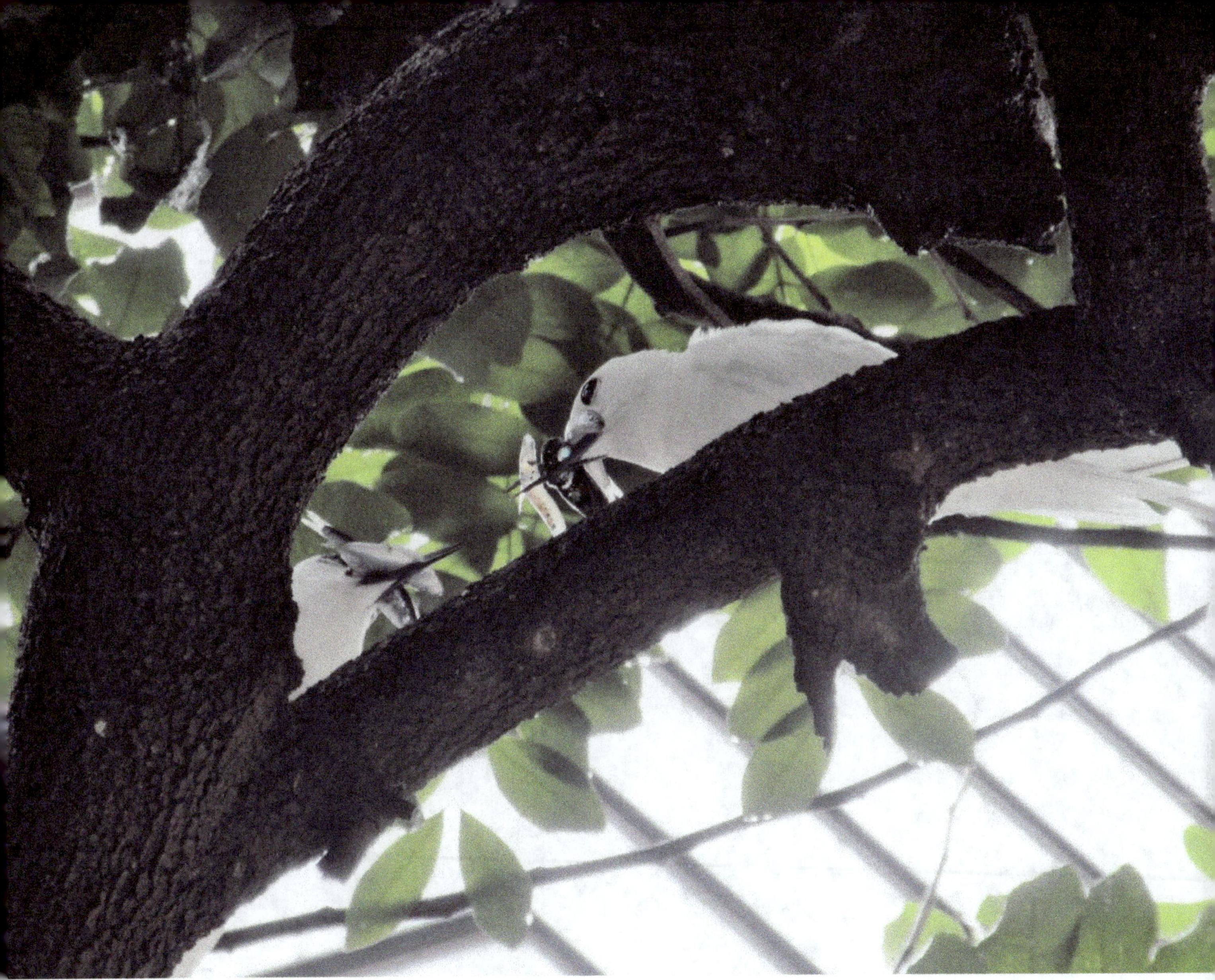

Day 42 after sighting: The parents bring fish for Skye.

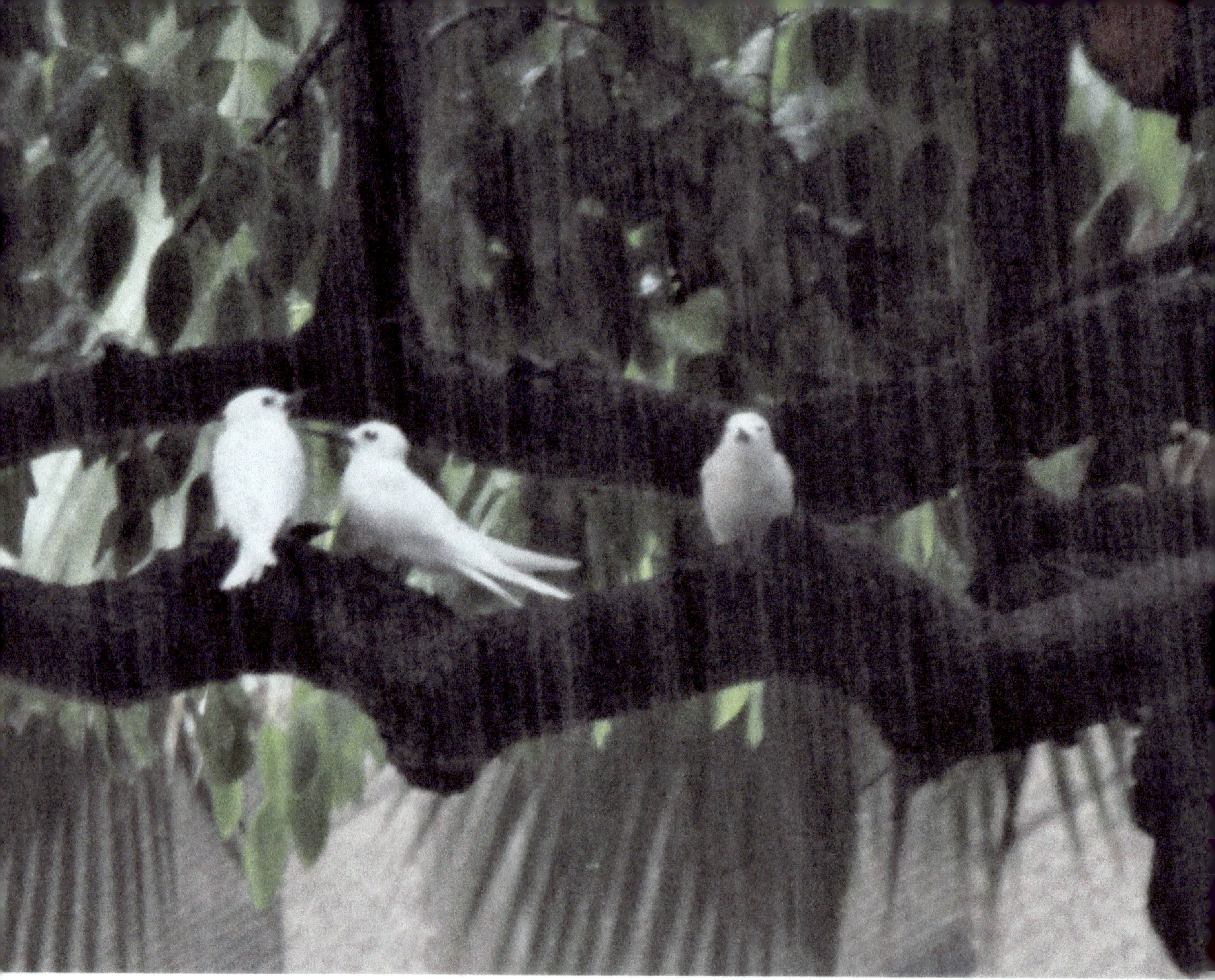

The family is caught in a sudden downpour.

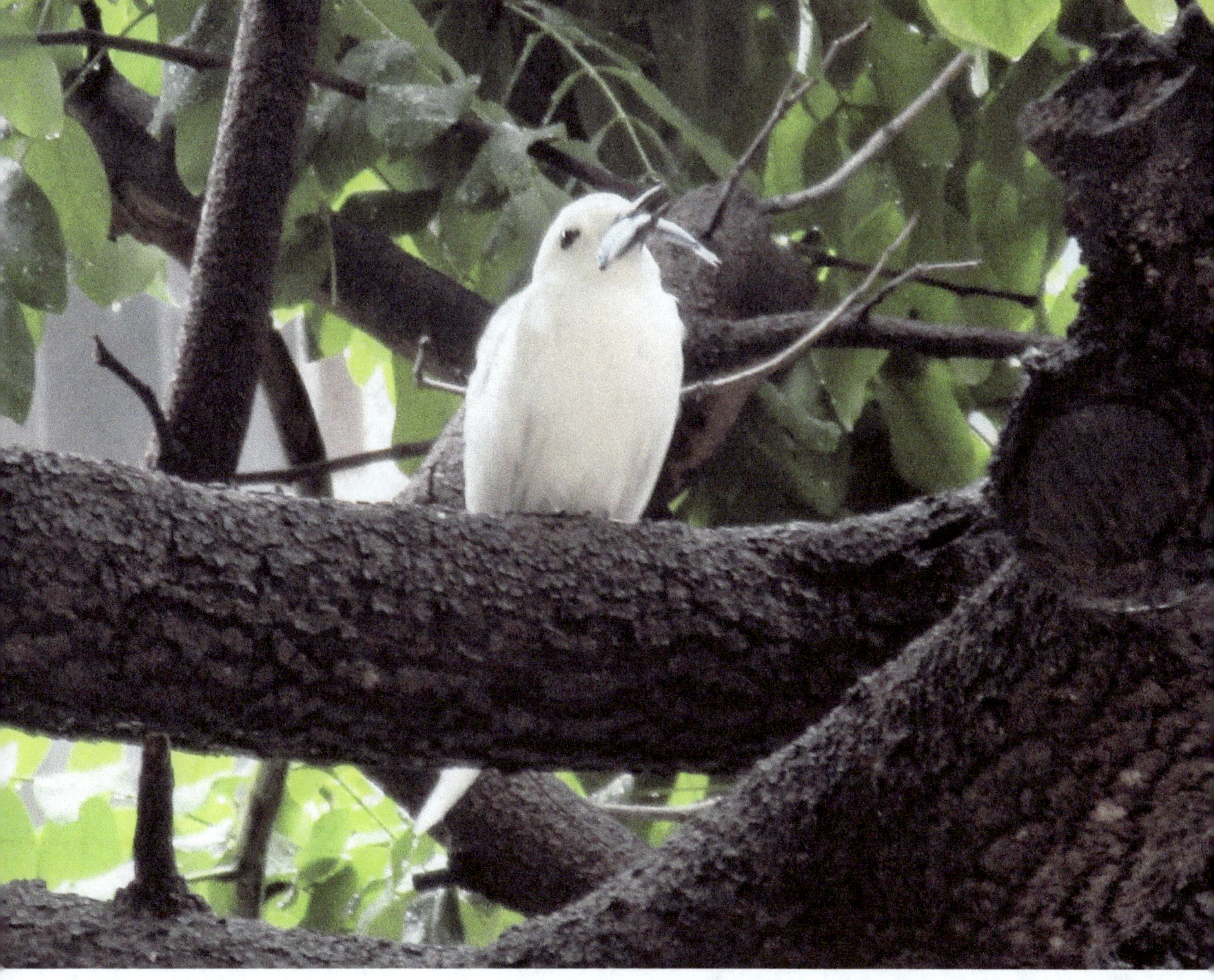

Day 44 after sighting: A parent with a fish patiently waits for Skye to return after fledging.

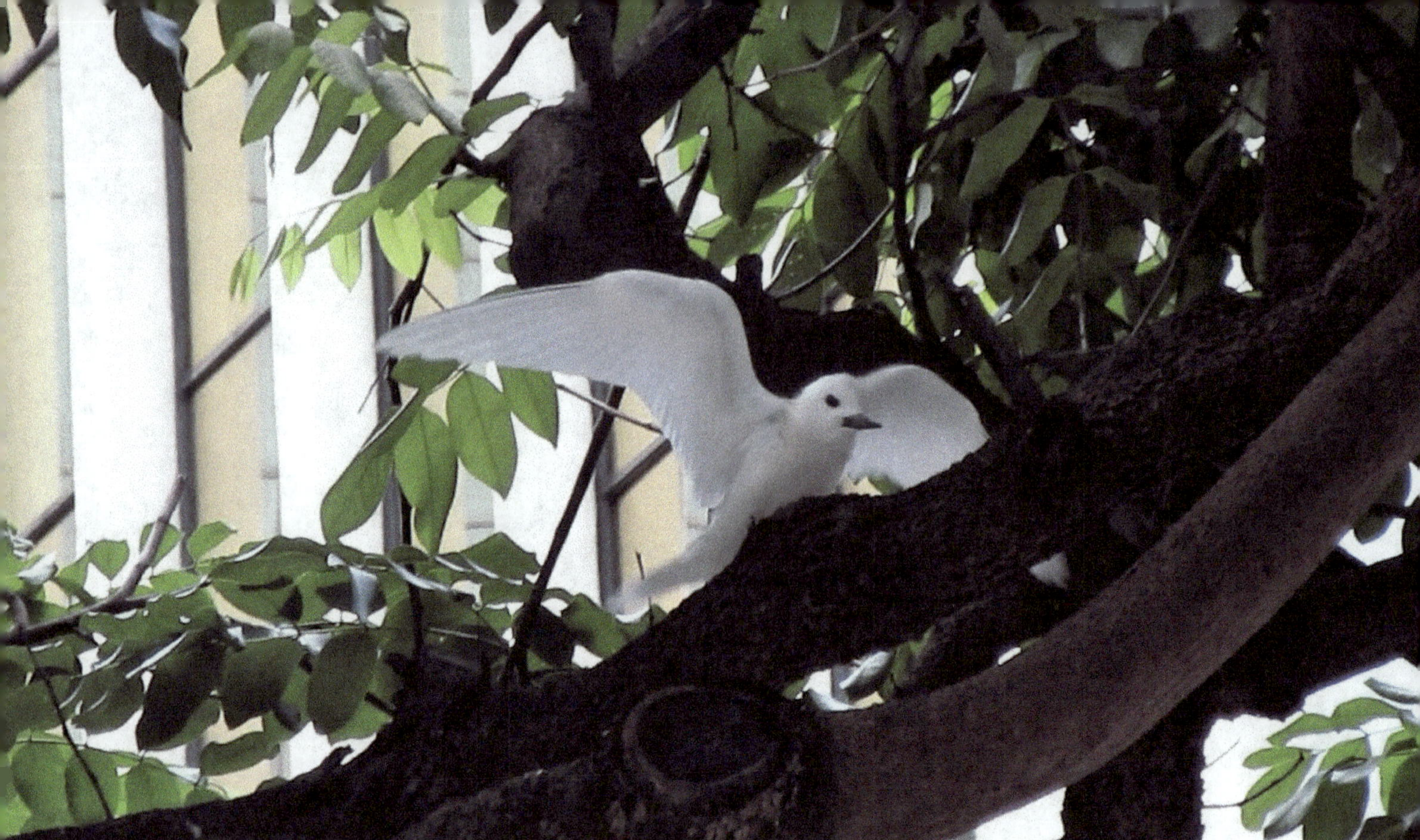

Day 46 after sighting: Skye returns to the tree after fledging.

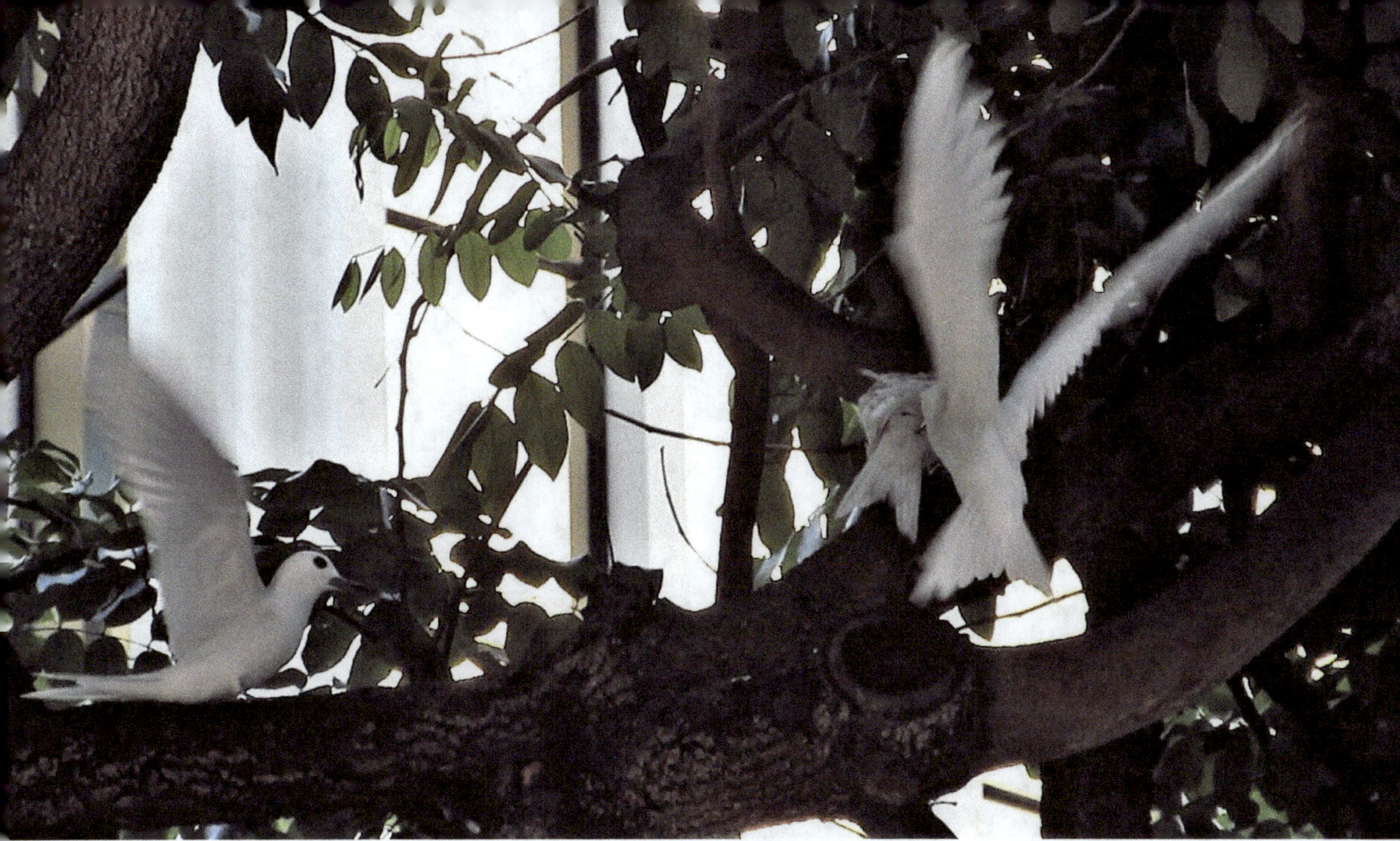

Day 47 after sighting: A parent returns and appears to poke Skye in the back.

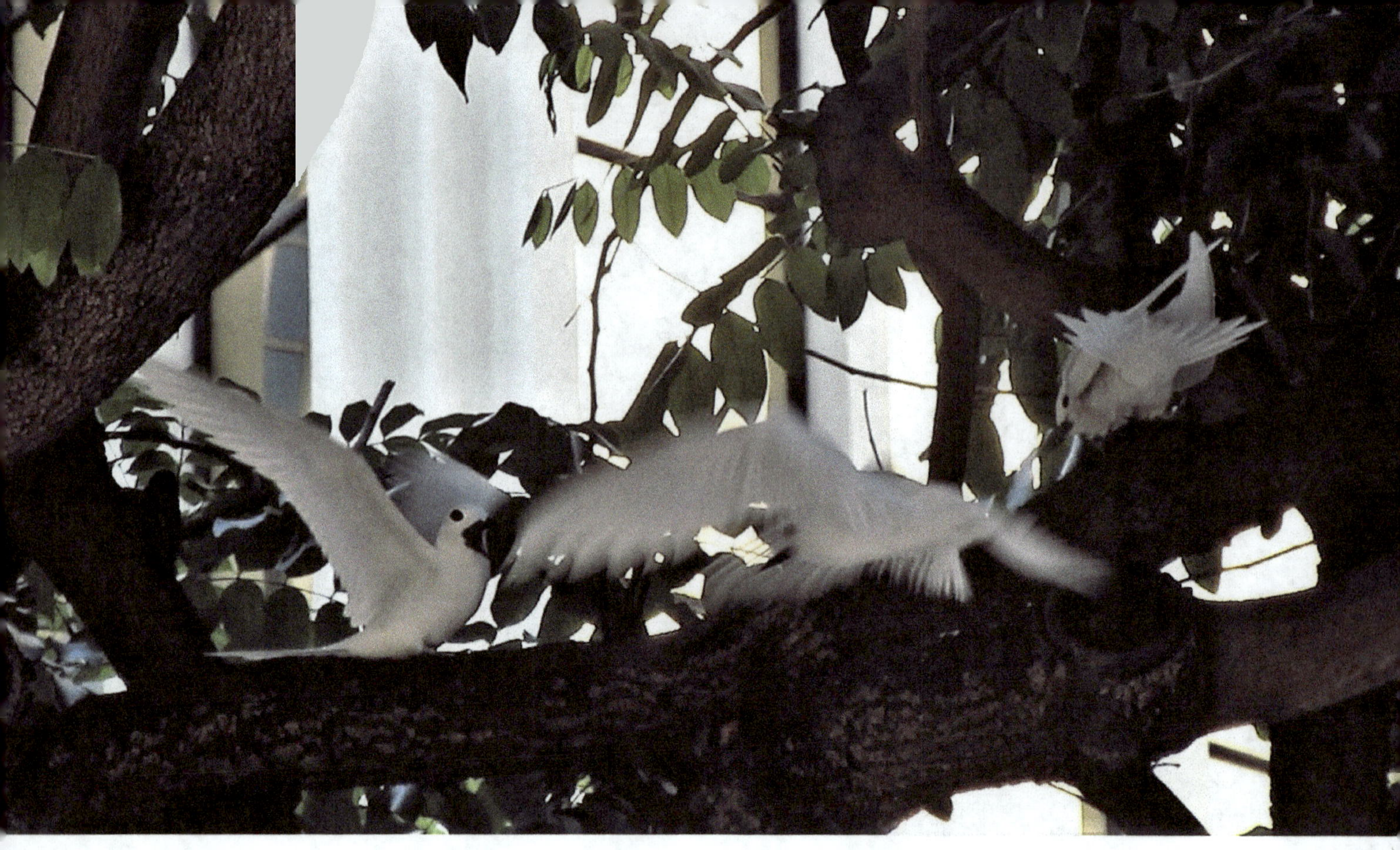

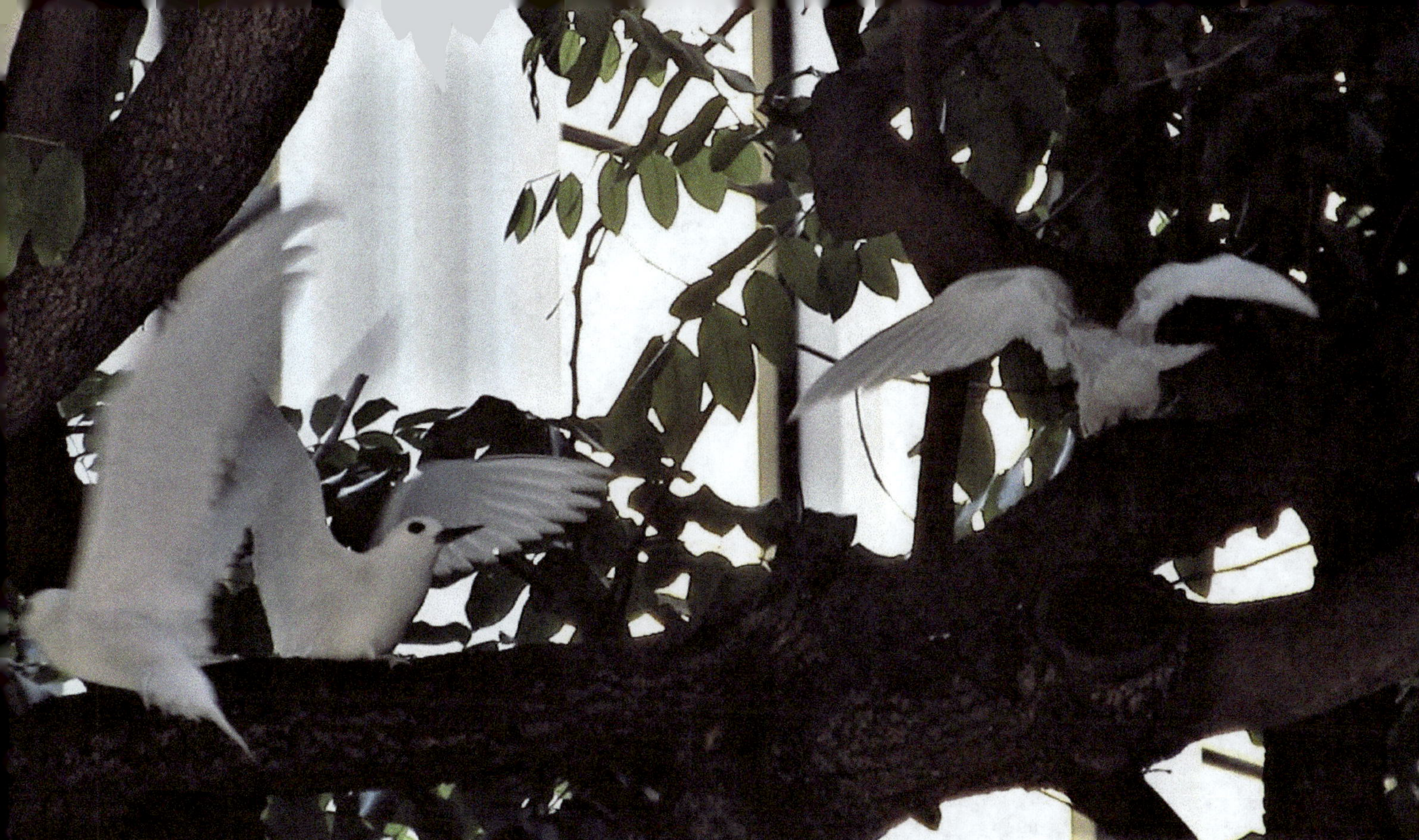

The parent immediately flies away.

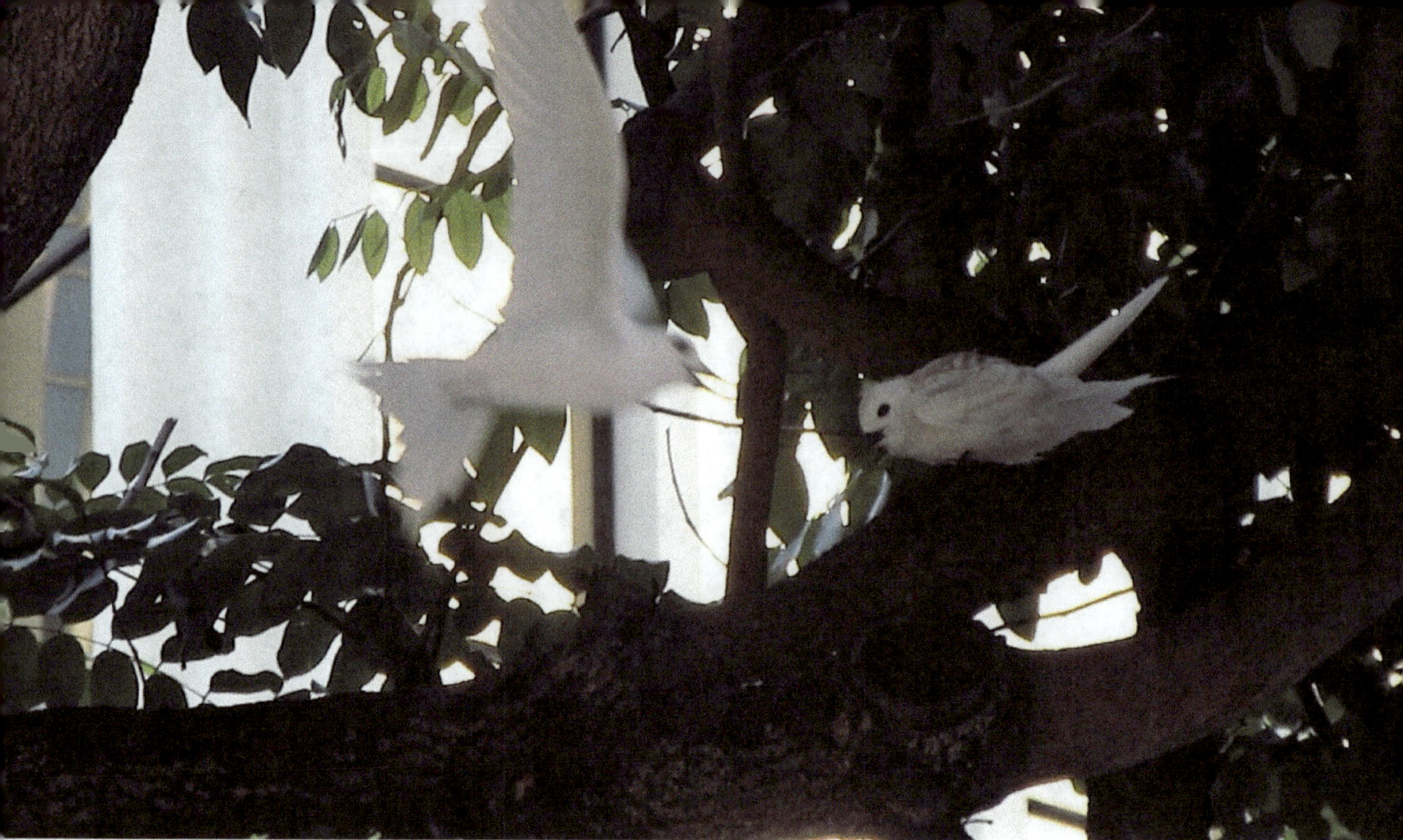

The other parent flies away, too.

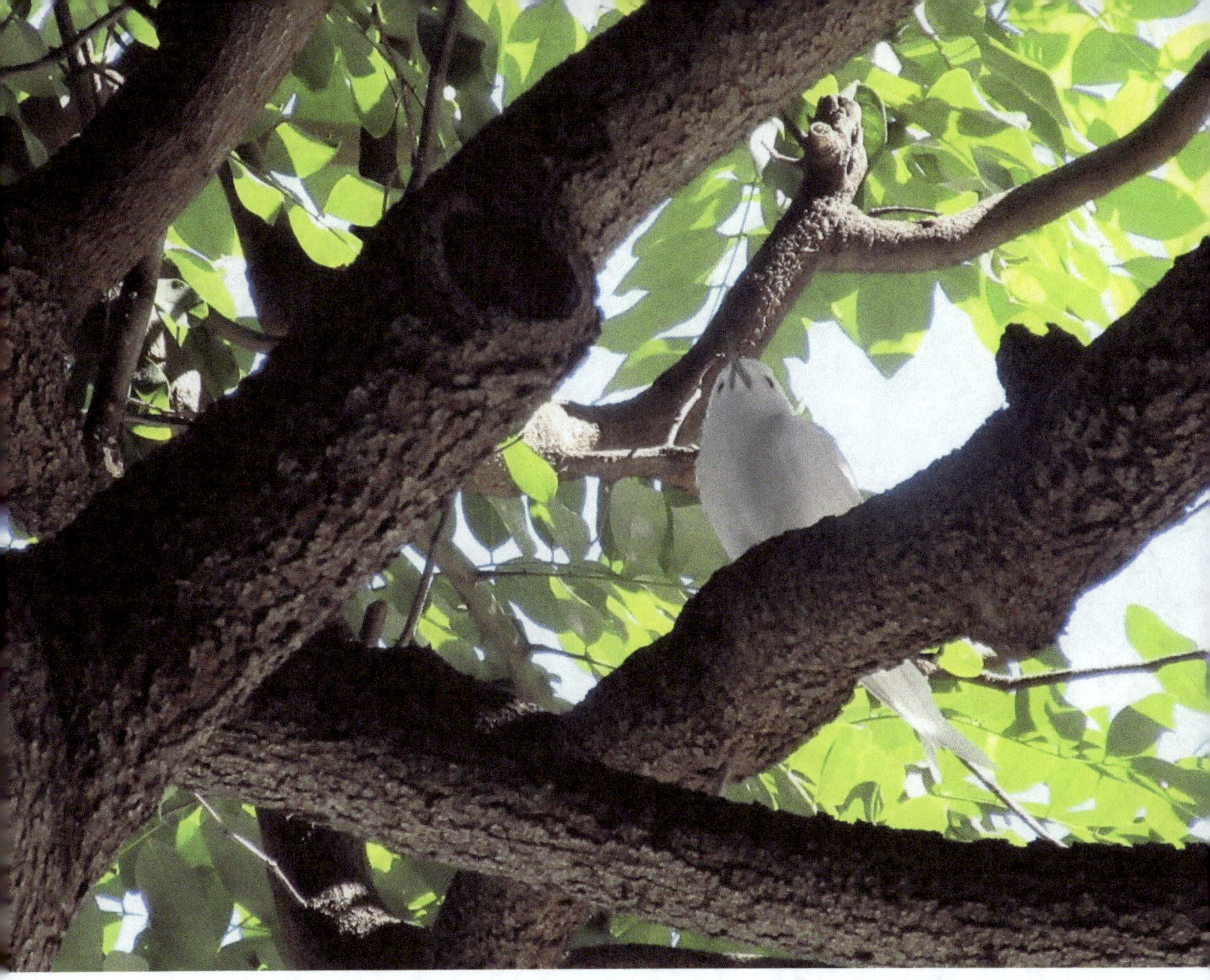

Day 56 after sighting: Skye returns to the tree.

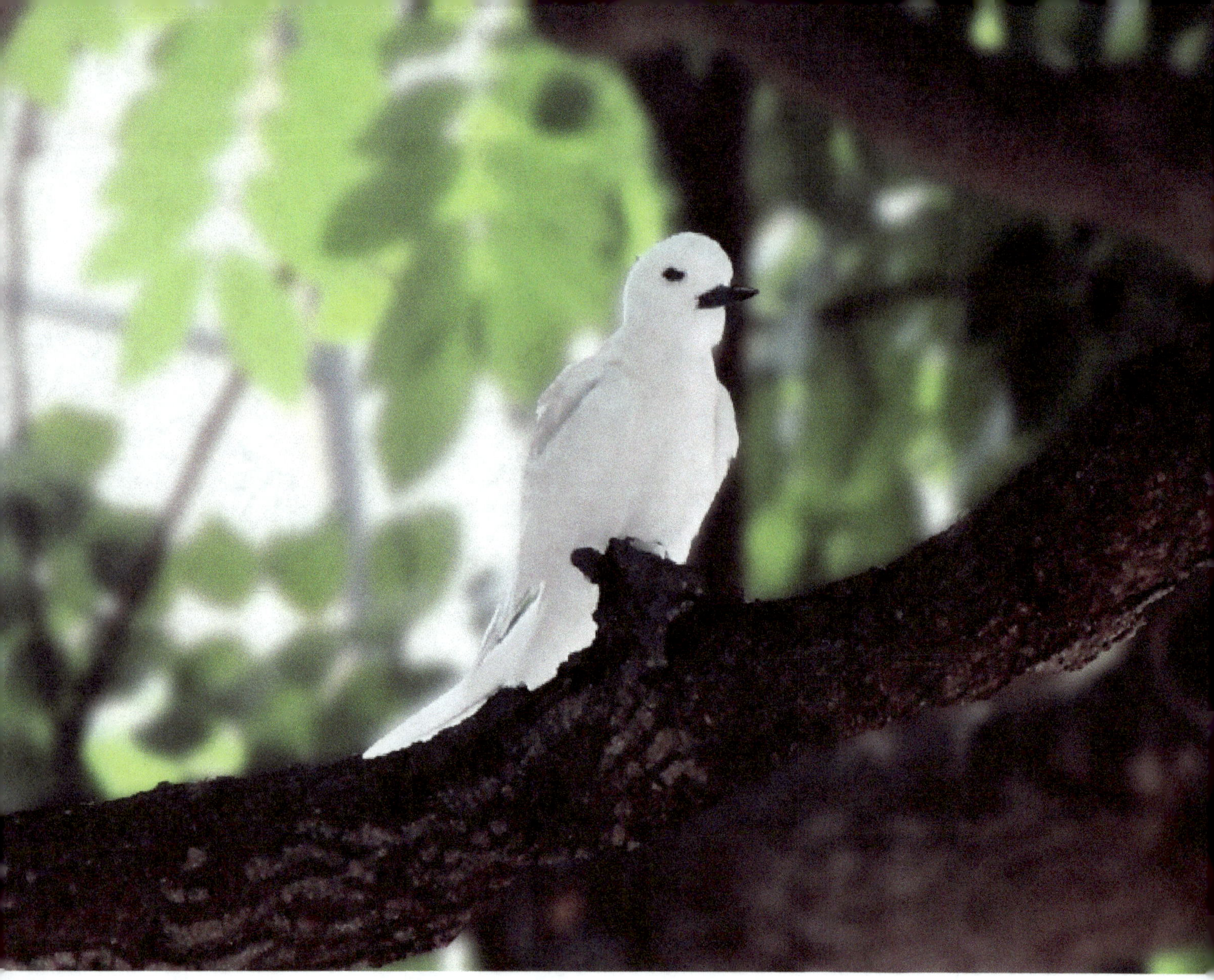

Day 72 after sighting: A last look at Skye

CHAPTER THREE

Sunny

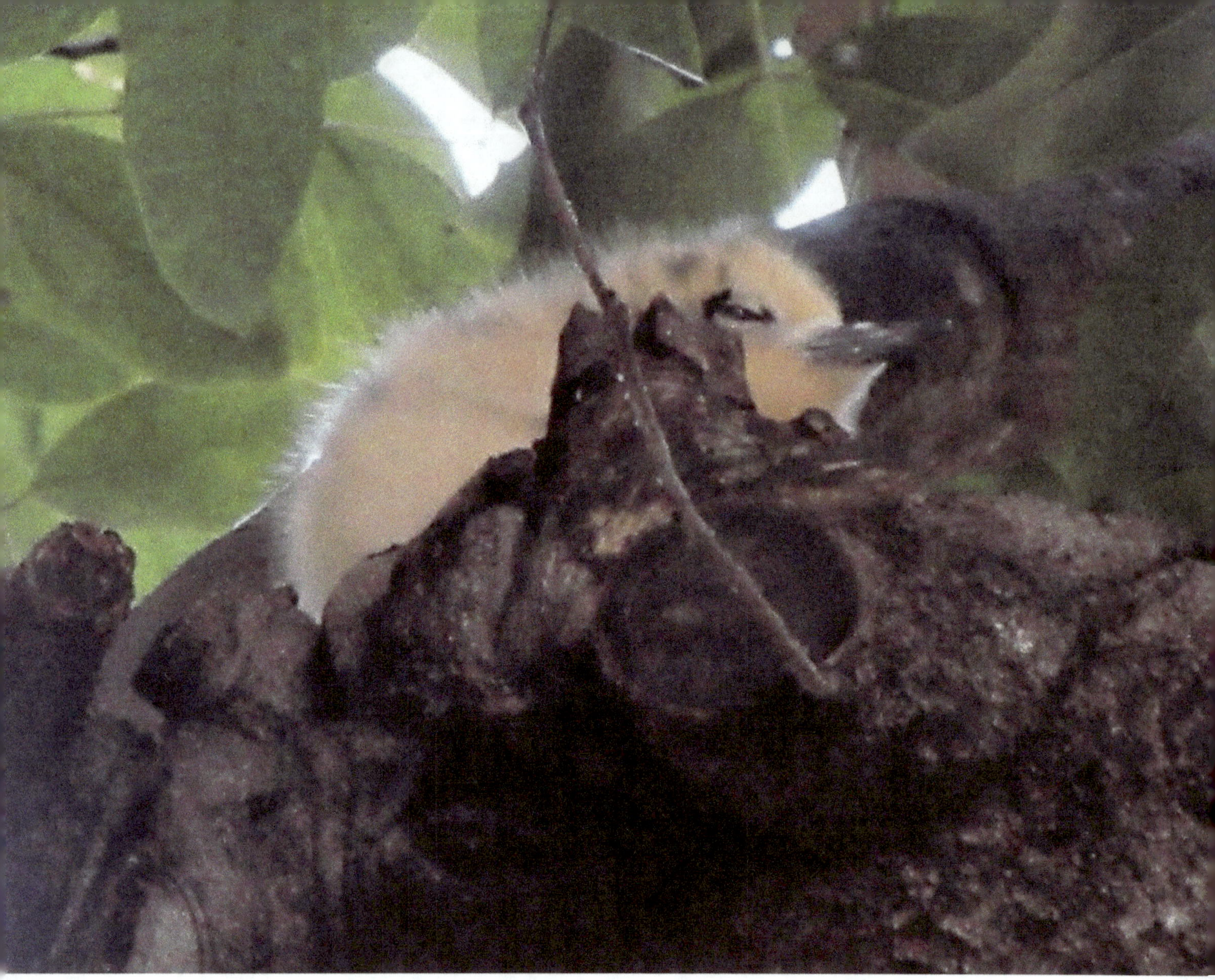

Sunny was born in another rainbow shower tree.

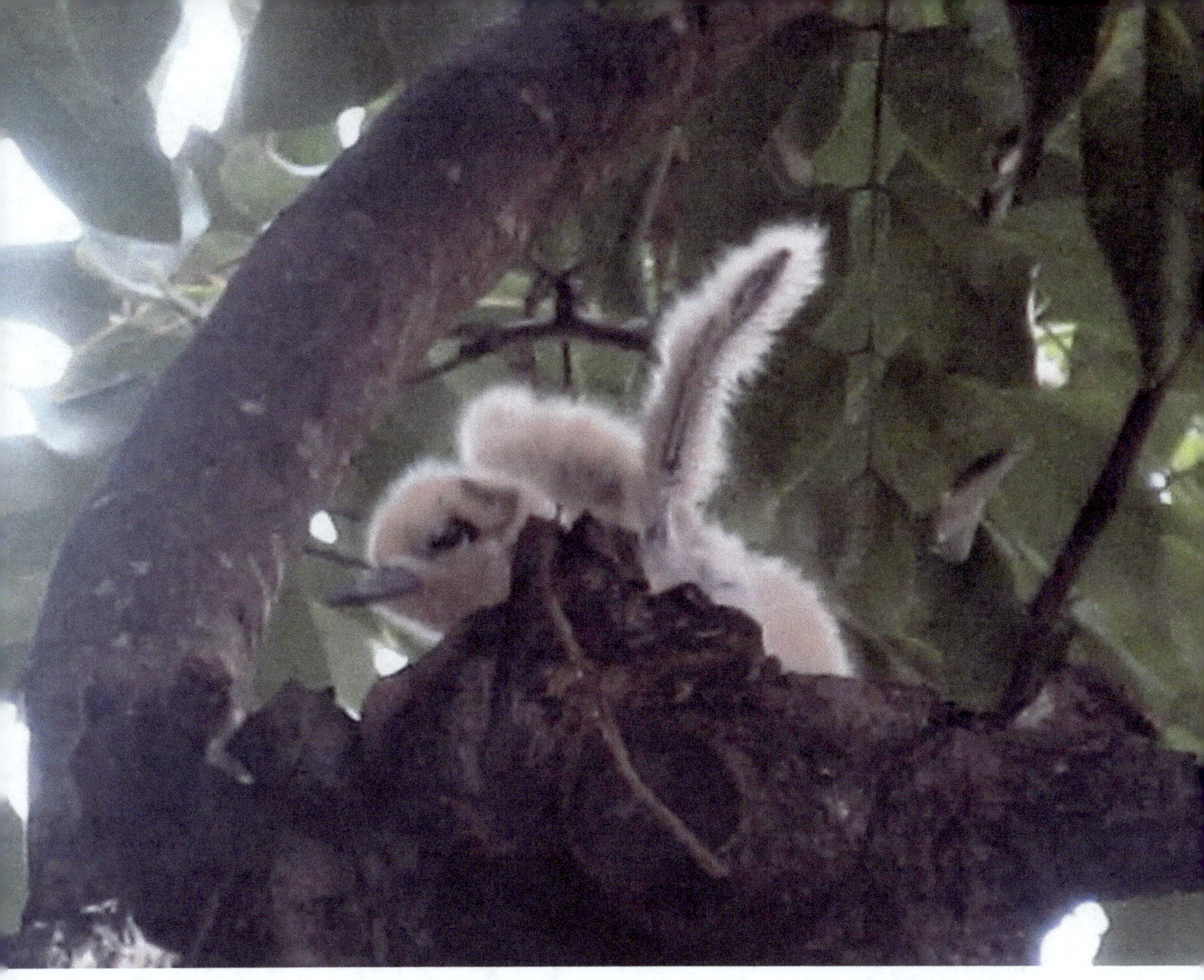

Day 2 after sighting

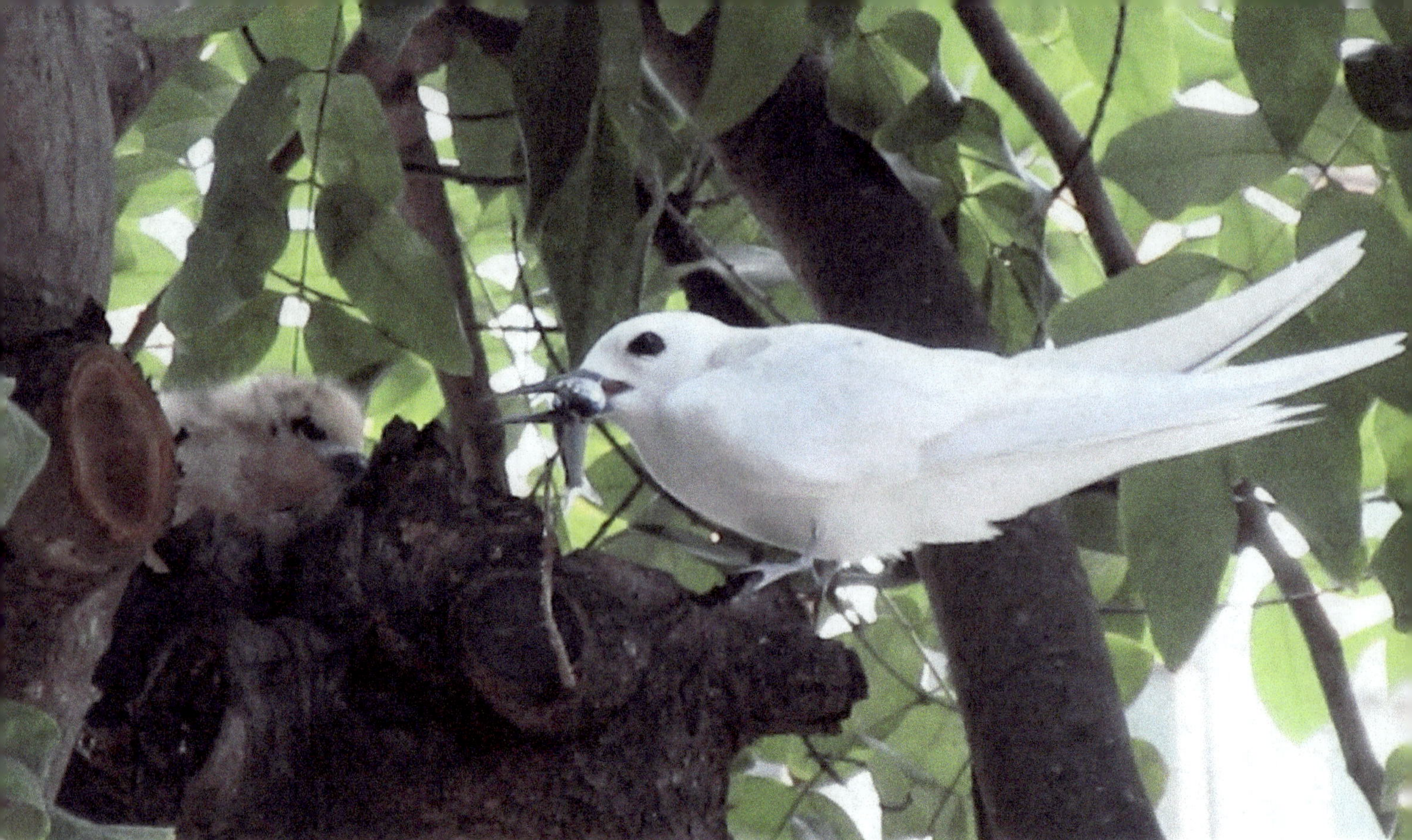

Day 4 after sighting: A parent brings a big fish for Sunny.

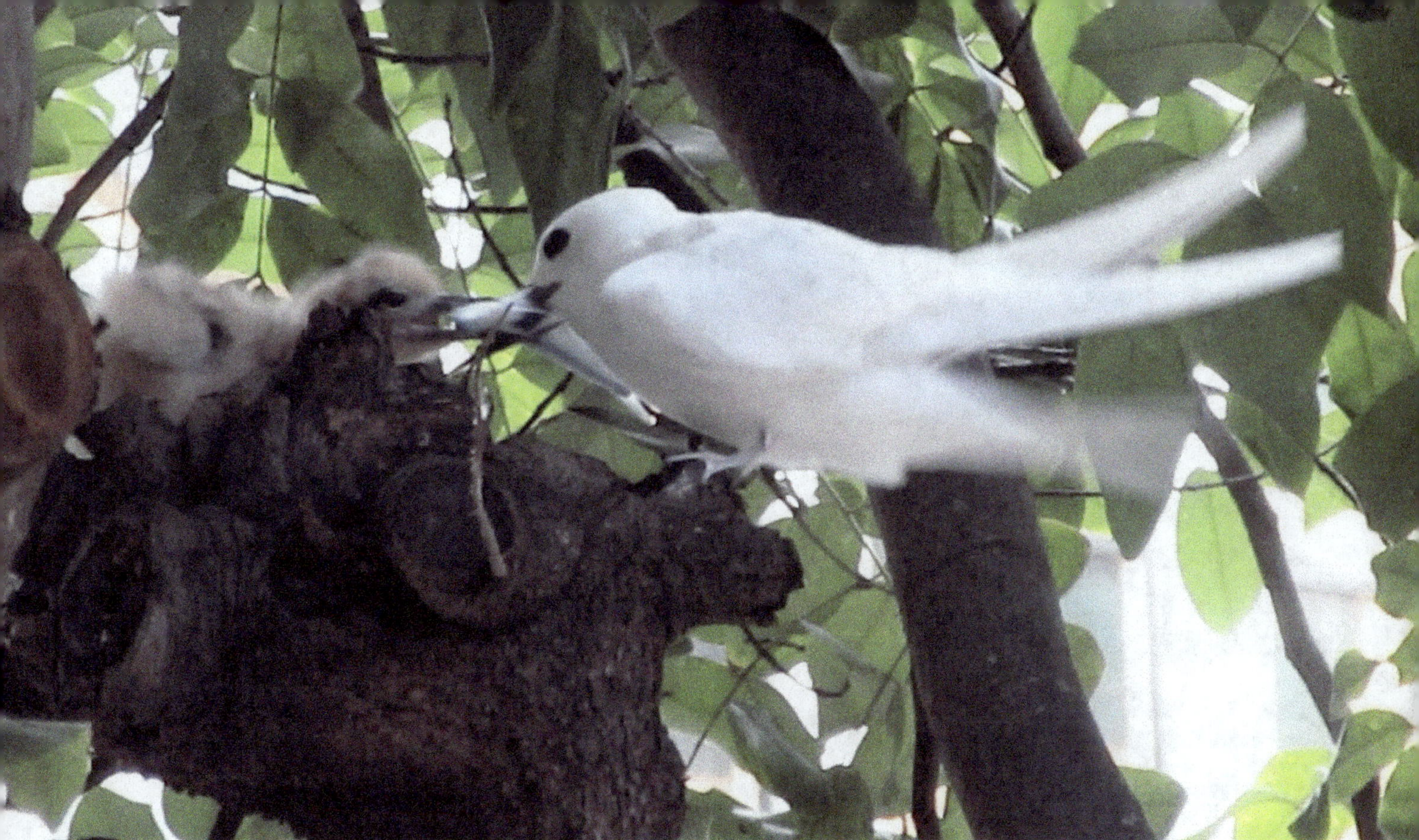

A careful transfer takes place.

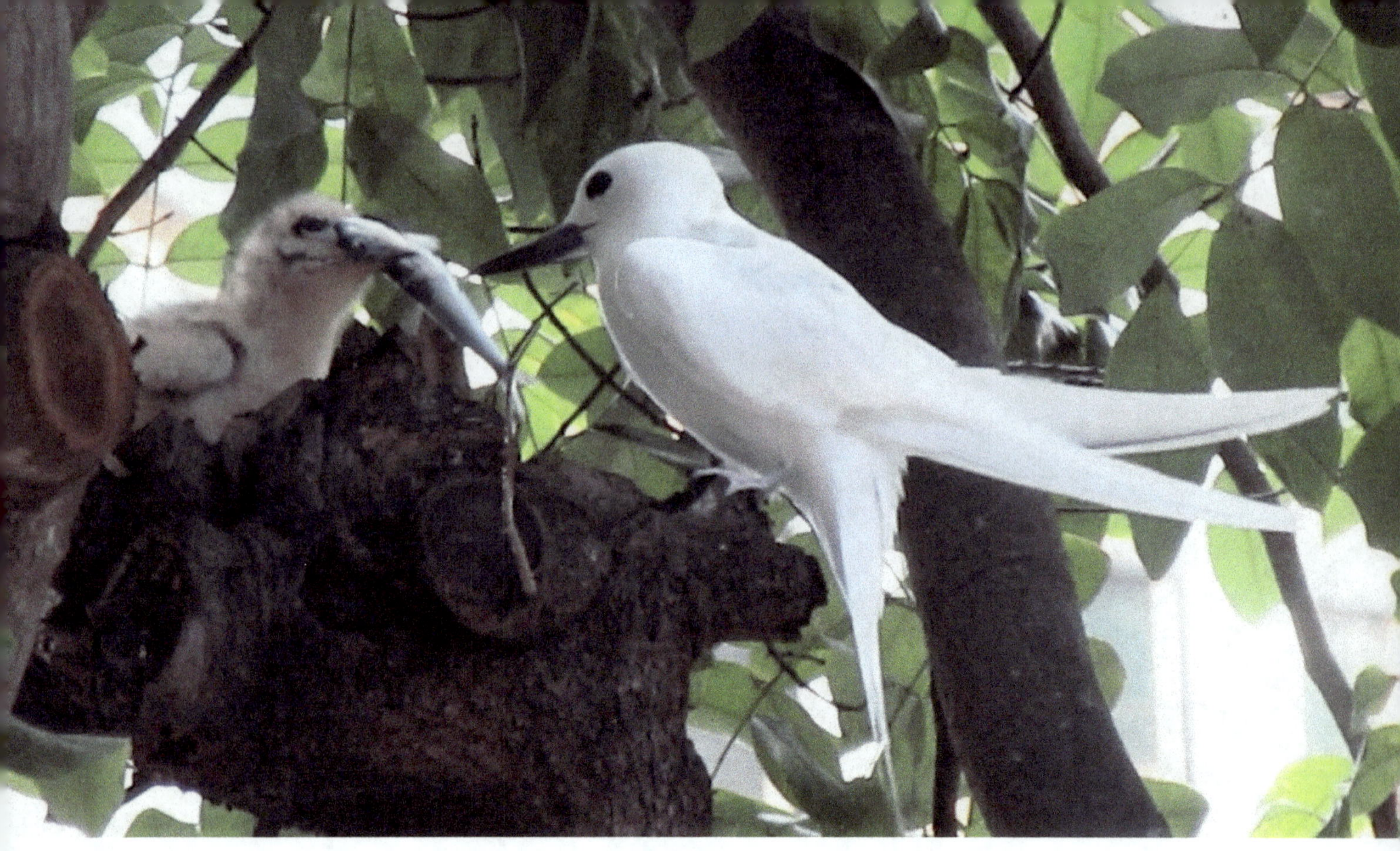

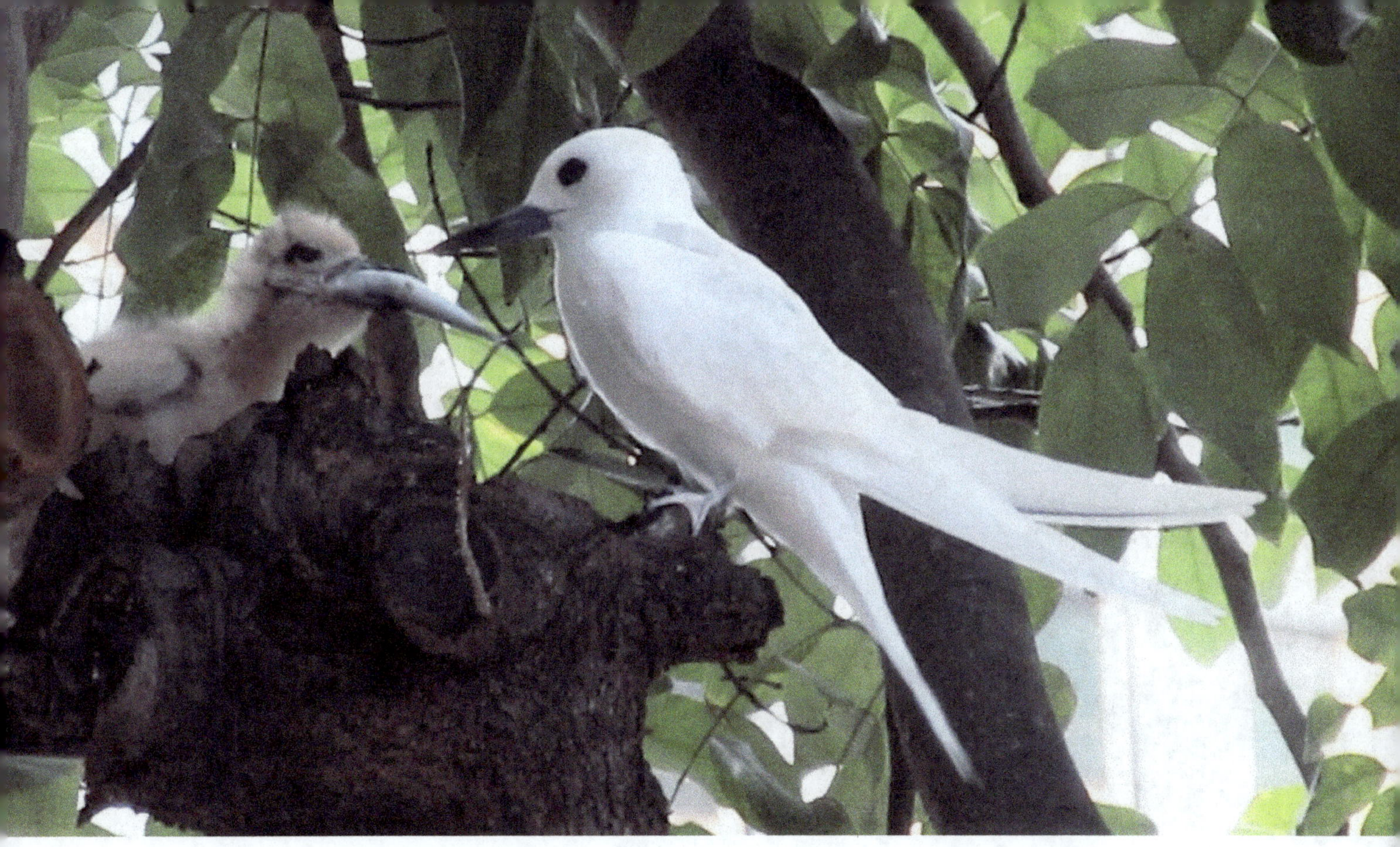

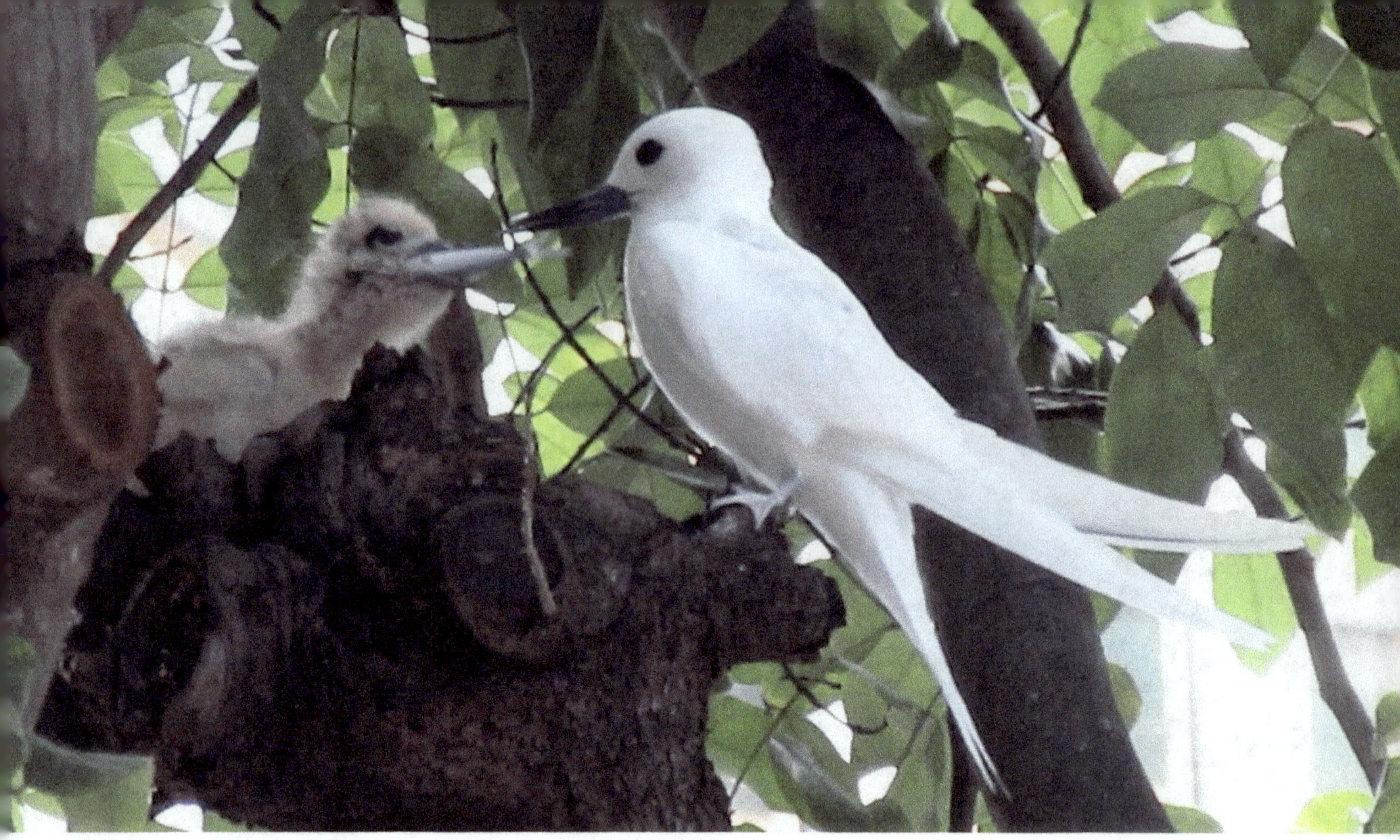

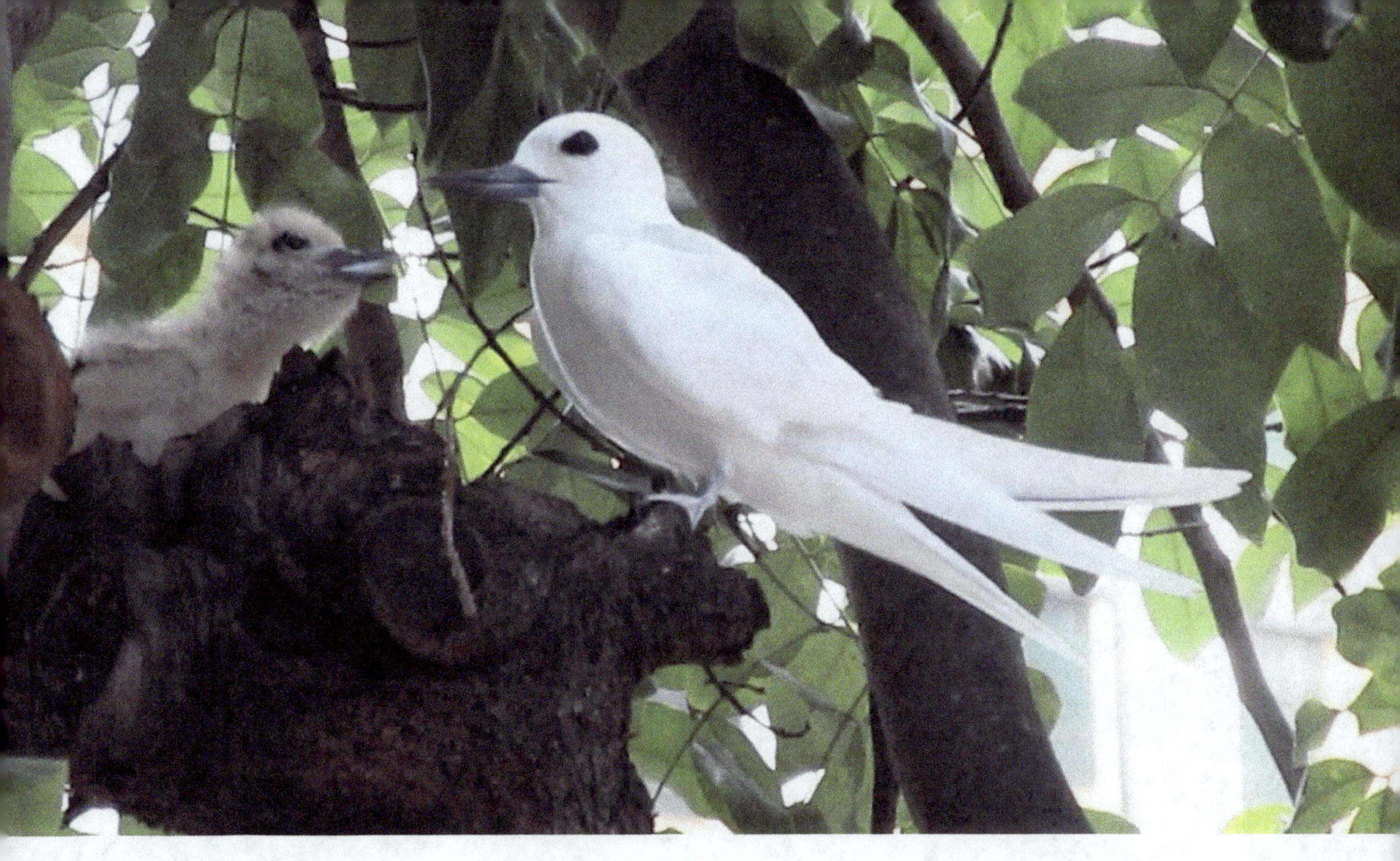

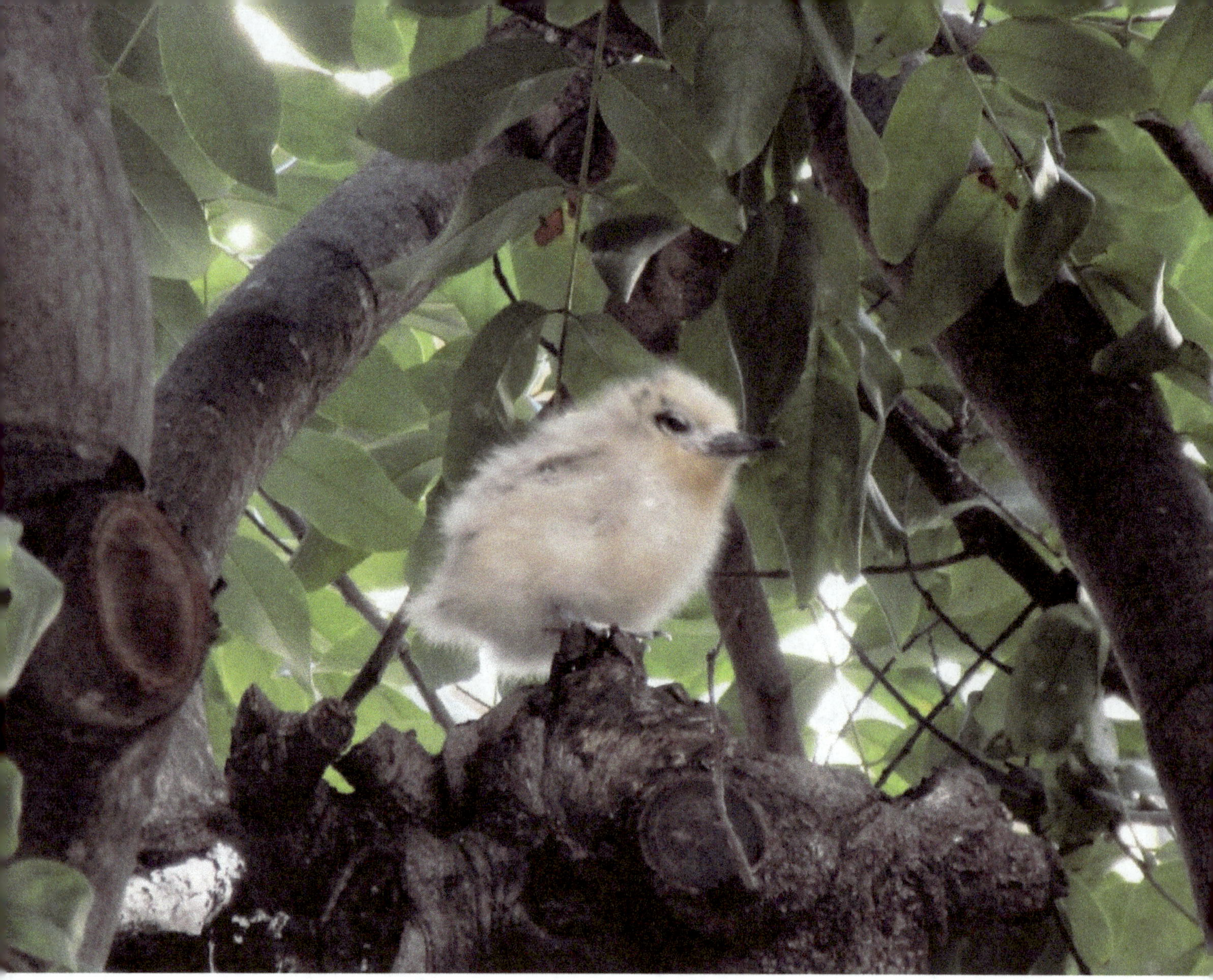

Day 7 after sighting

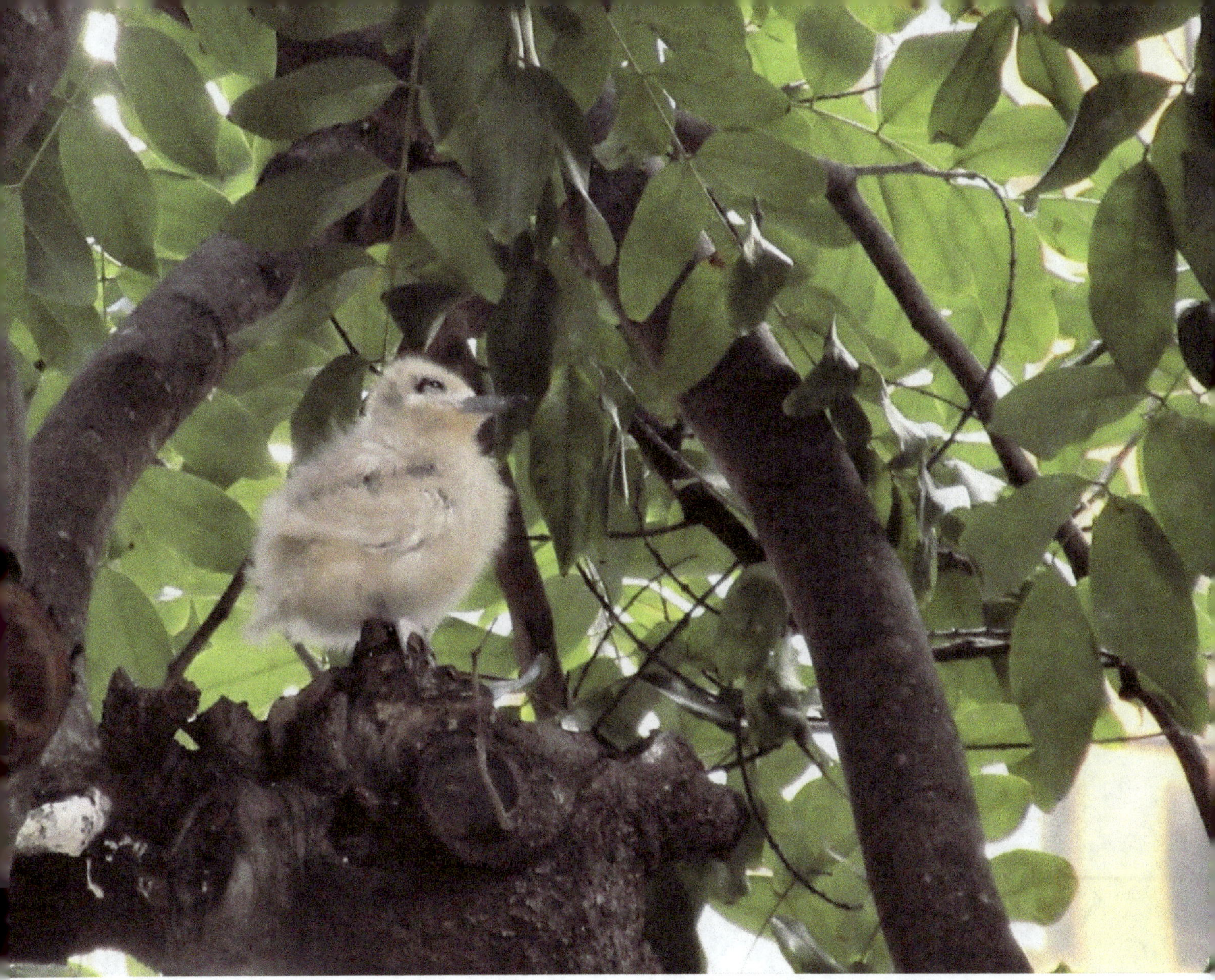

Day 11 after sighting

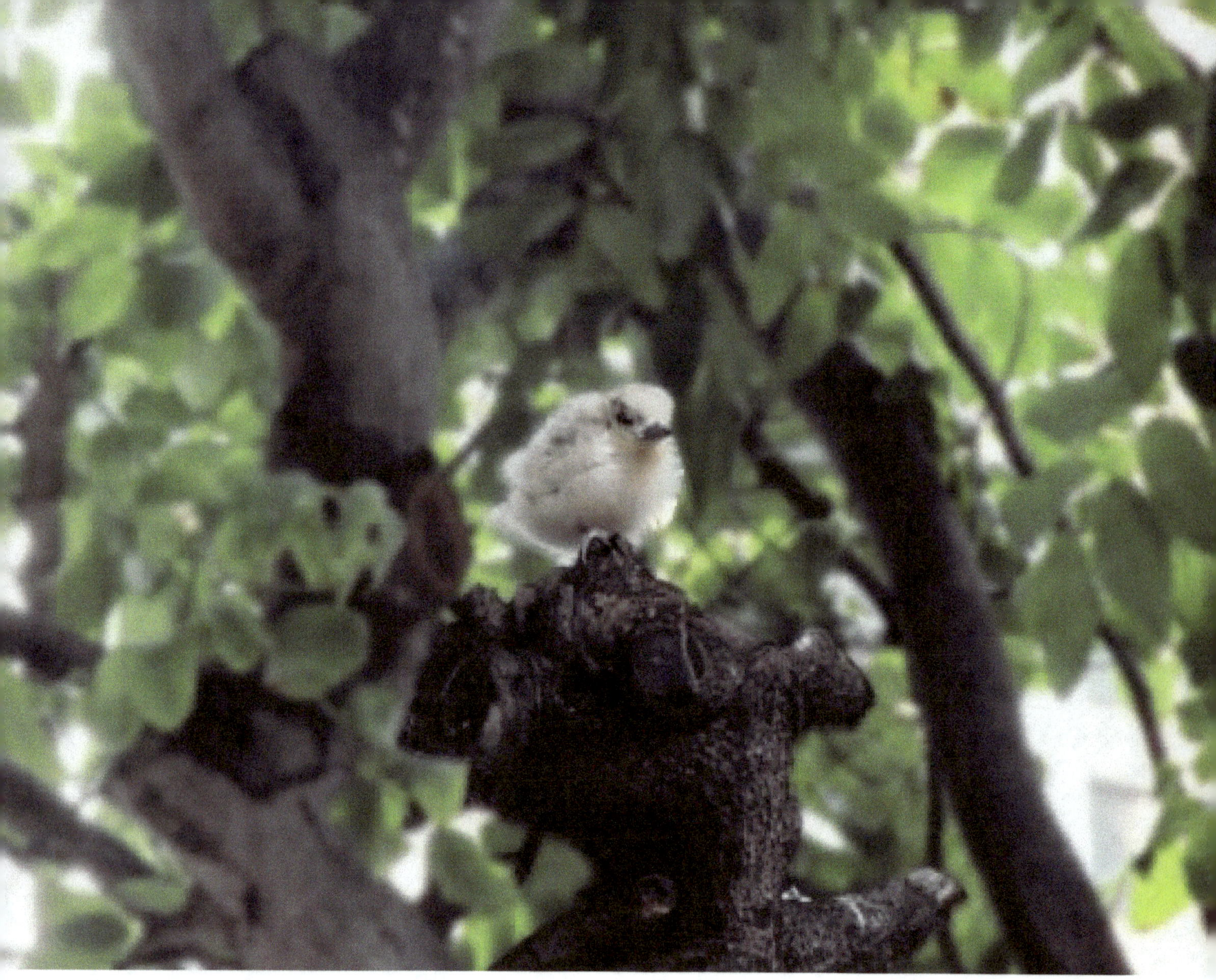

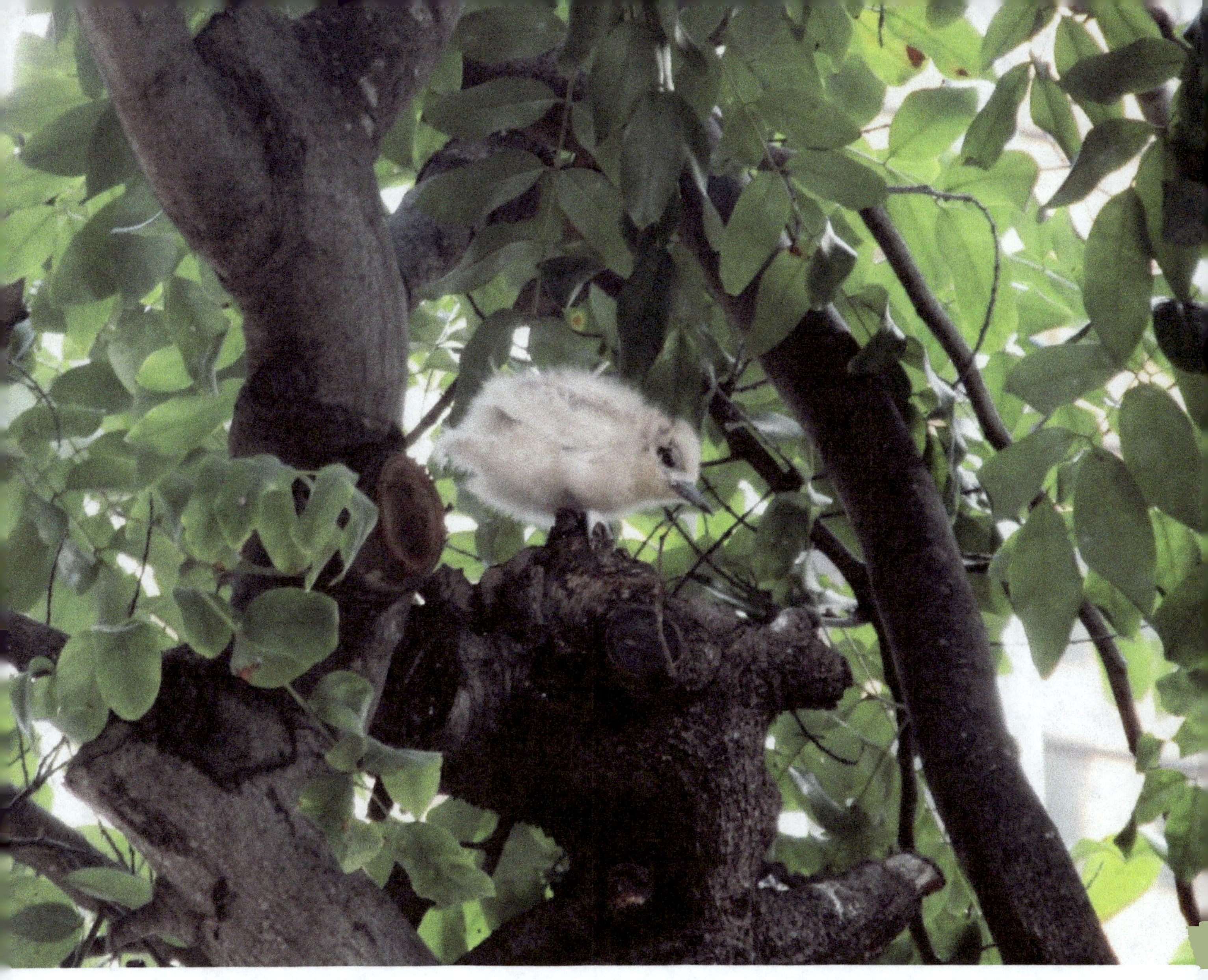

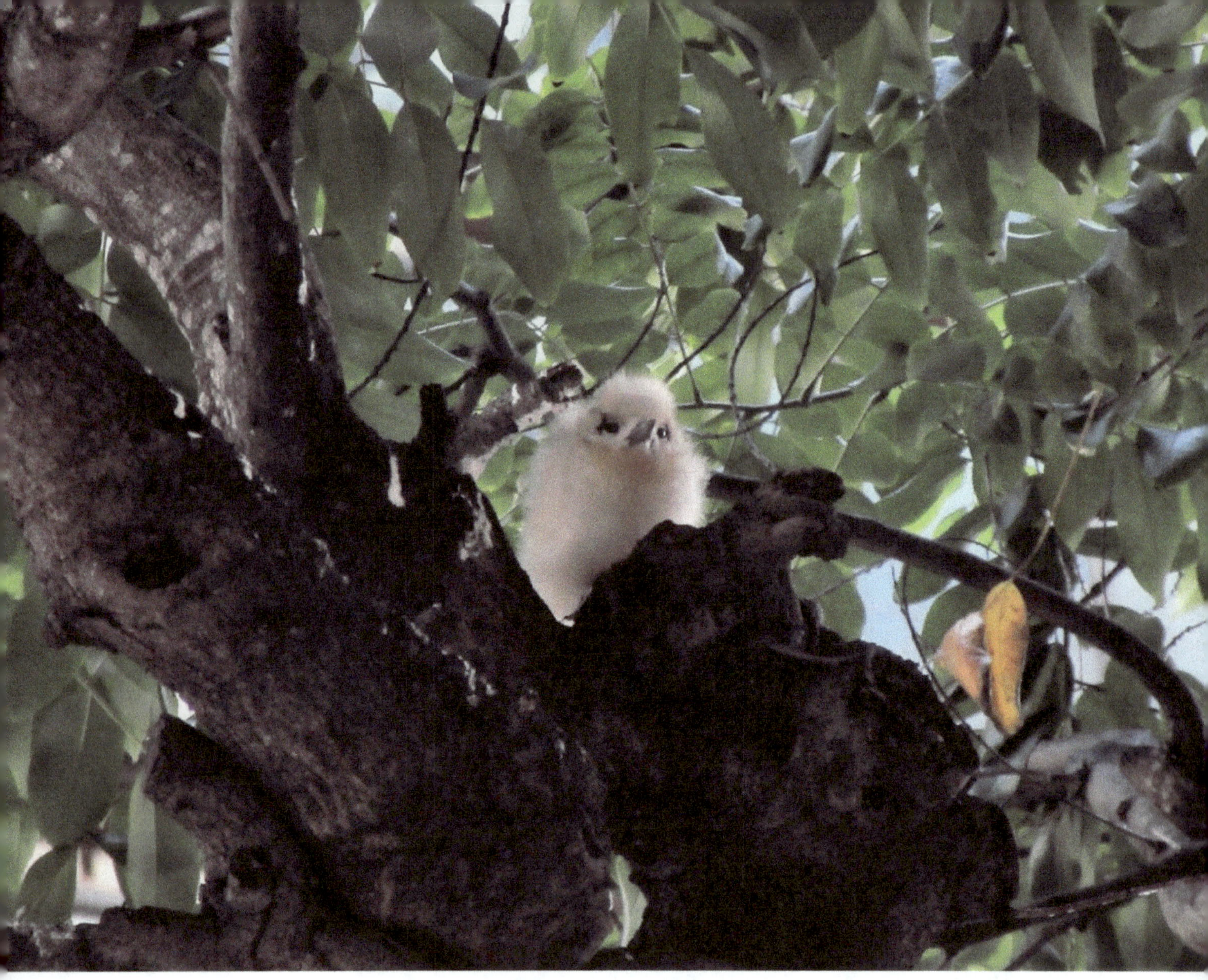

Day 13 after sighting

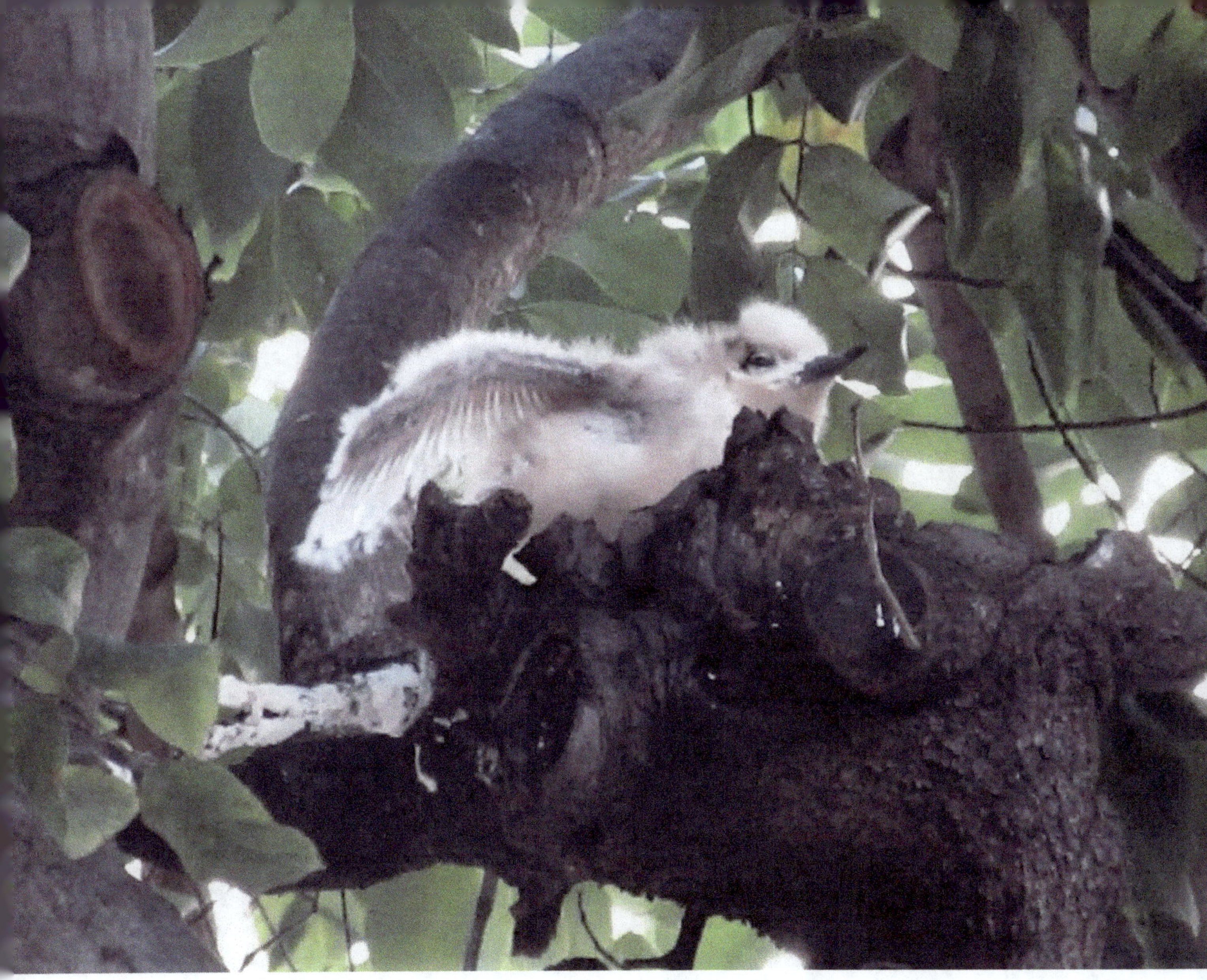

Day 14 after sighting

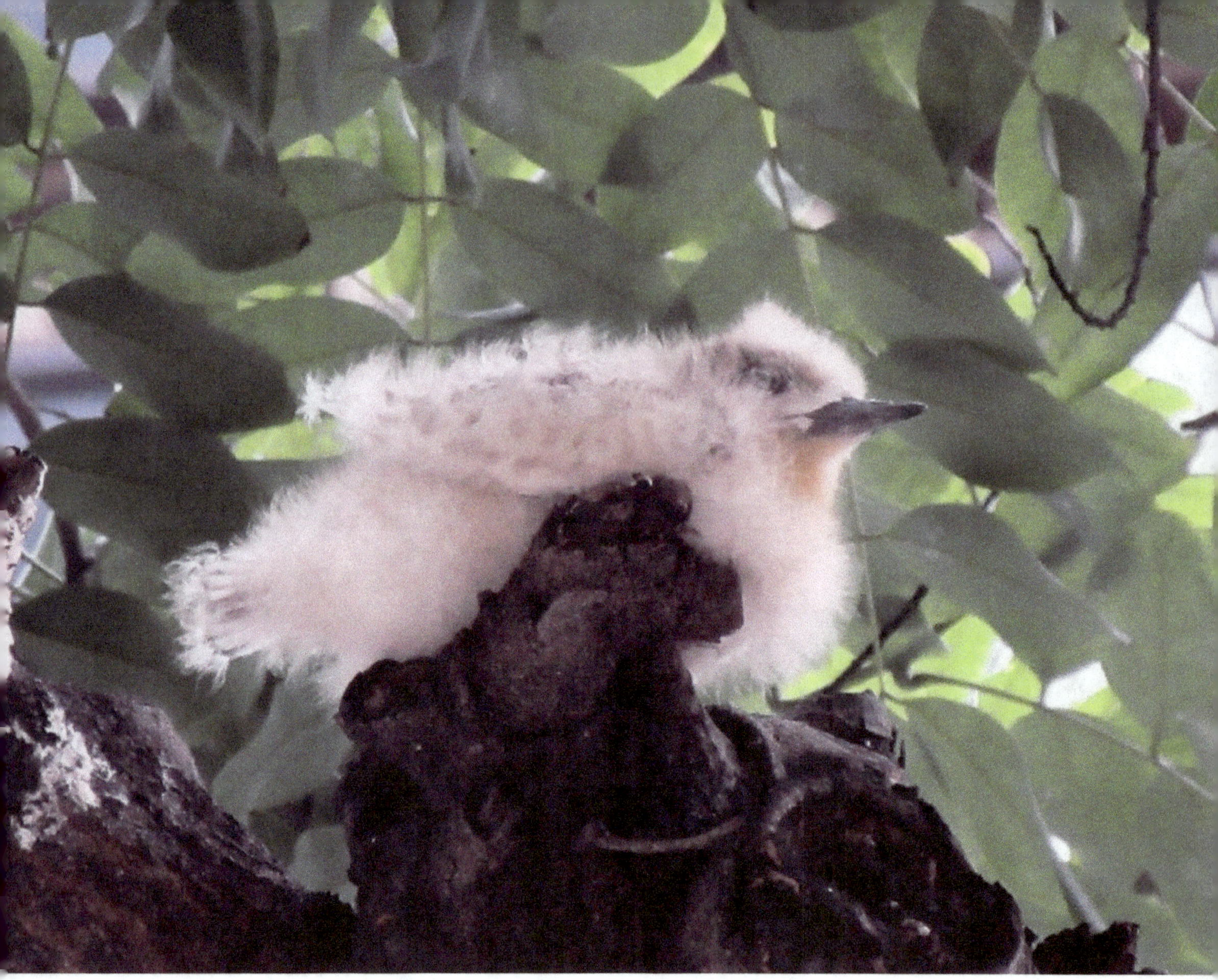

Day 15 after sighting: Sleepy Sunny

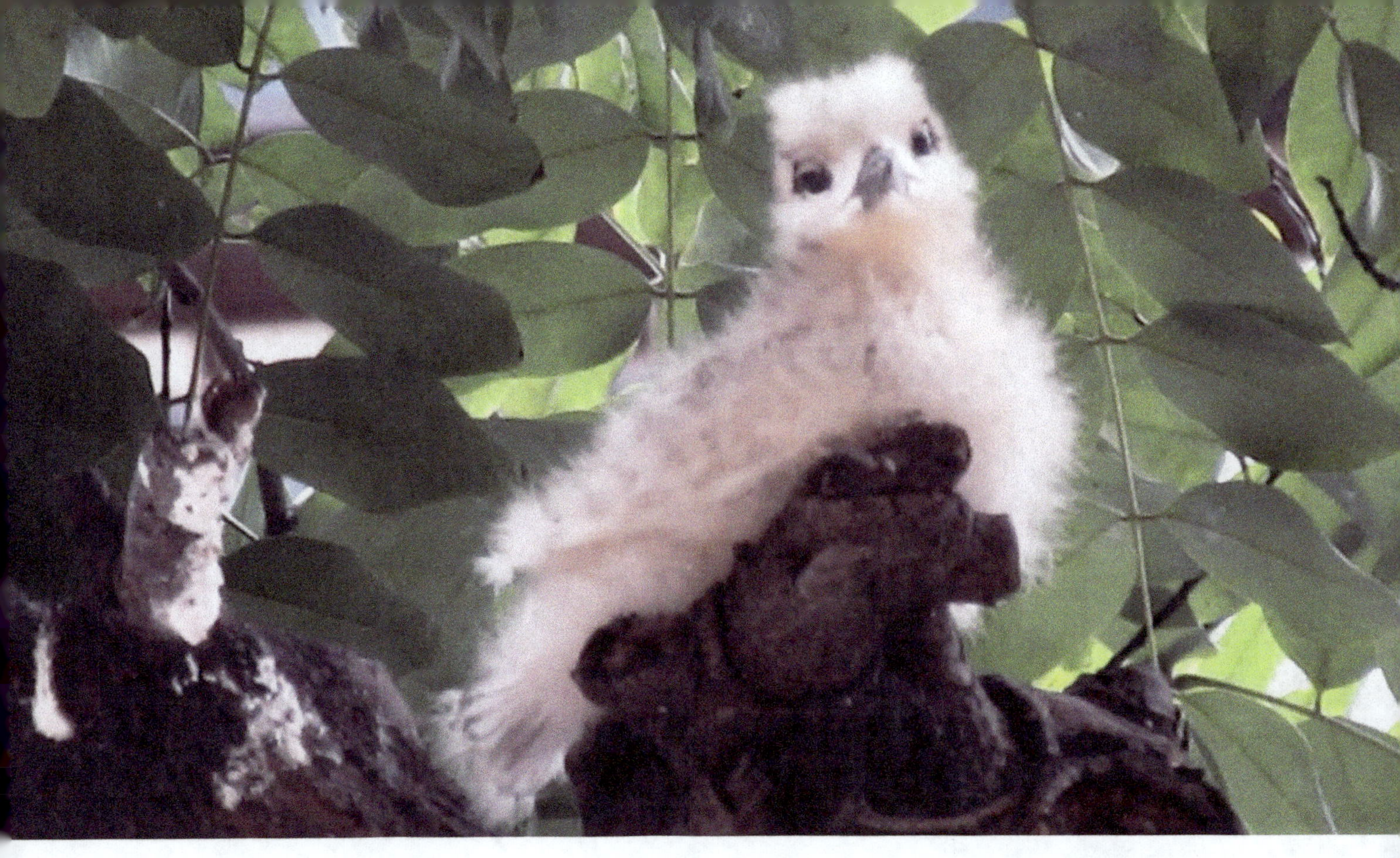

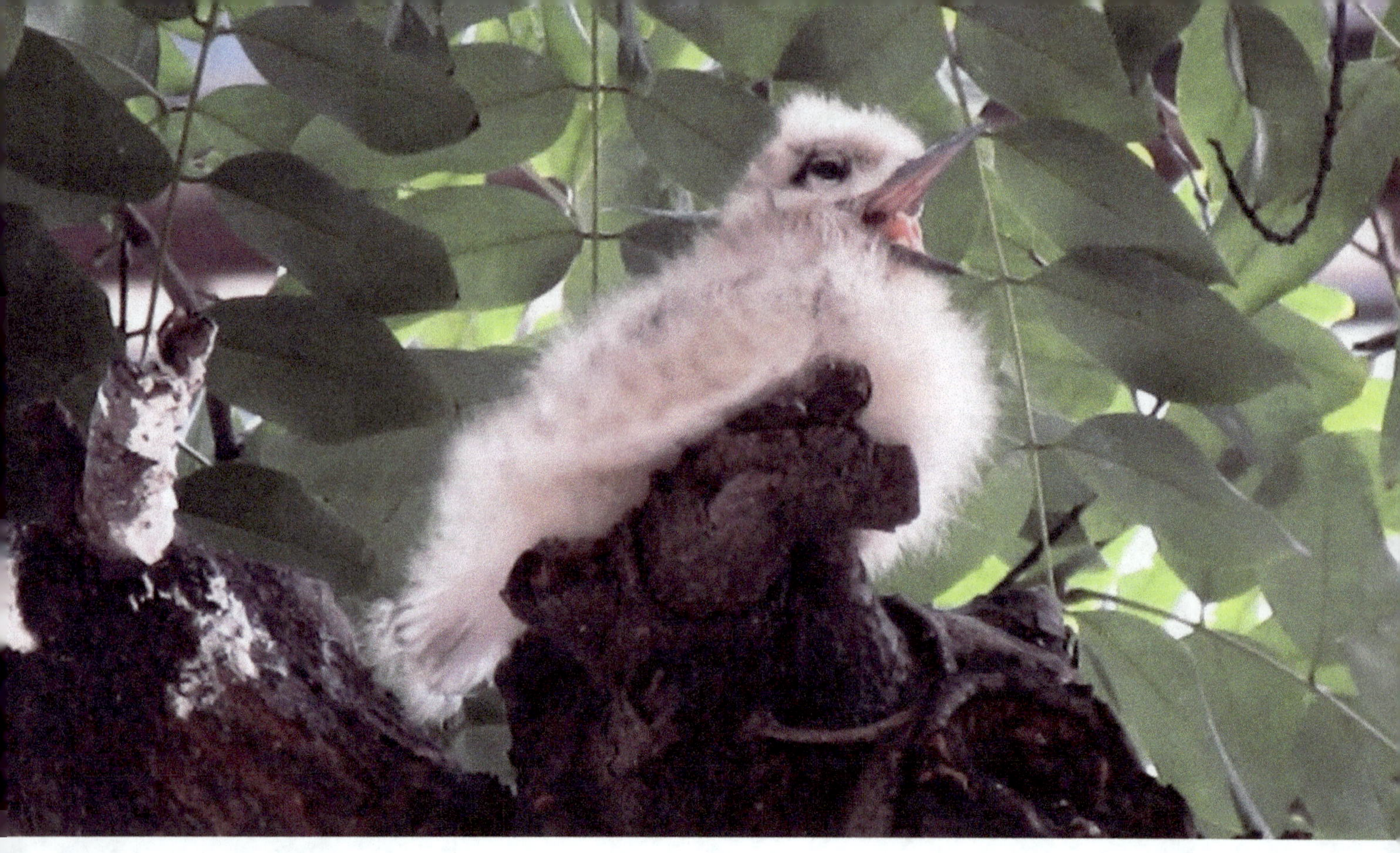

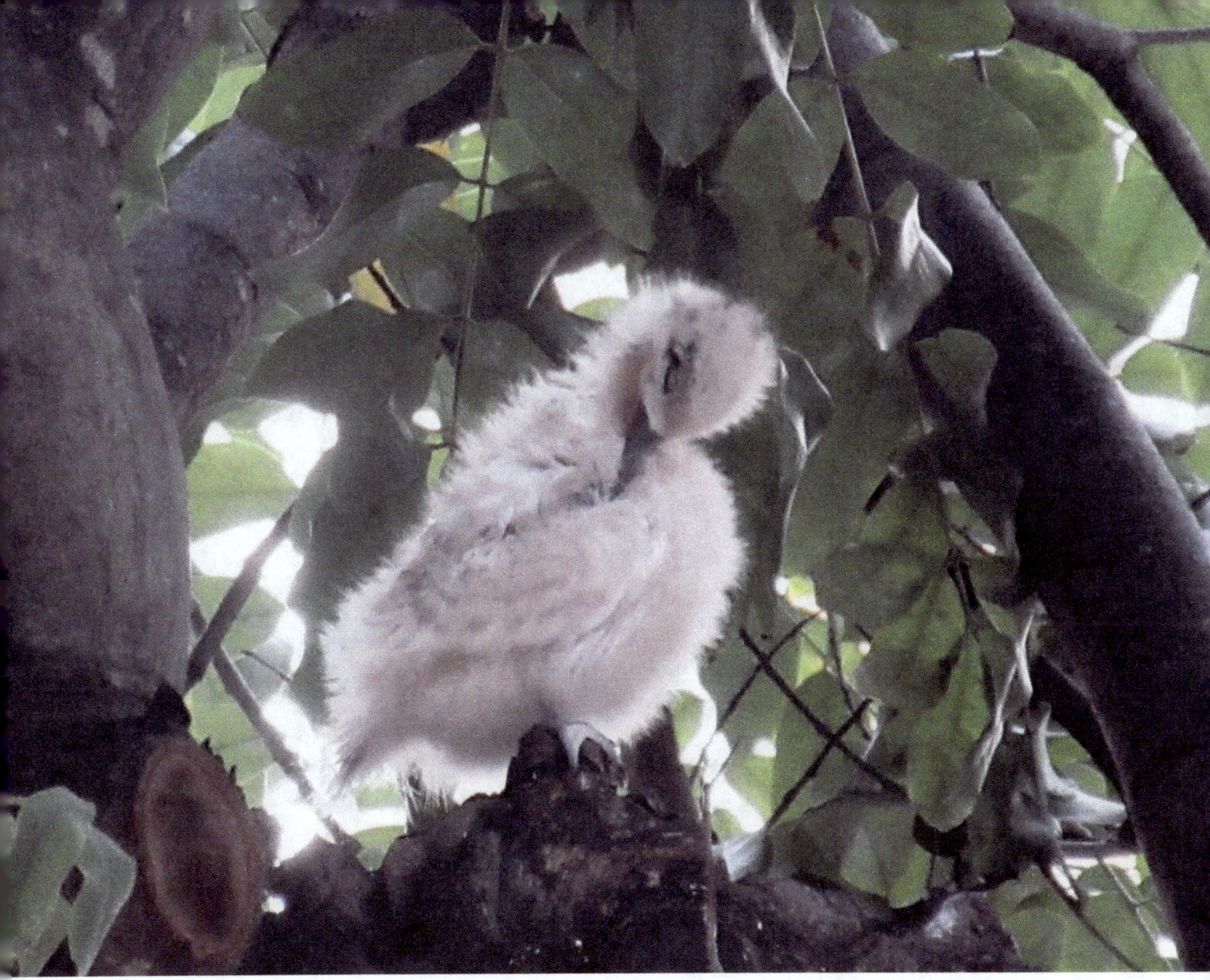

Day 16 after sighting

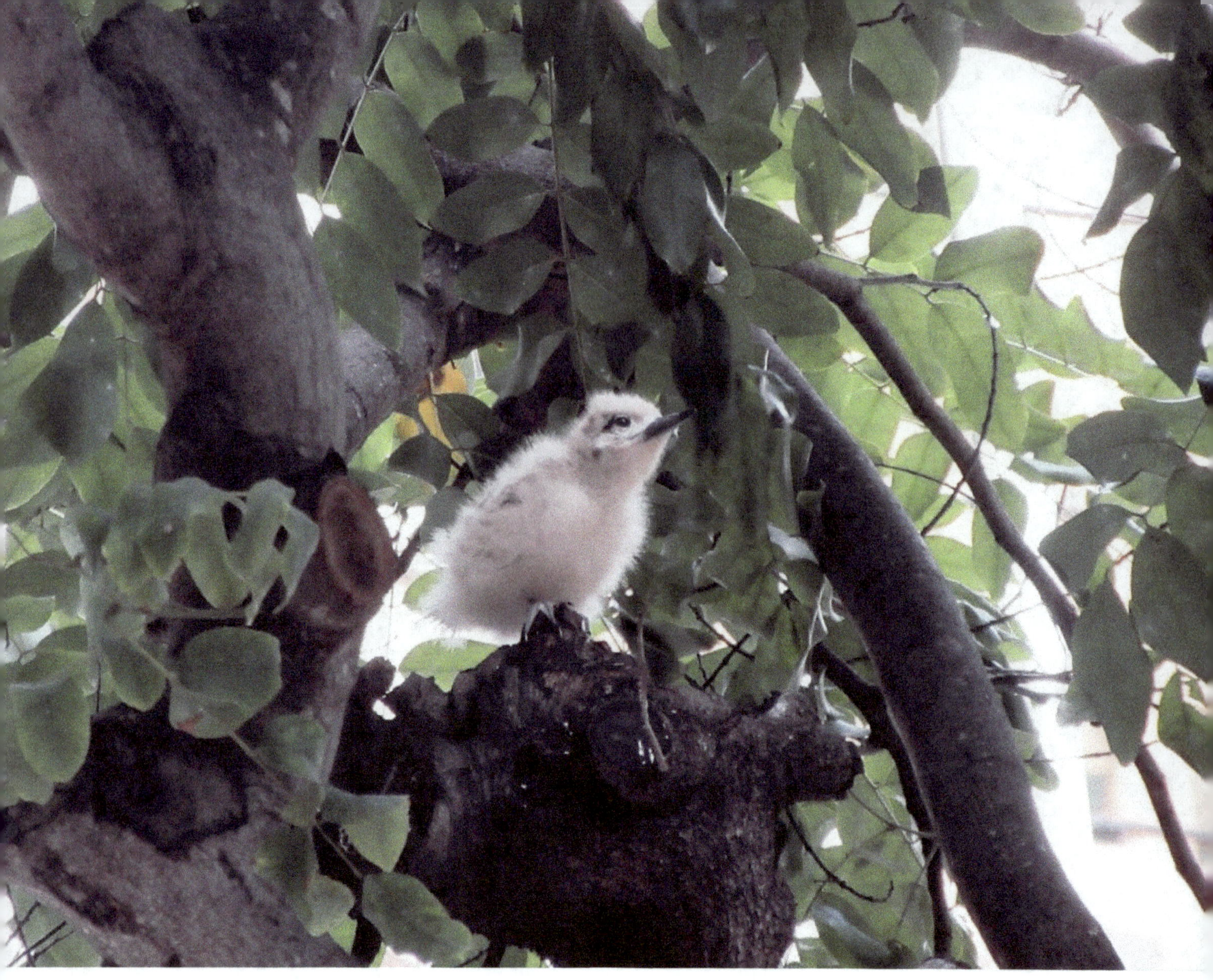

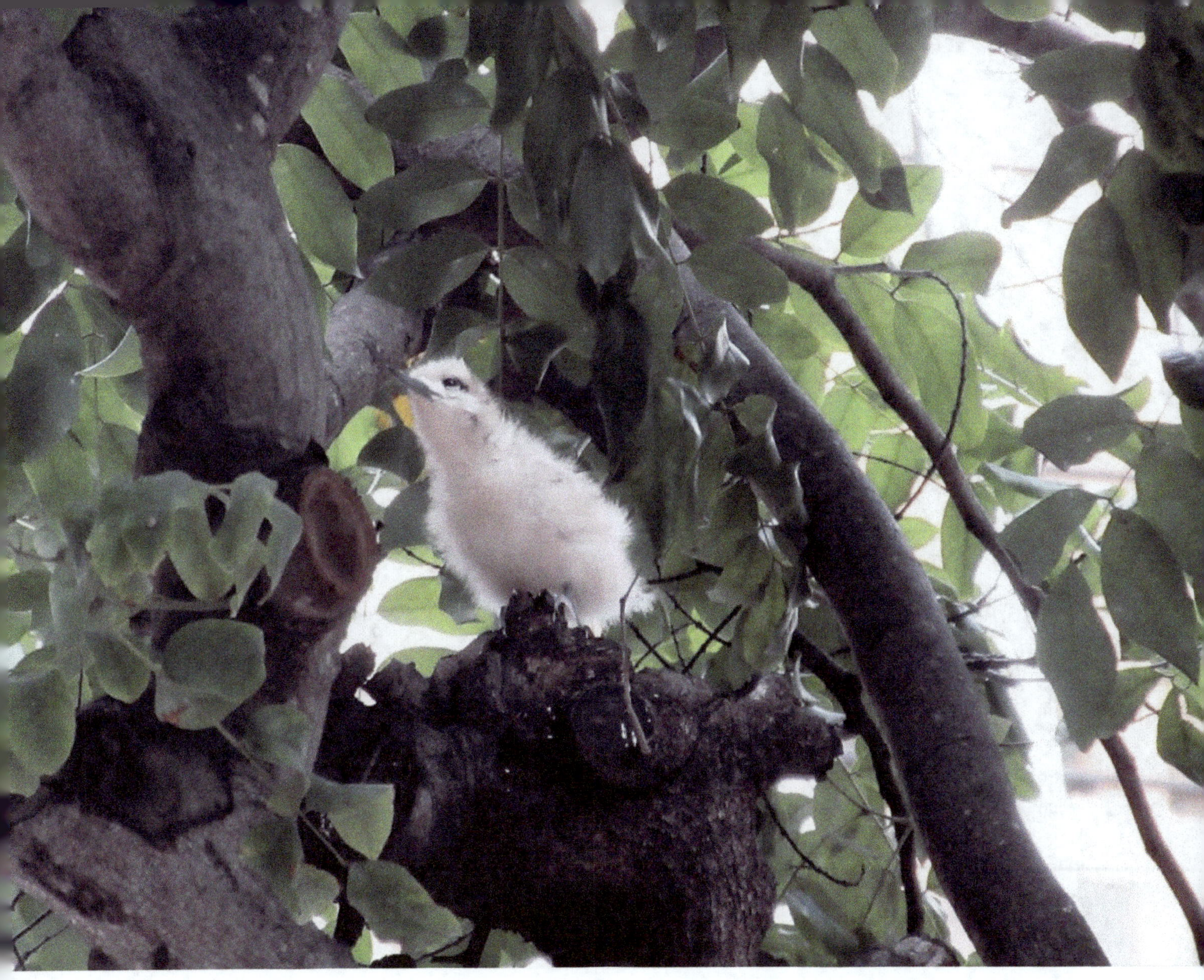

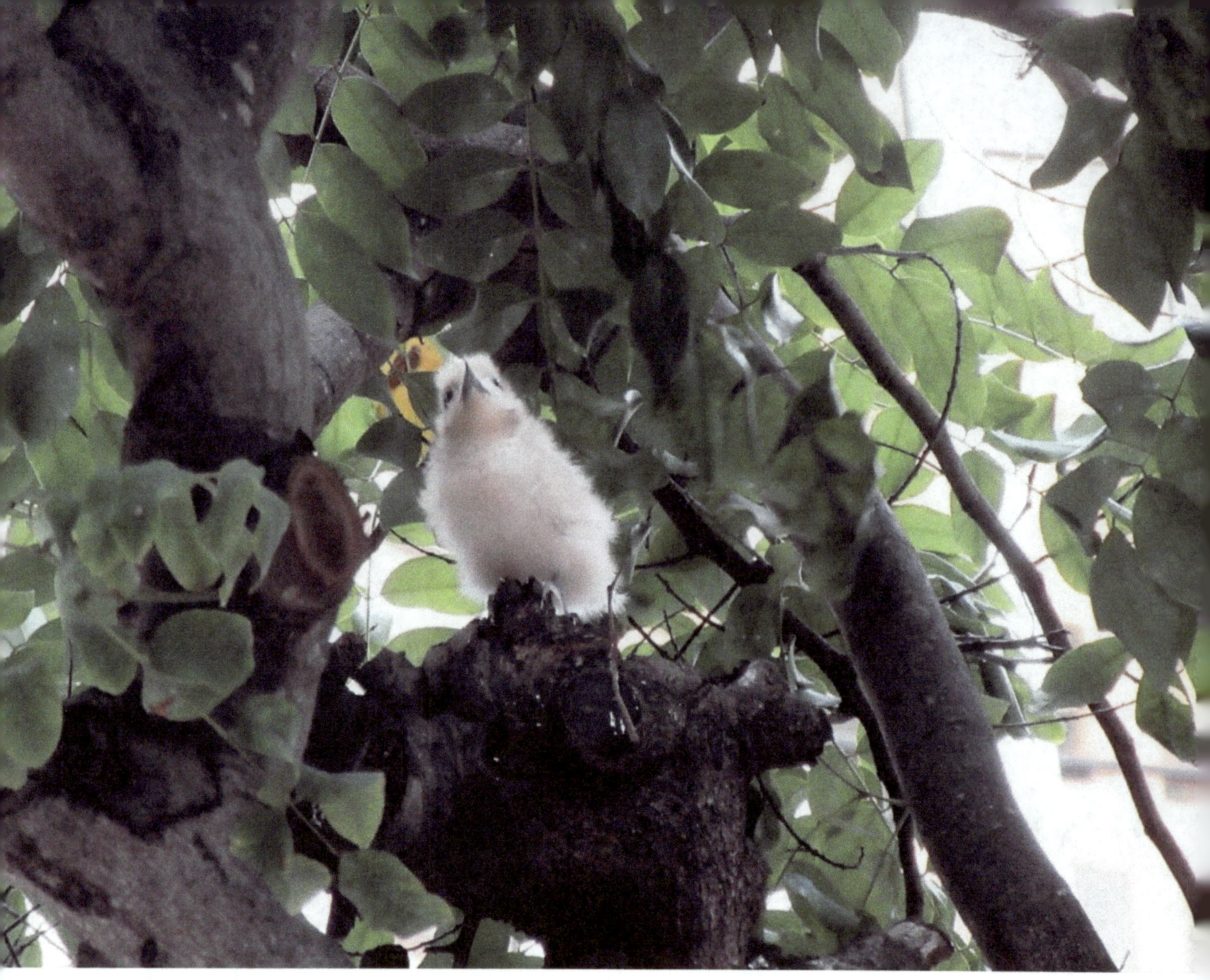

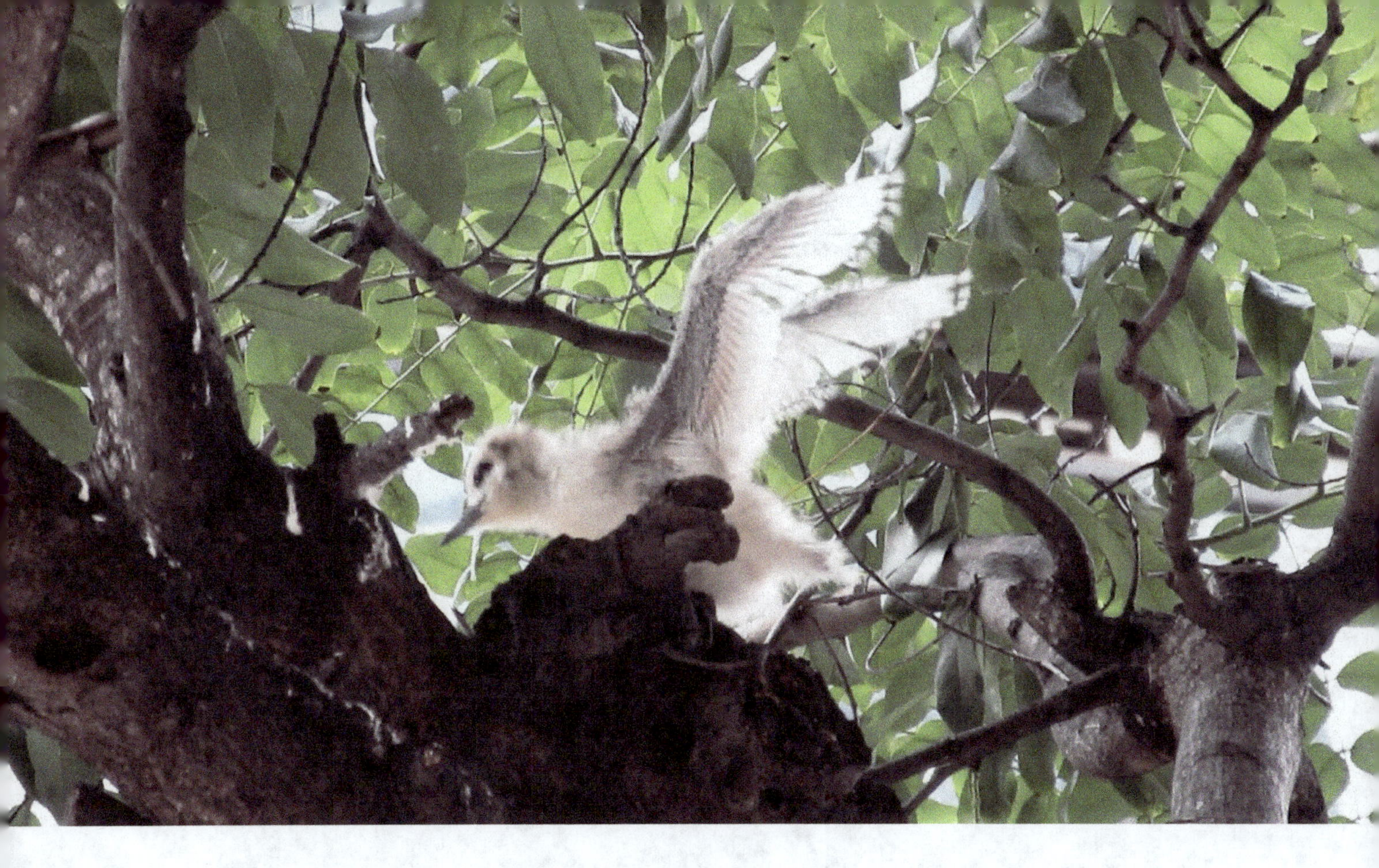

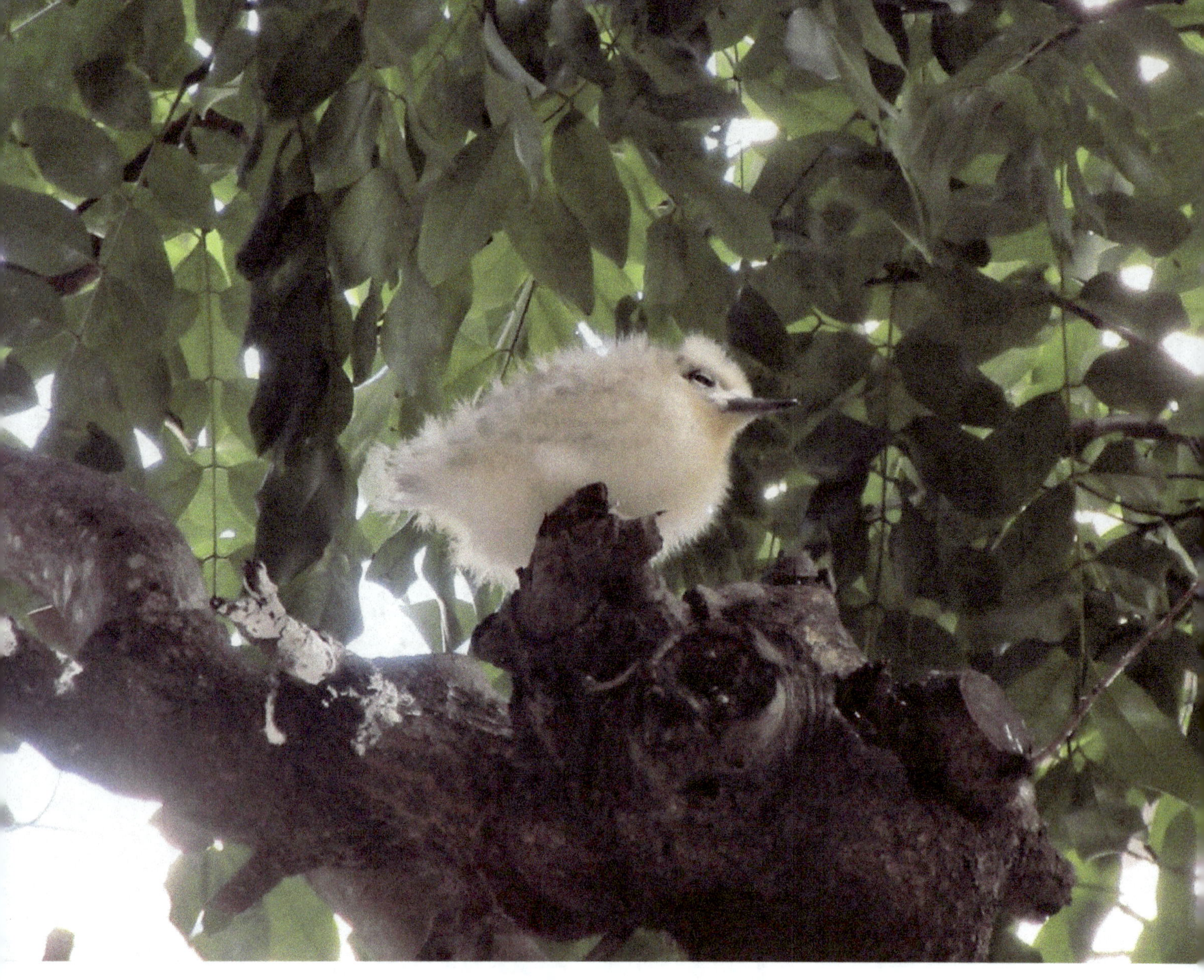

Day 18 after sighting

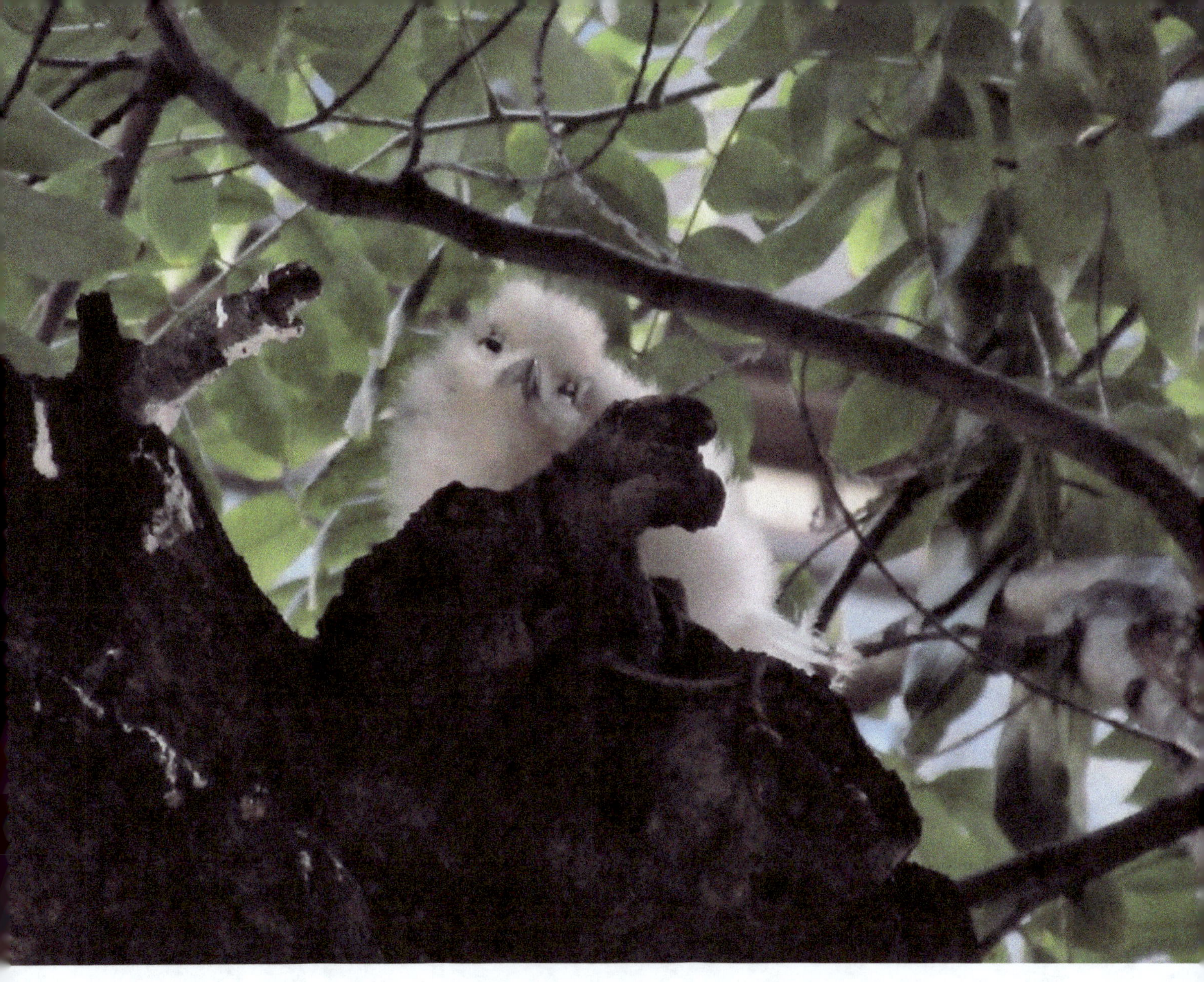

Day 19 after sighting

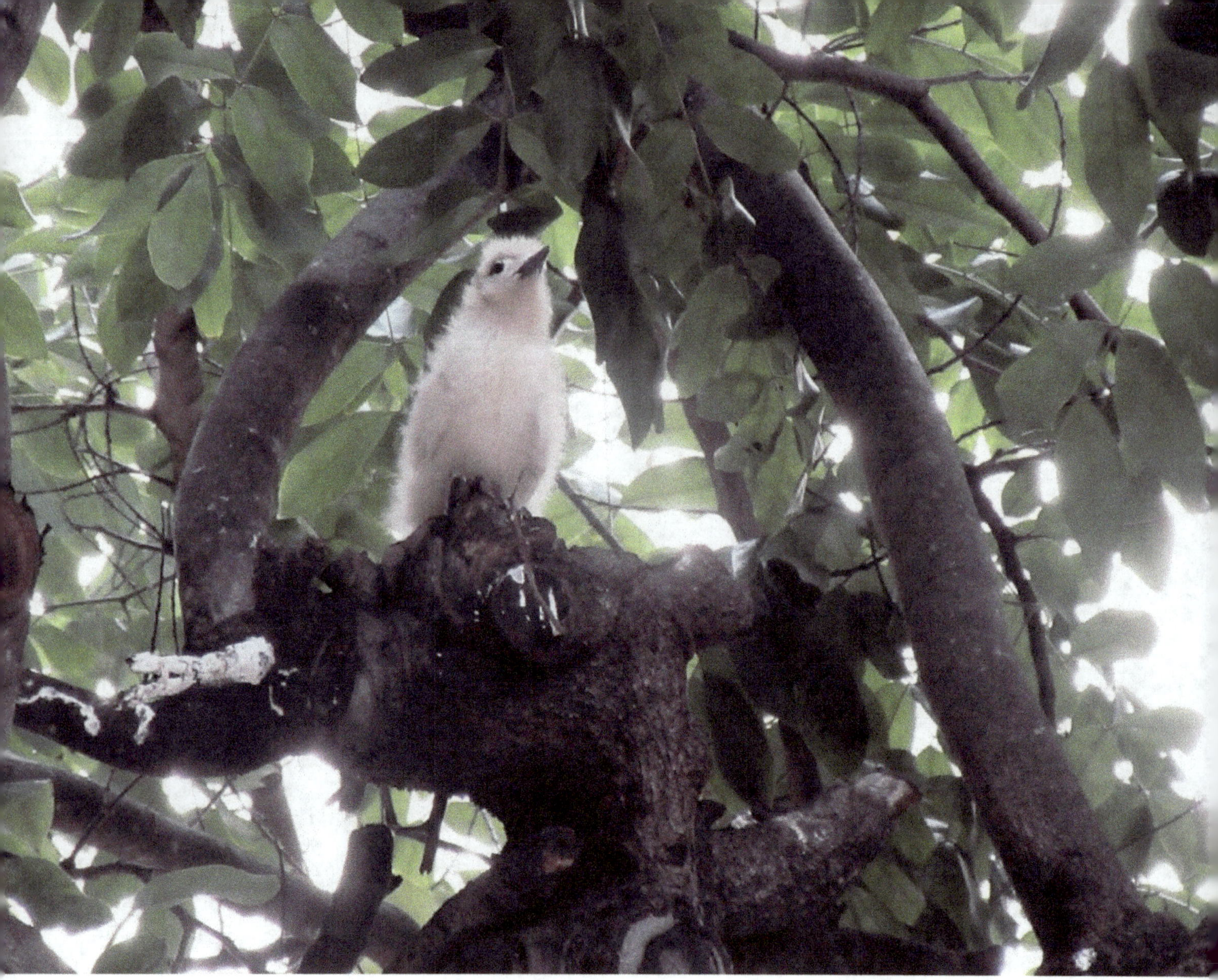

Day 21 after sighting

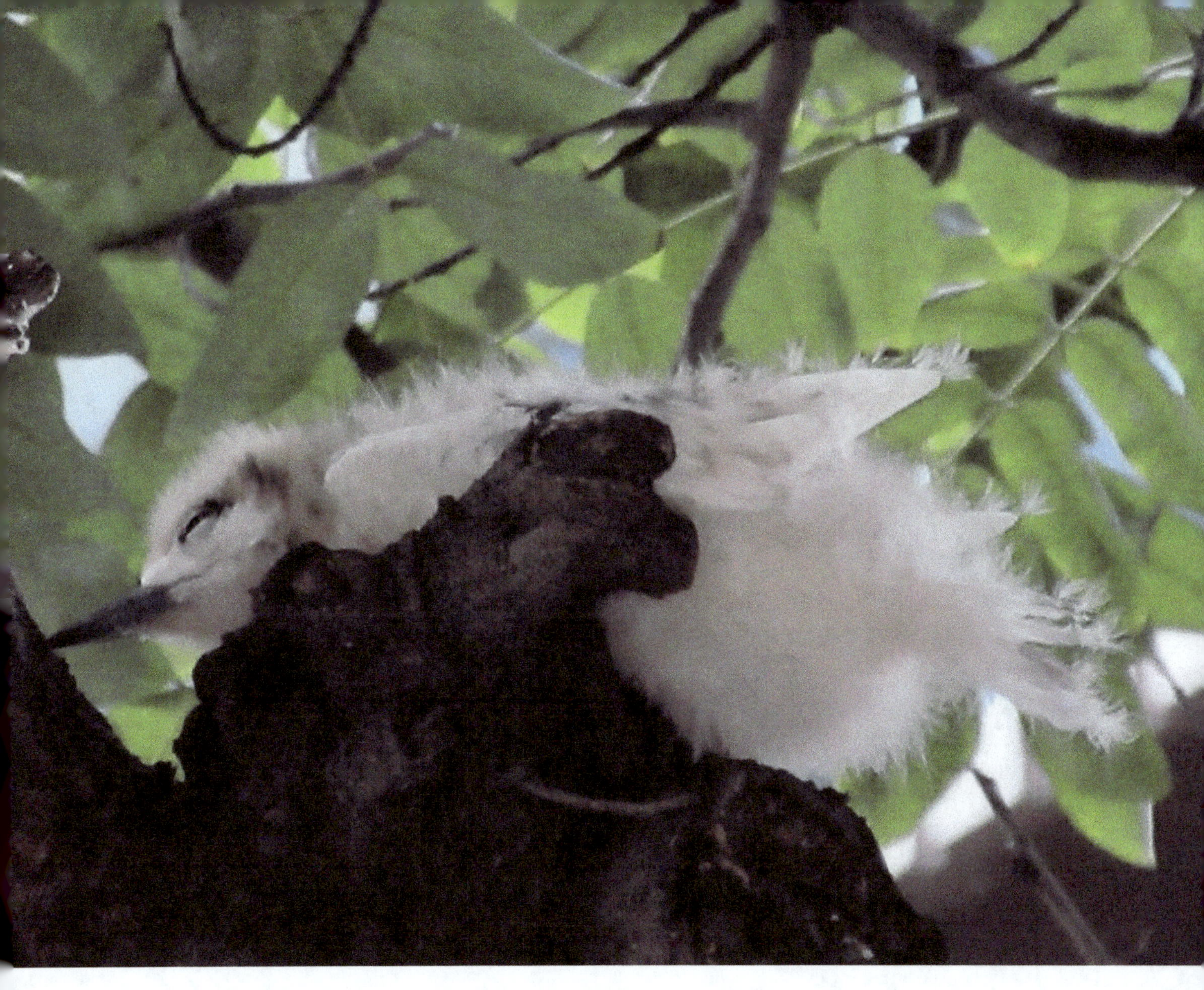

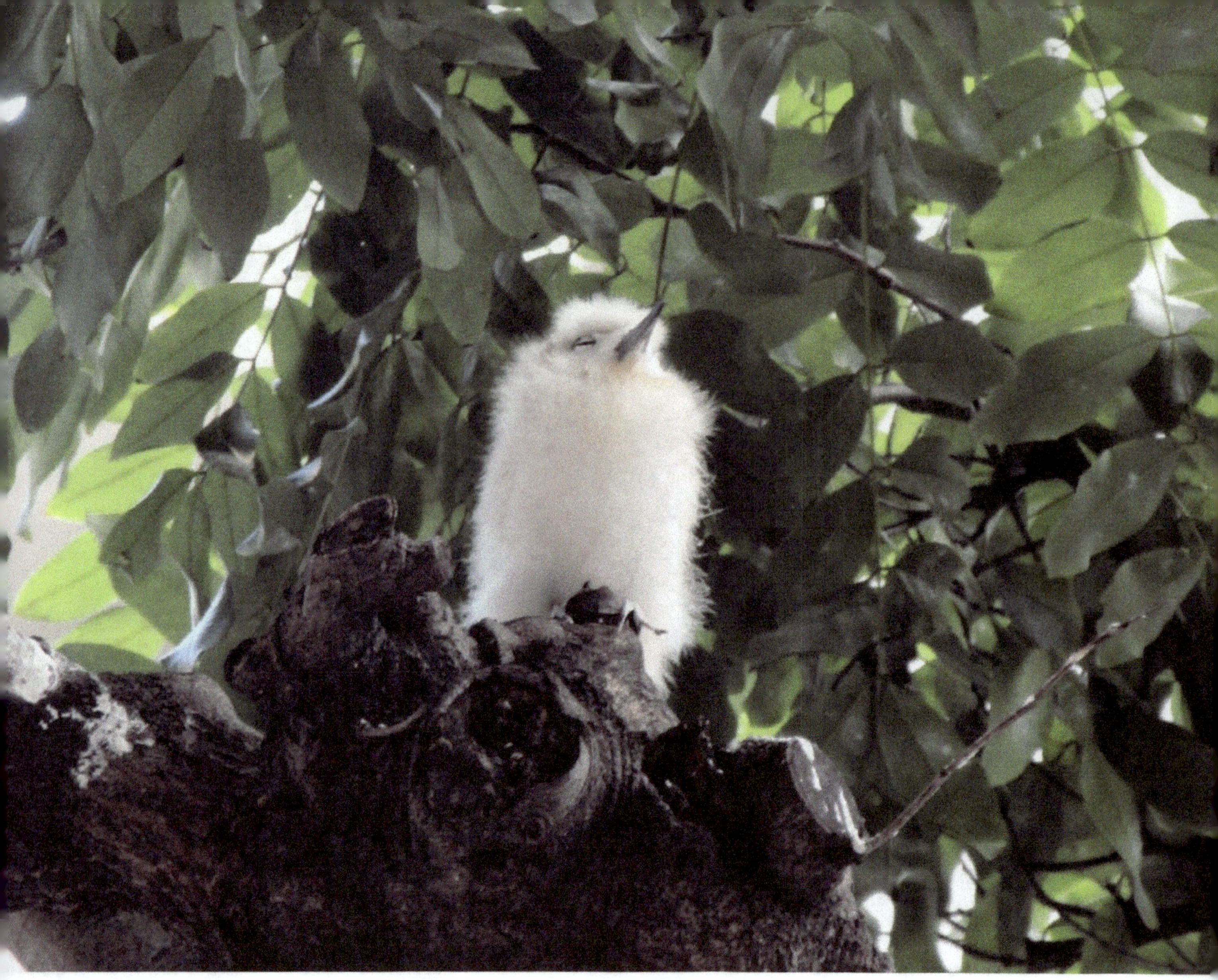

Day 25 after sighting

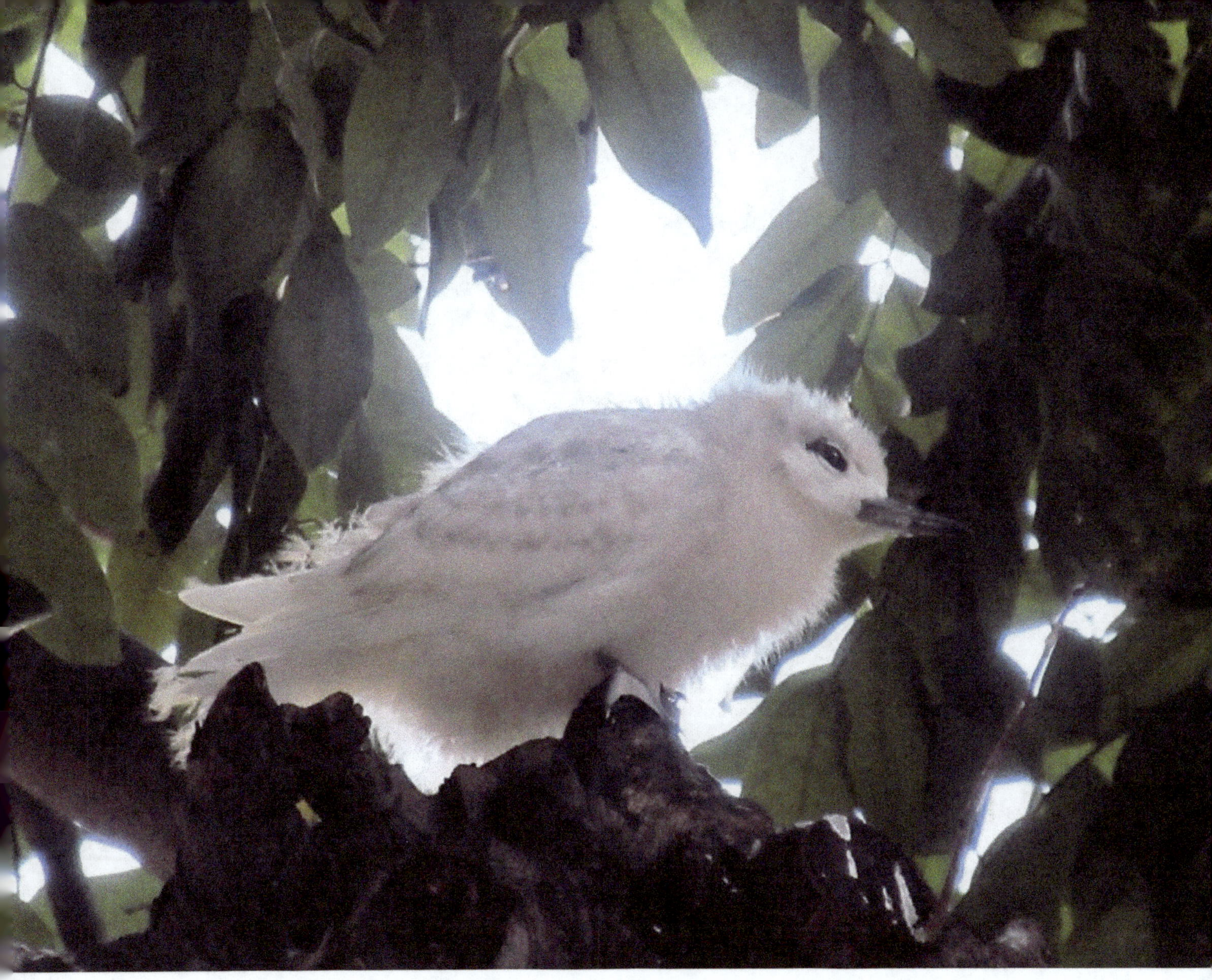

Day 27 after sighting

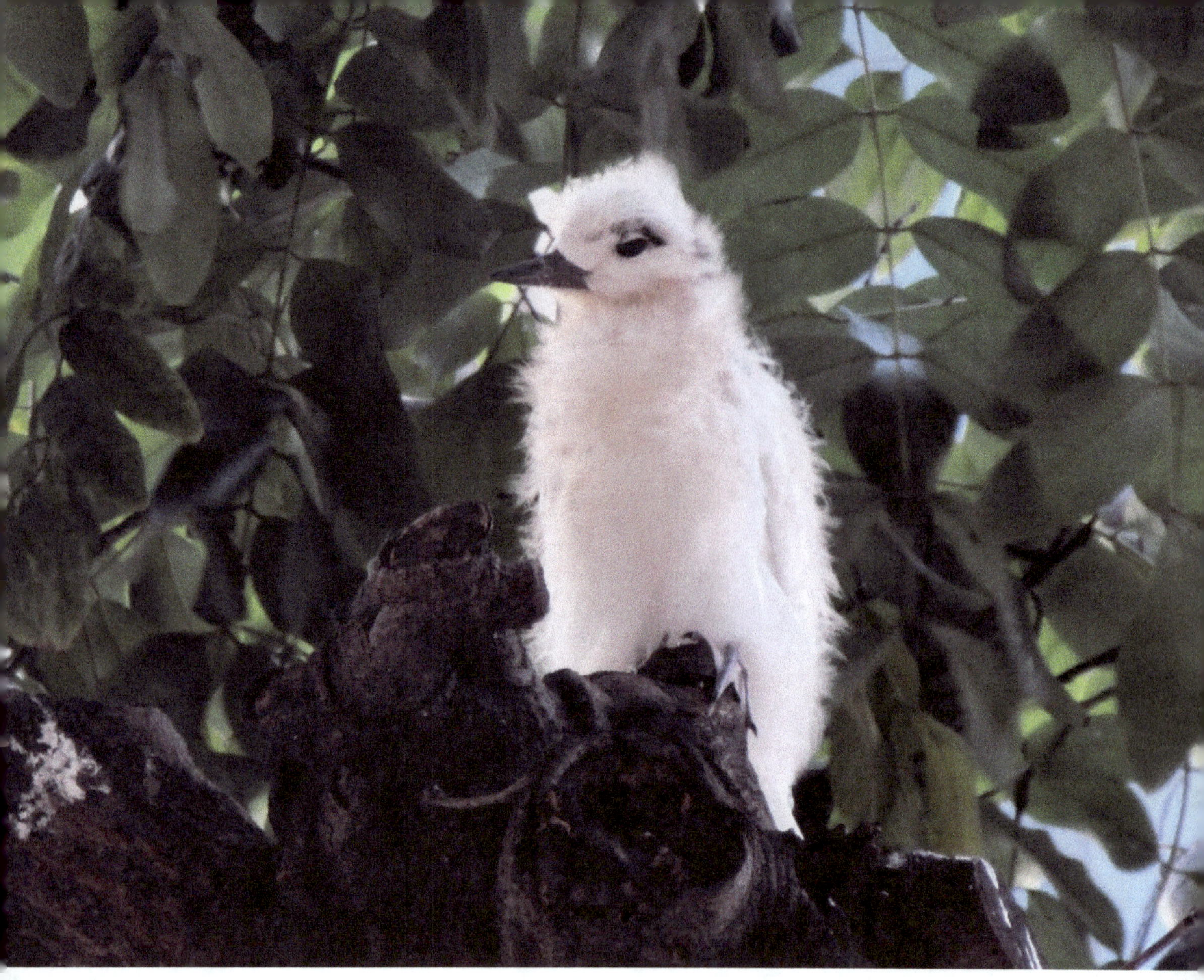

Day 28 after sighting

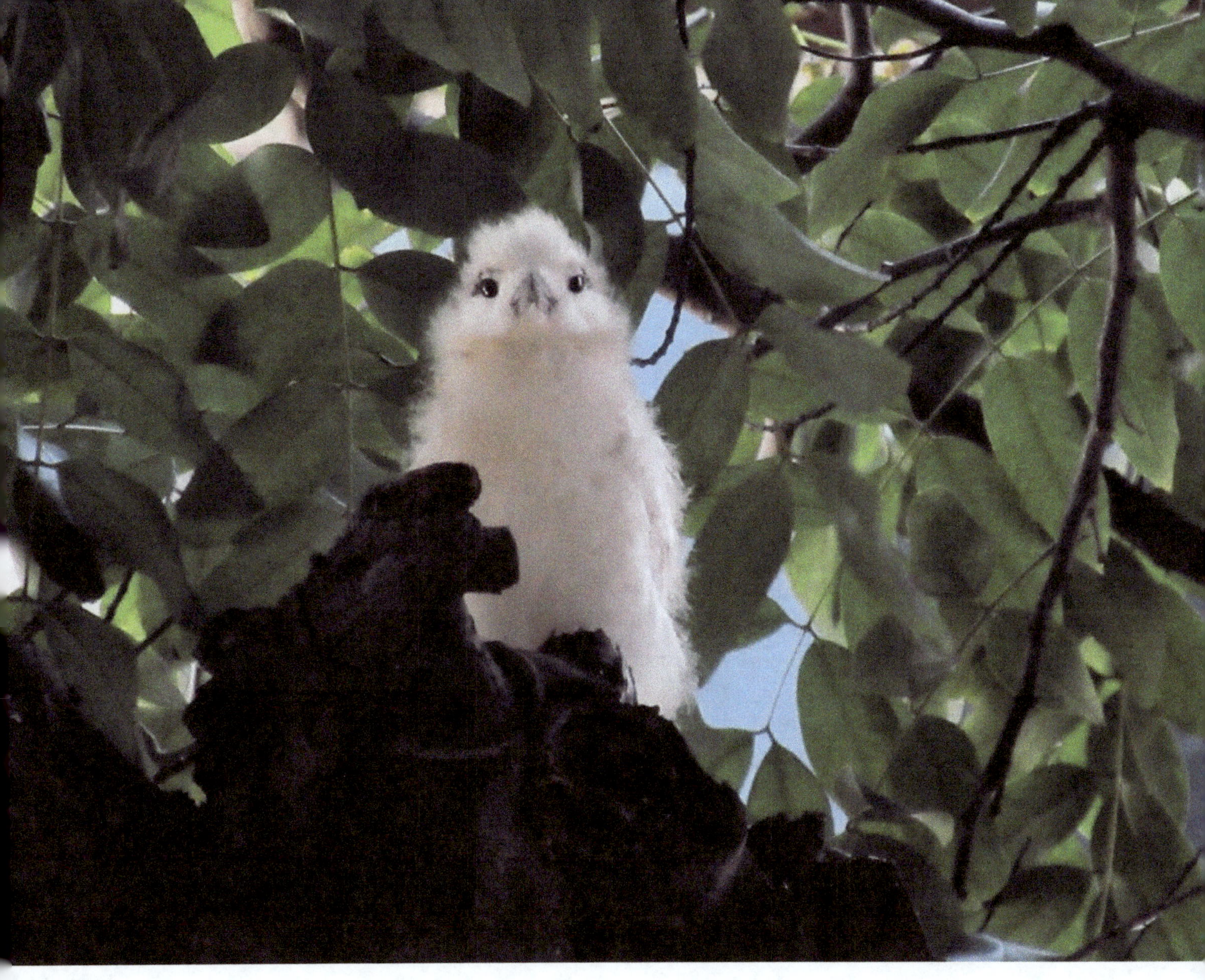

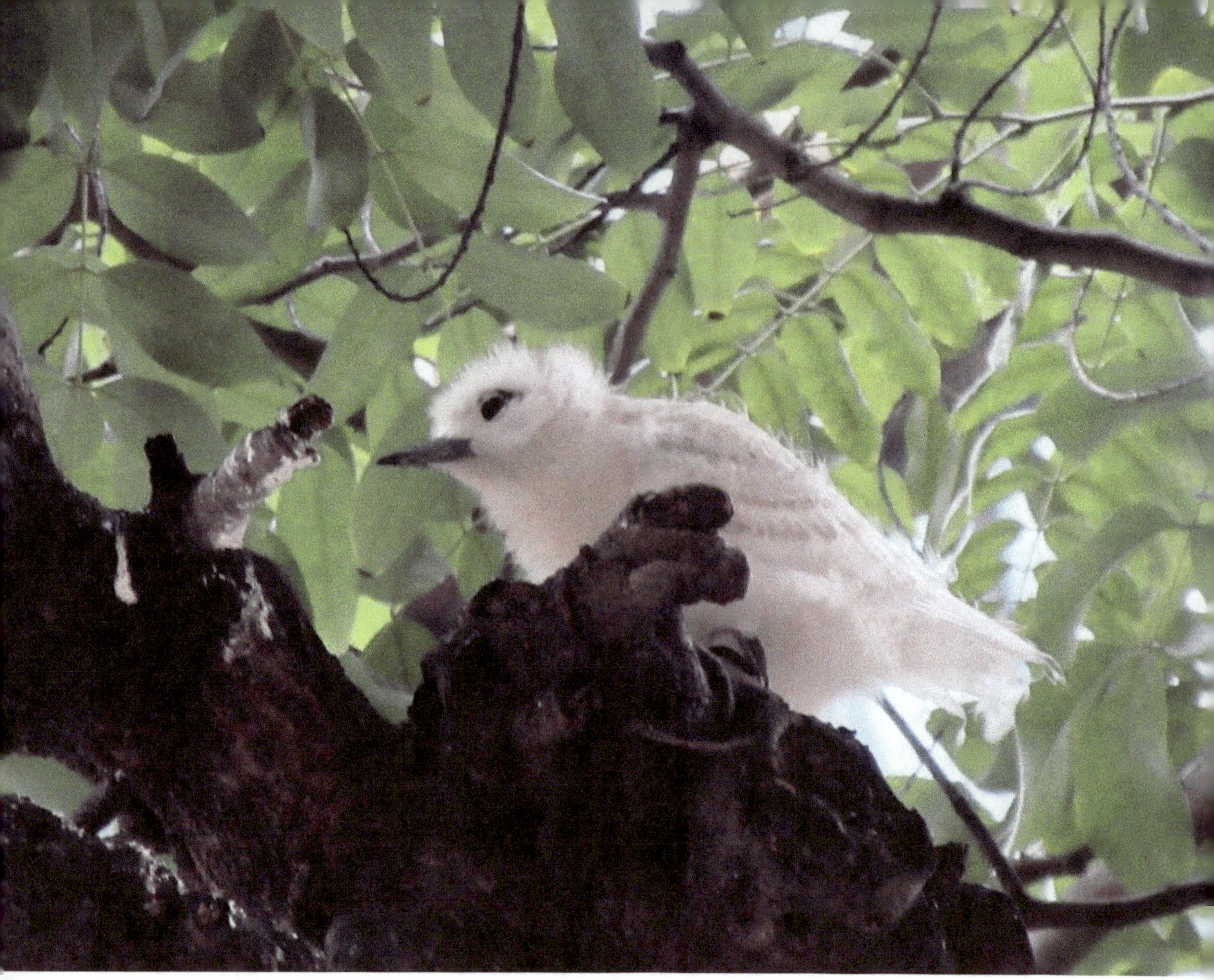

Day 30 after sighting

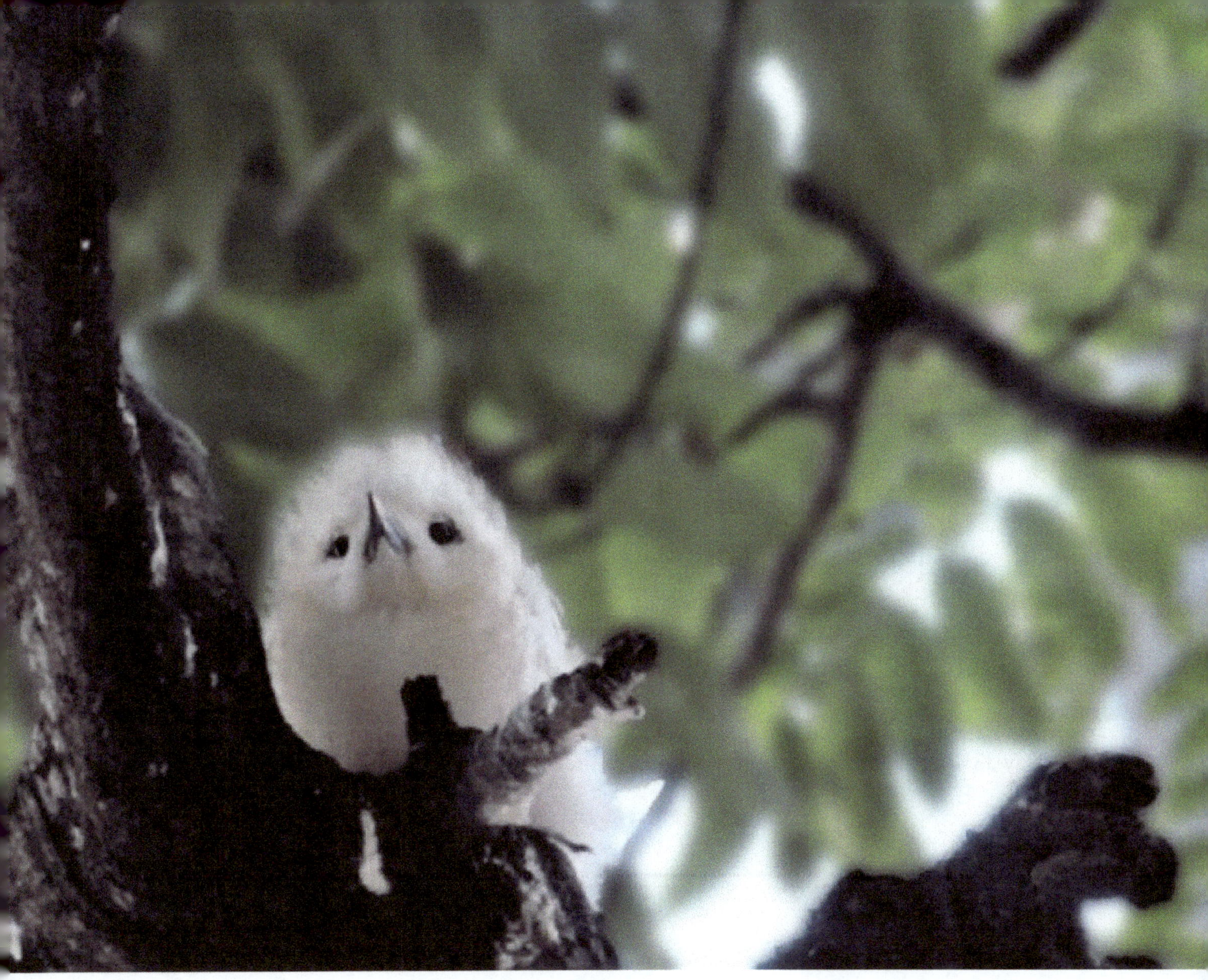

Day 32 after sighting

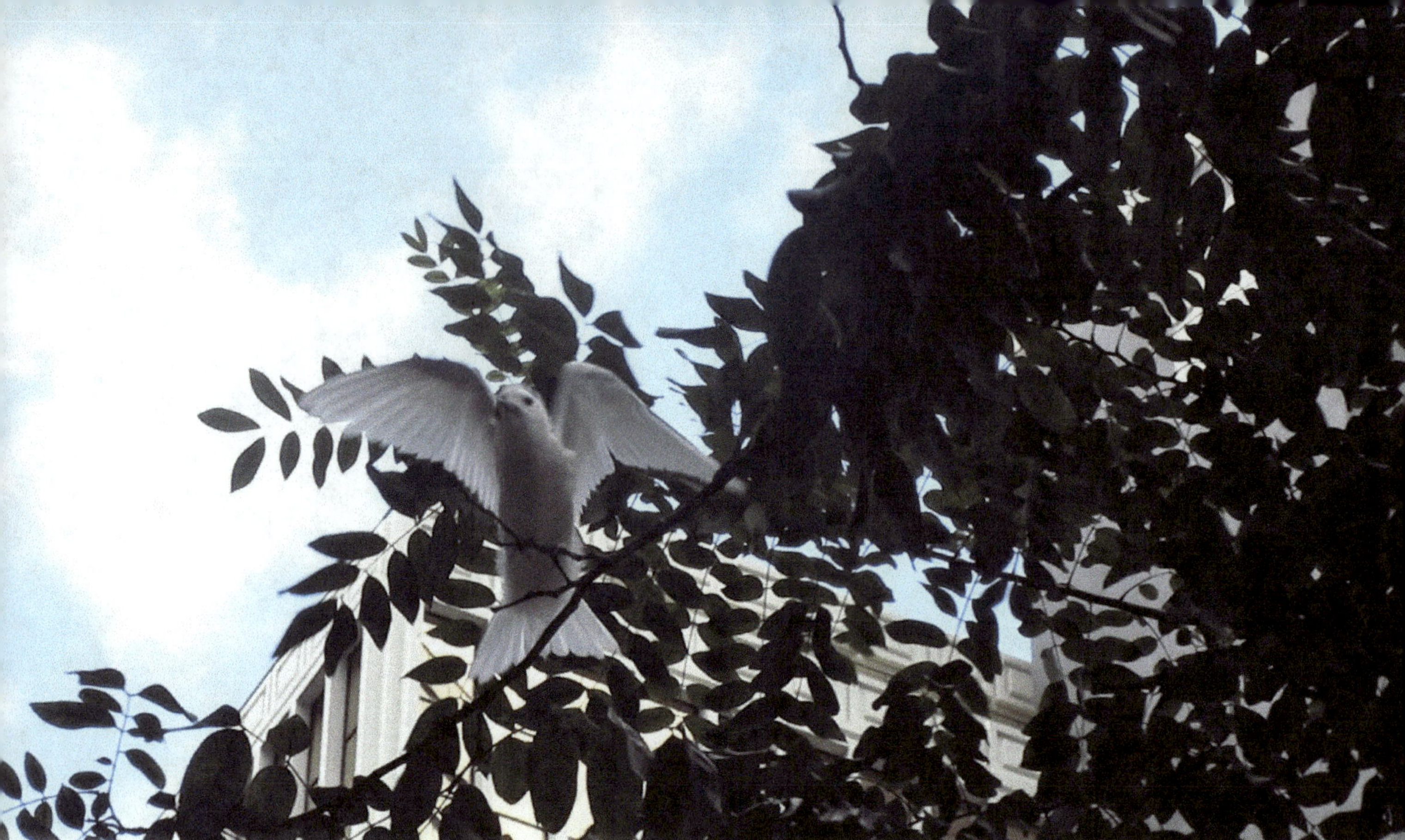

Day 33 after sighting: Sunny moves from the breeding branch to an outer branch of the tree.

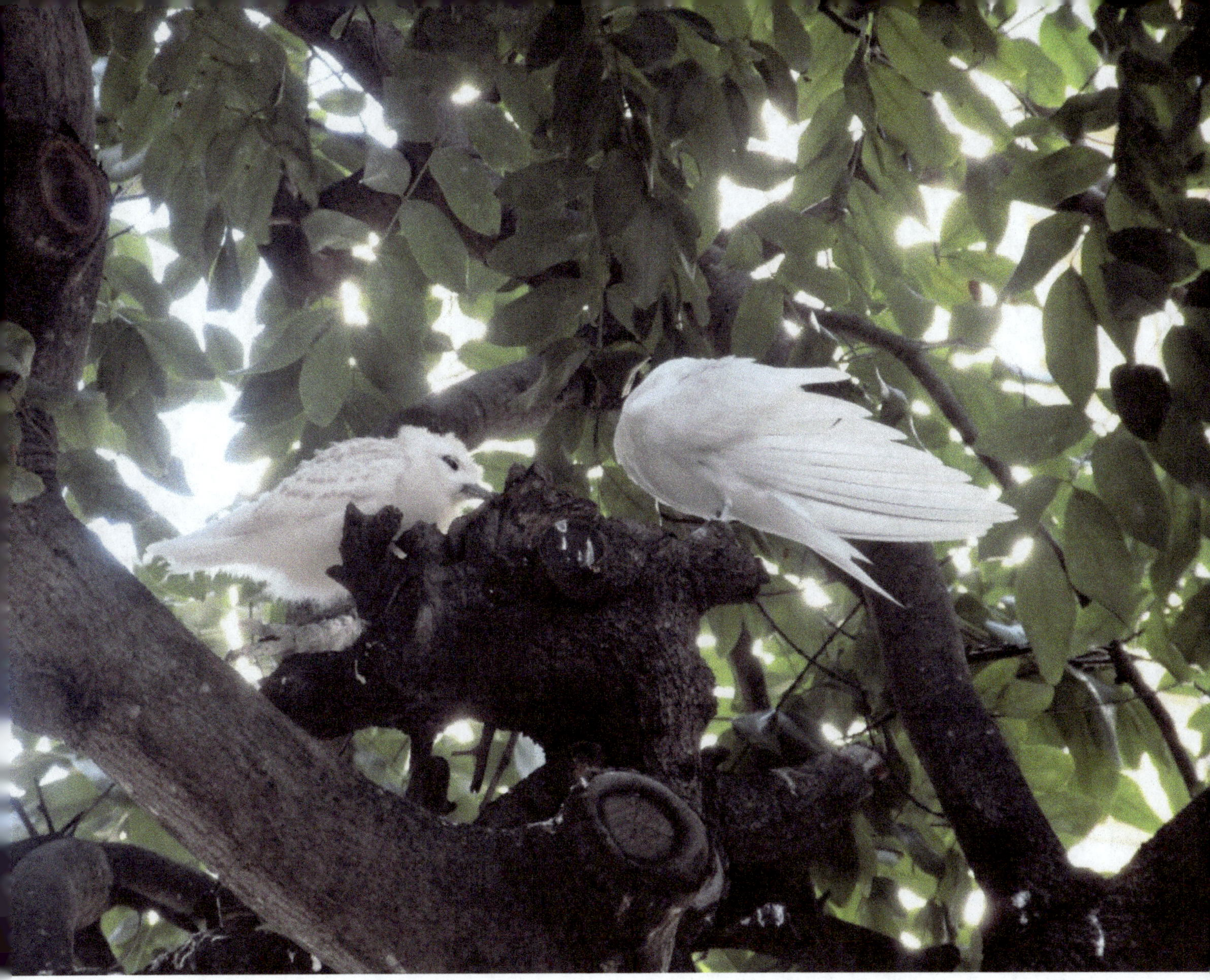

Day 35 after sighting: Sunny and a parent at the breeding branch

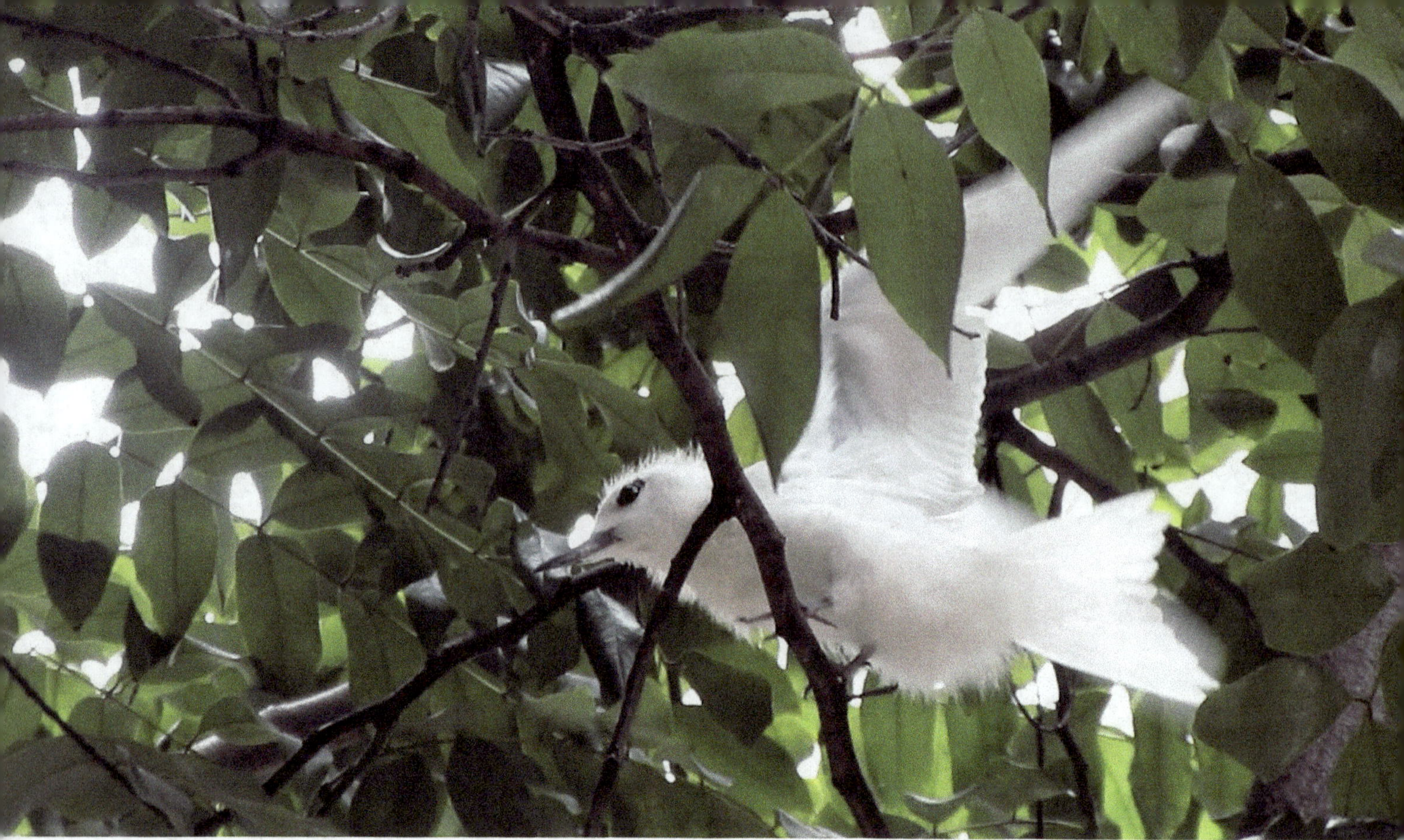

Day 42 after sighting: Sunny balances on a branch.

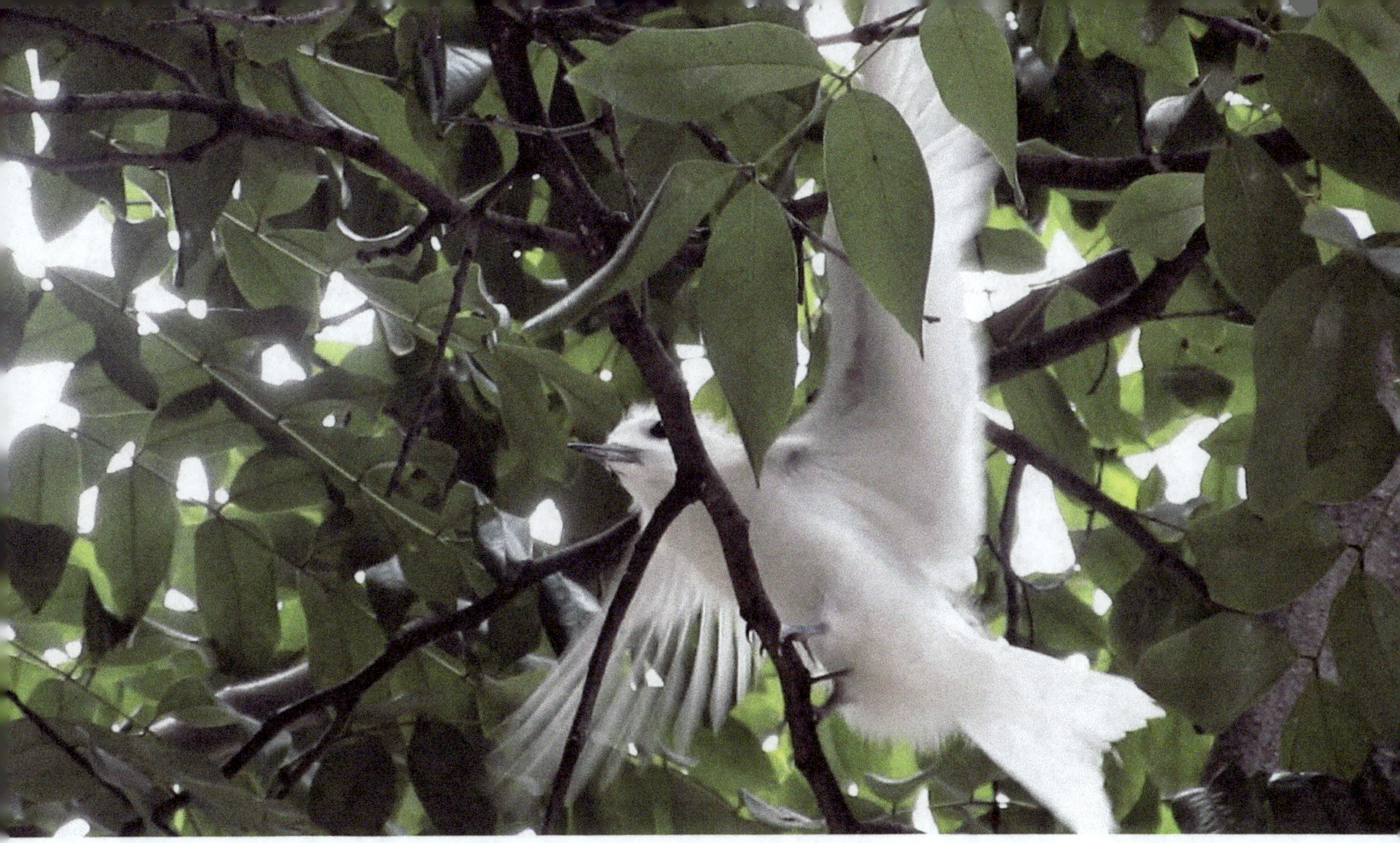

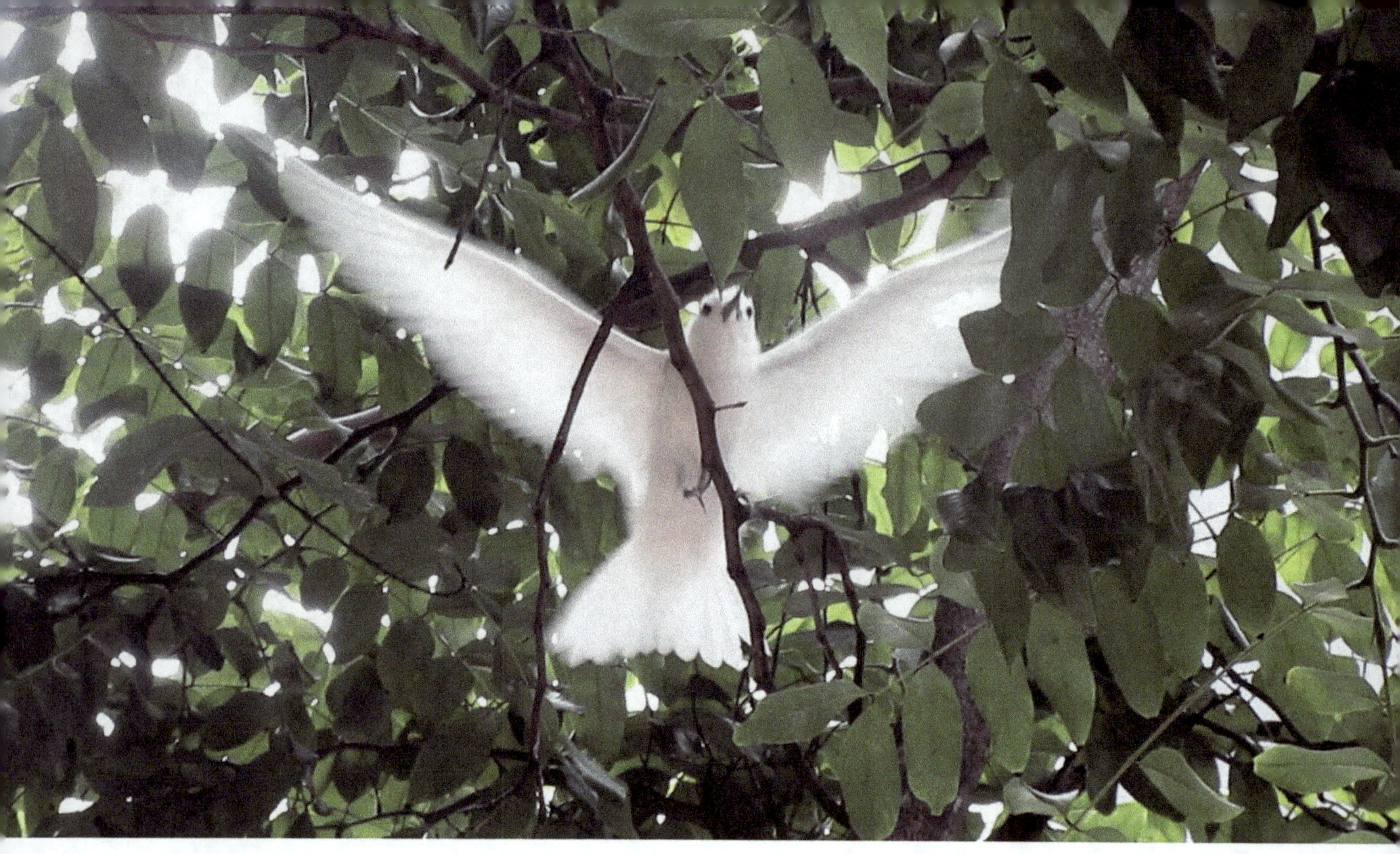

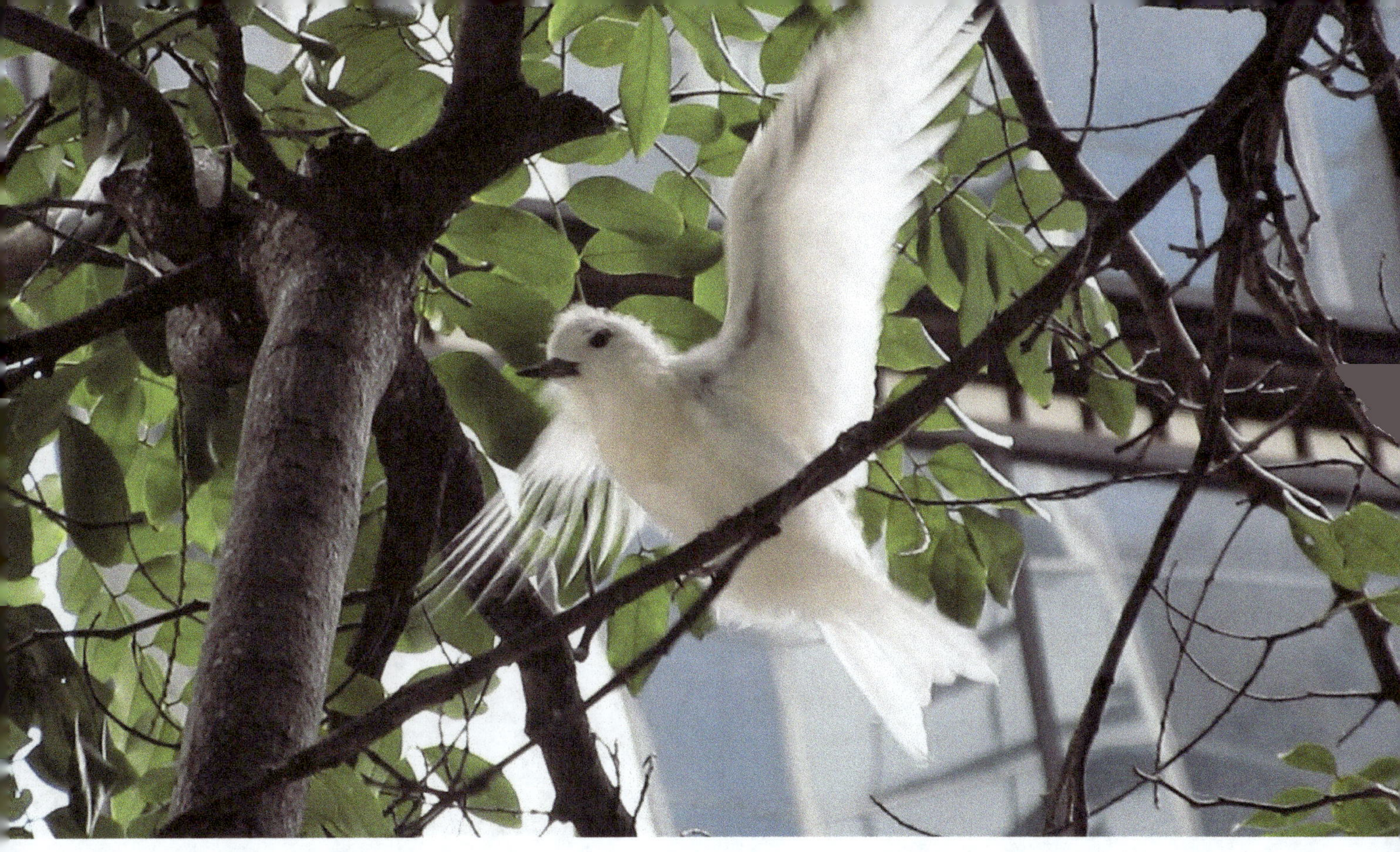

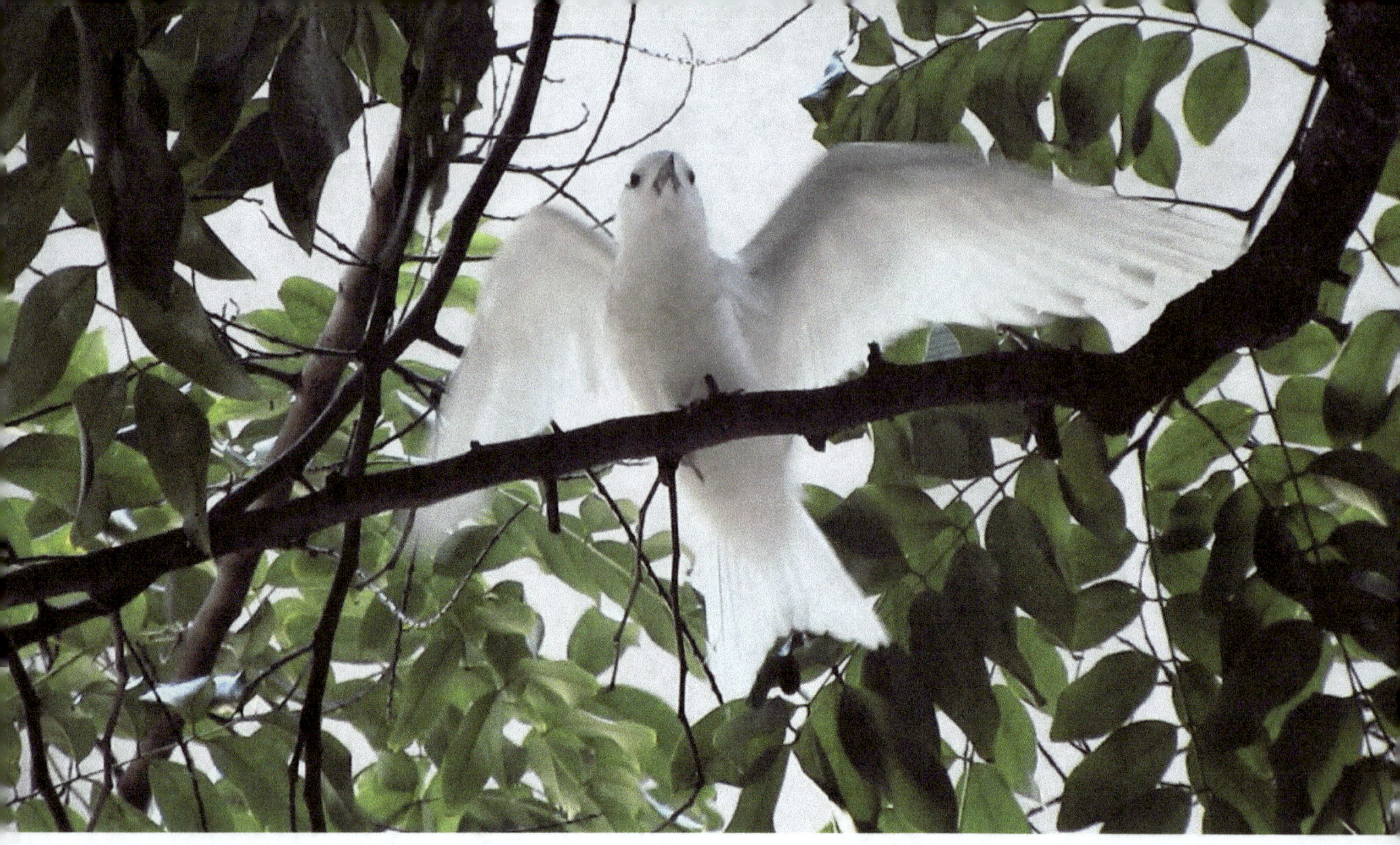

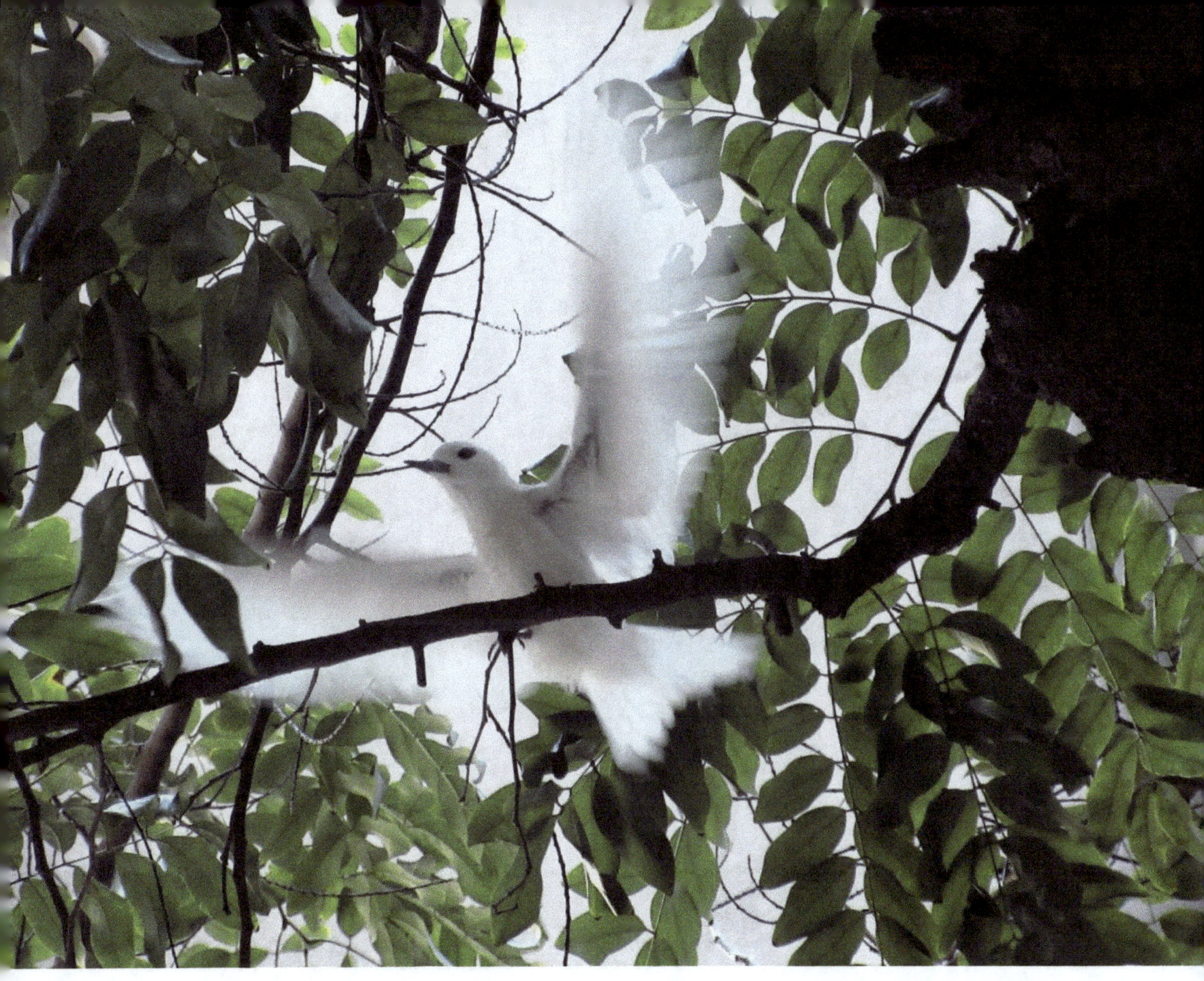

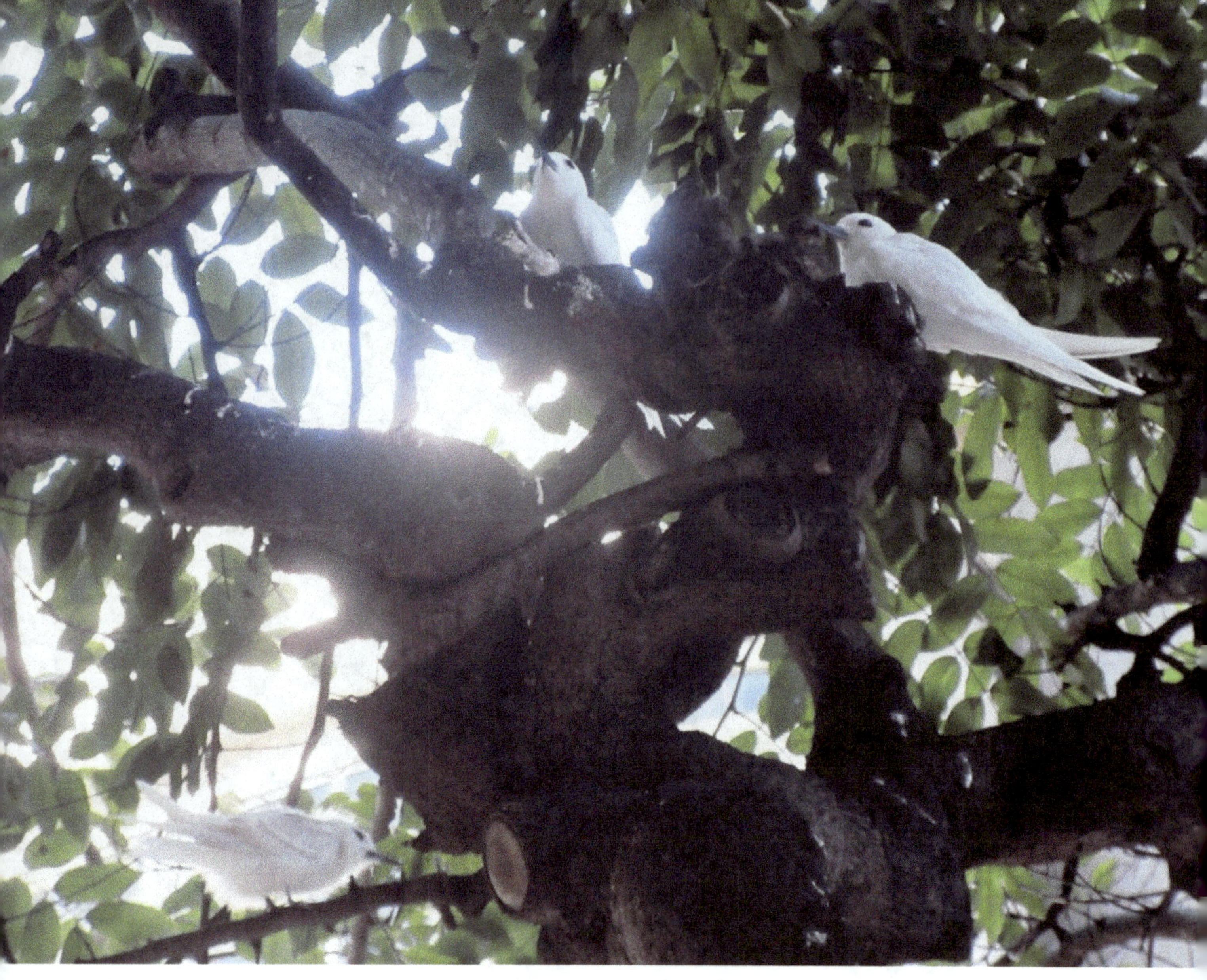

Day 43 after sighting: Sunny and the parents near the breeding branch

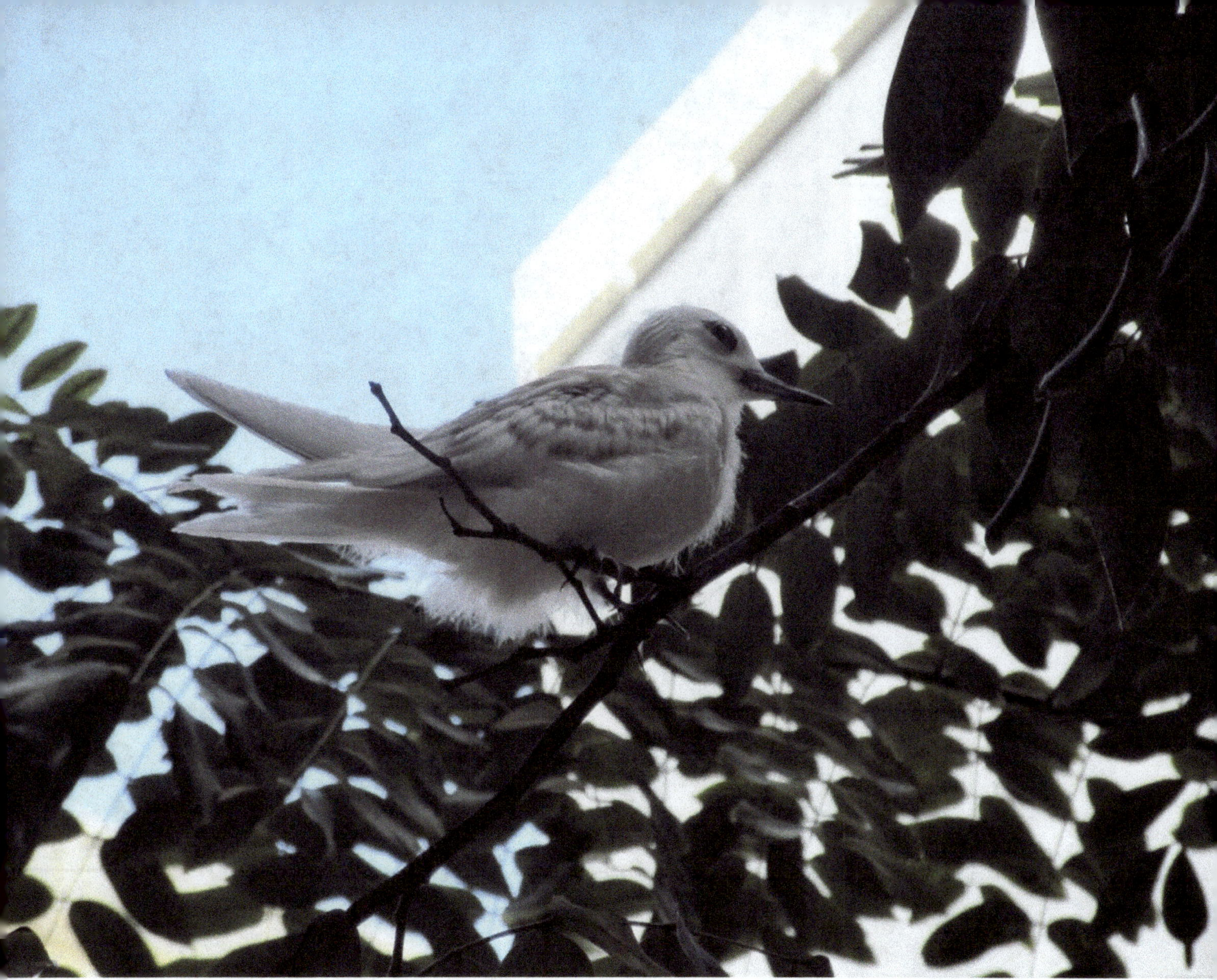

Sunny hangs on to an outer branch of the tree.

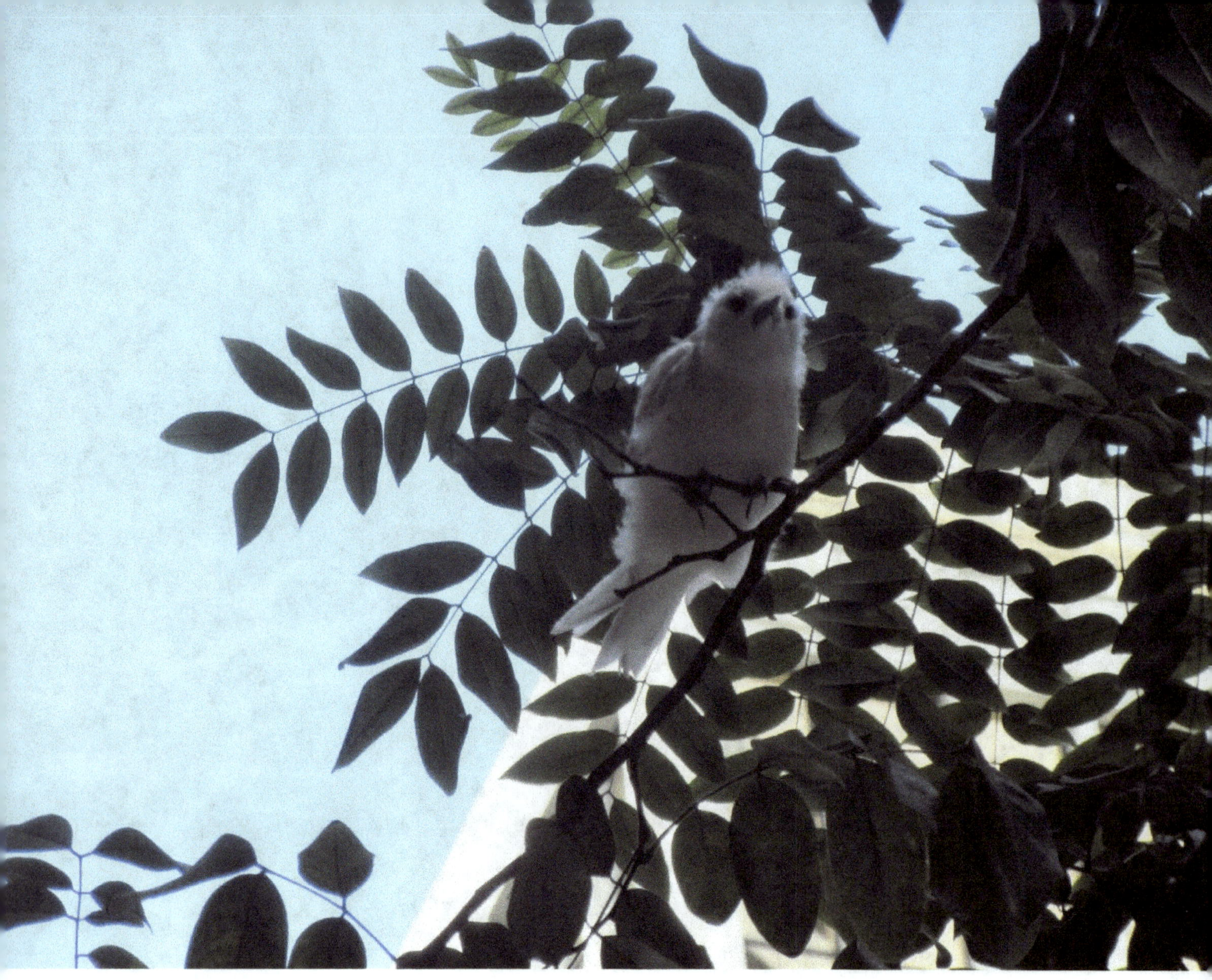

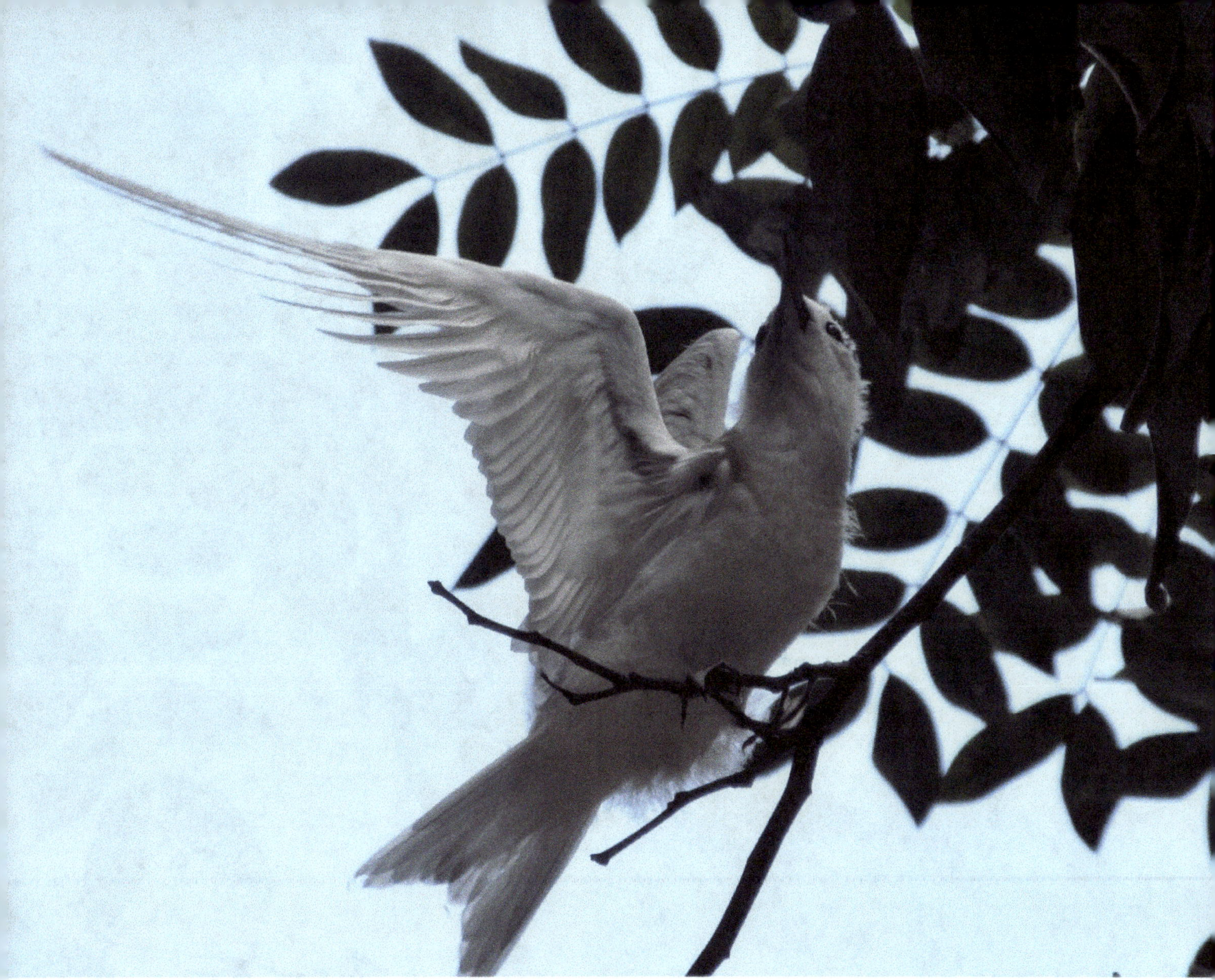

Day 44 after sighting

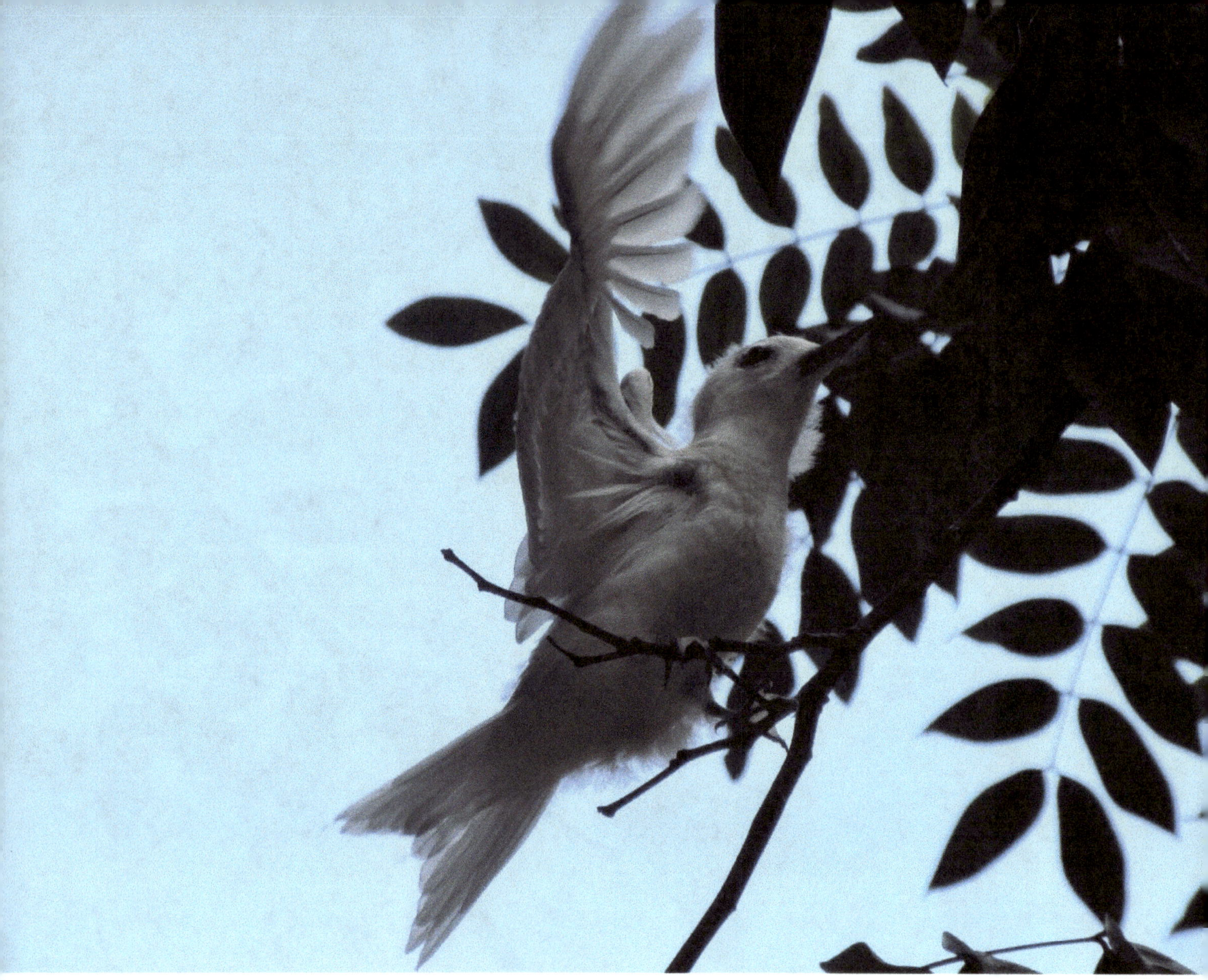

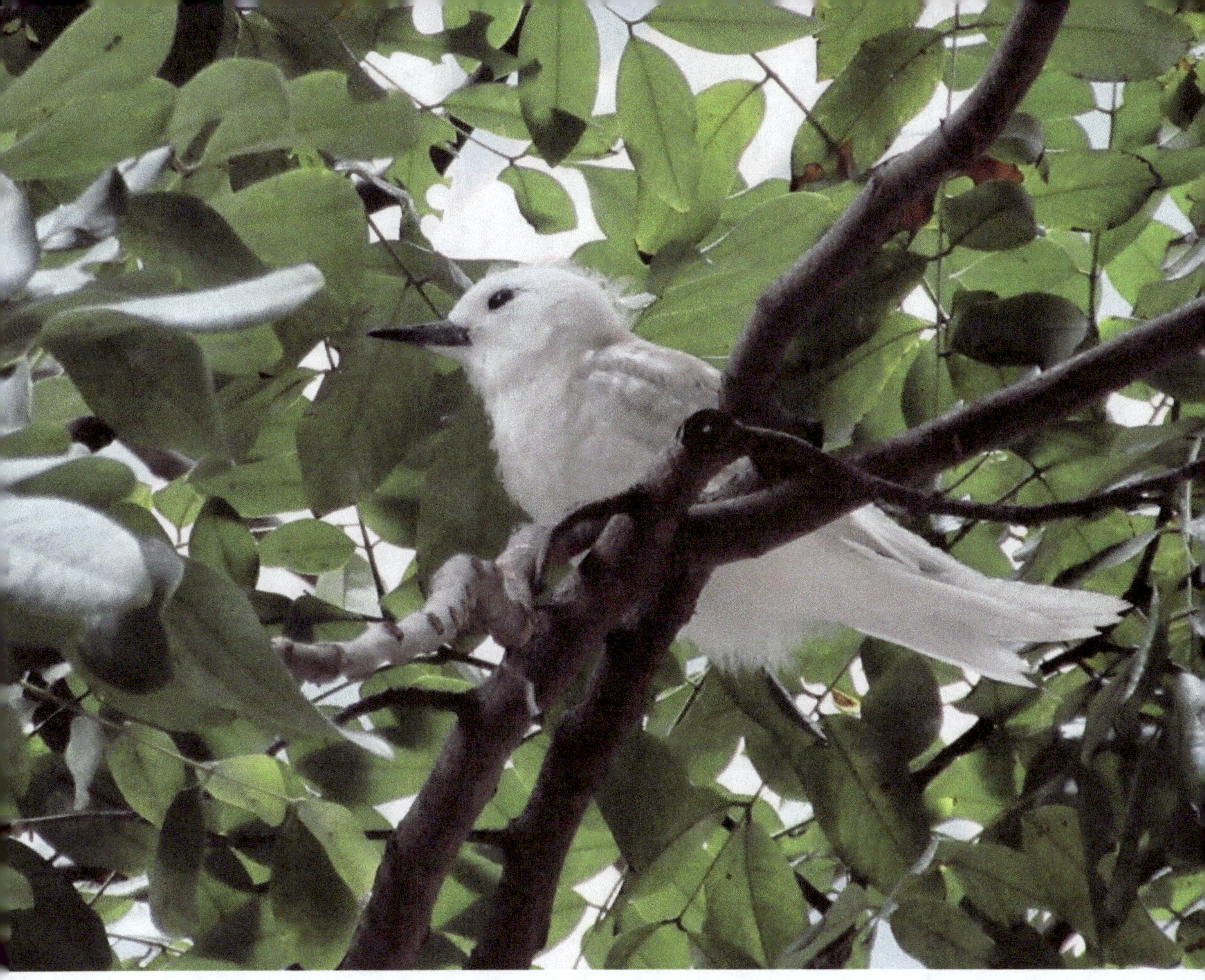

Day 46 after sighting

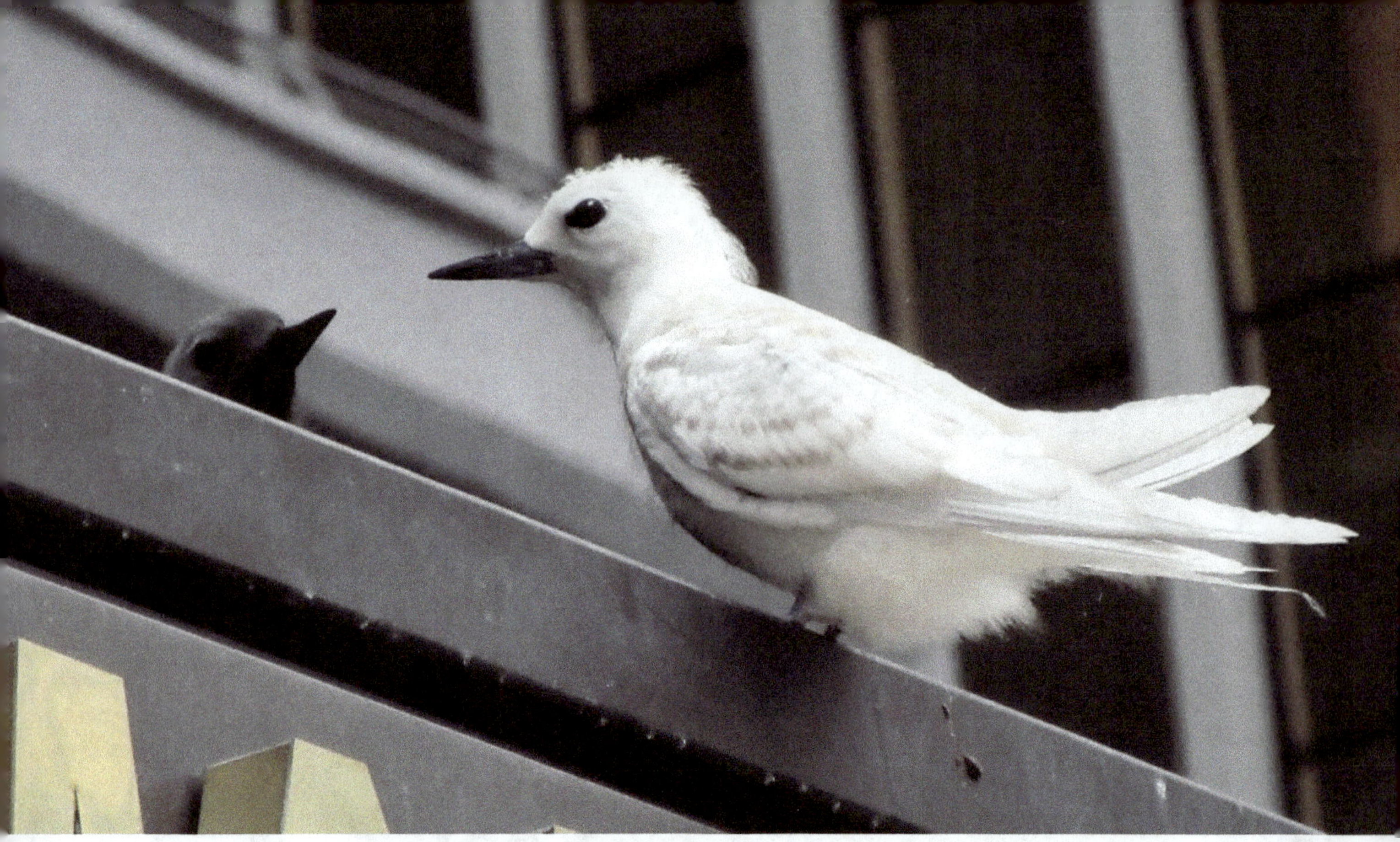

Sunny sees a reflection after flying to a nearby building.

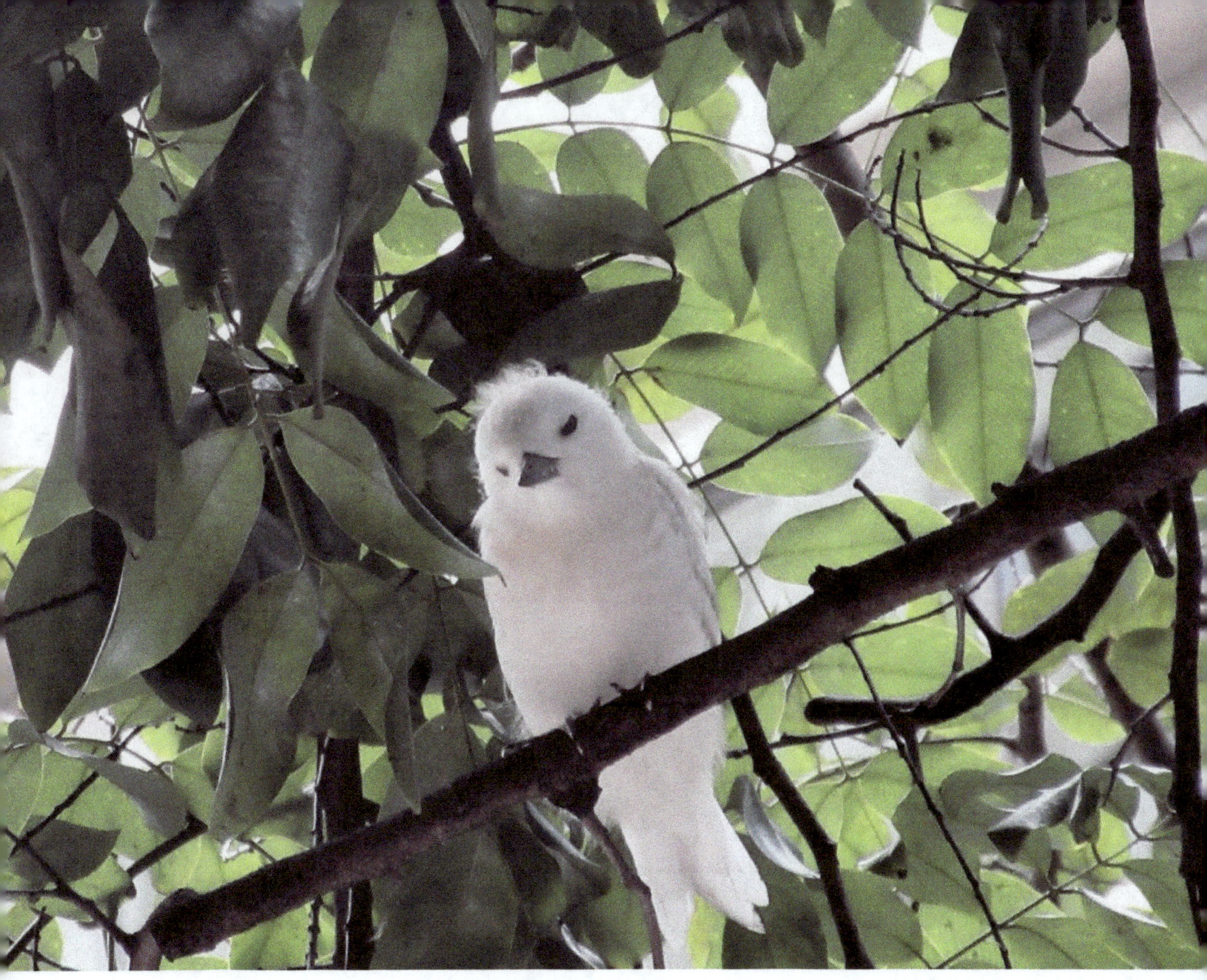

Day 48 after sighting

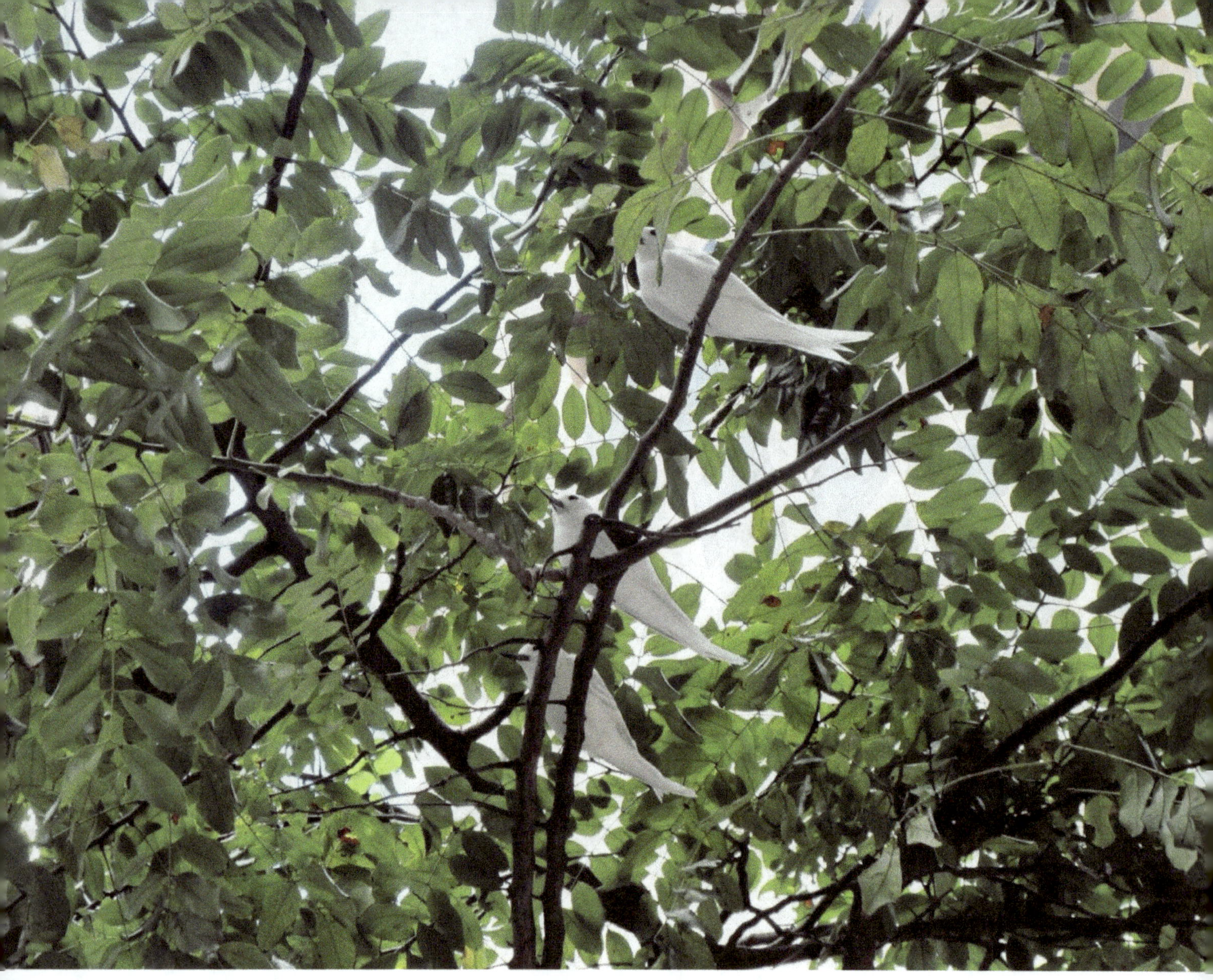

Day 56 after sighting: Sunny and the parents

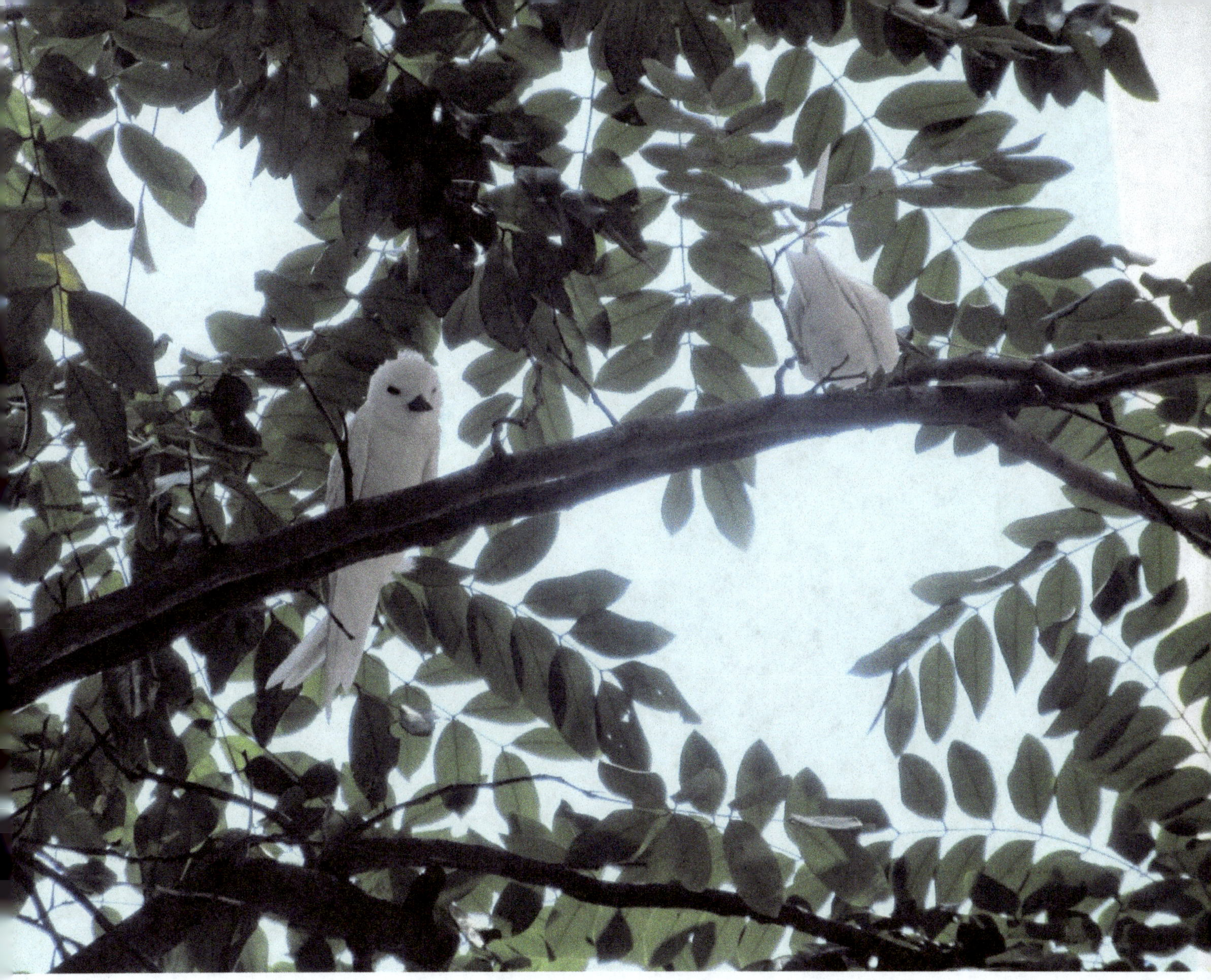

Day 57 after sighting: Sunny and a parent

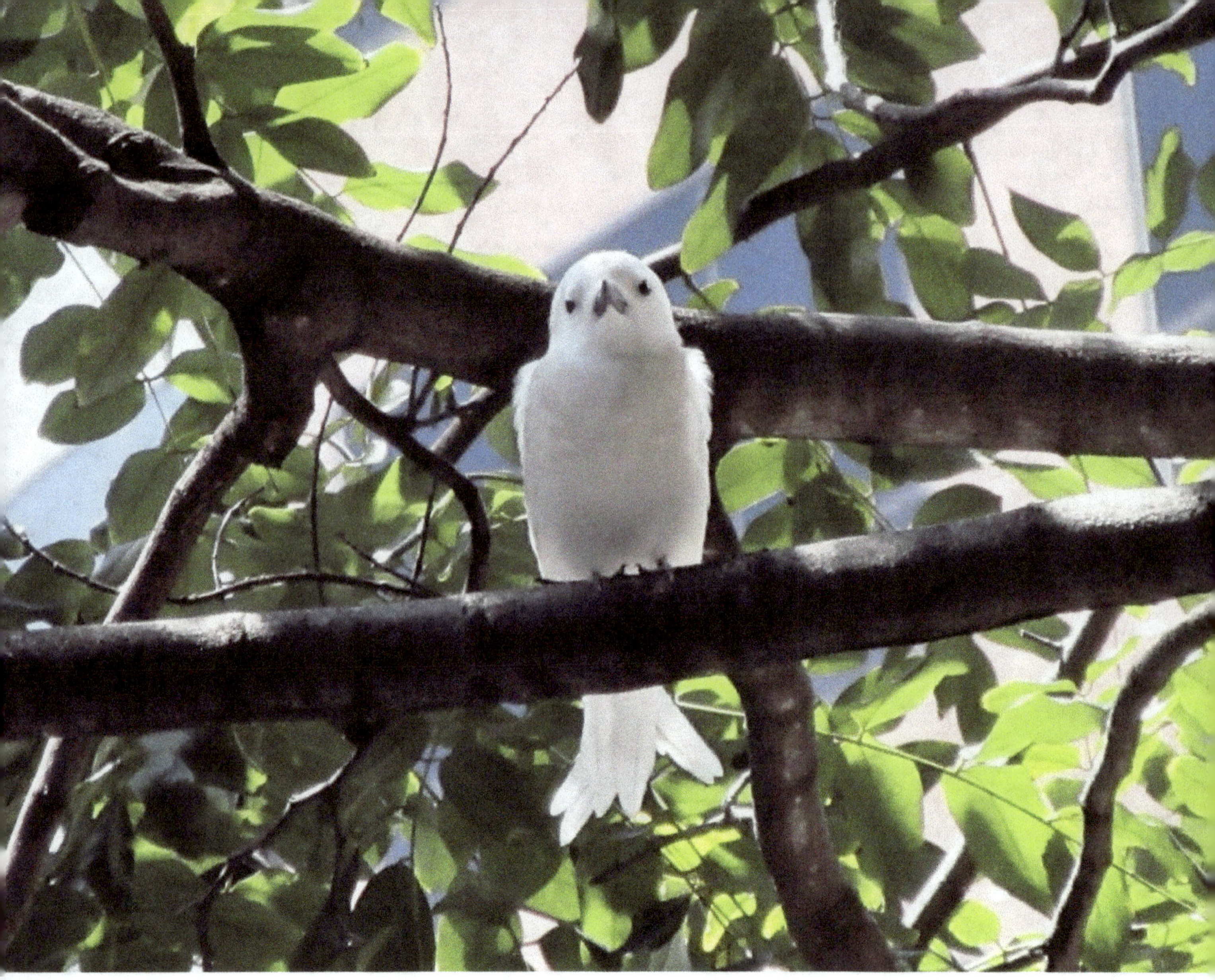

Day 65 after sighting

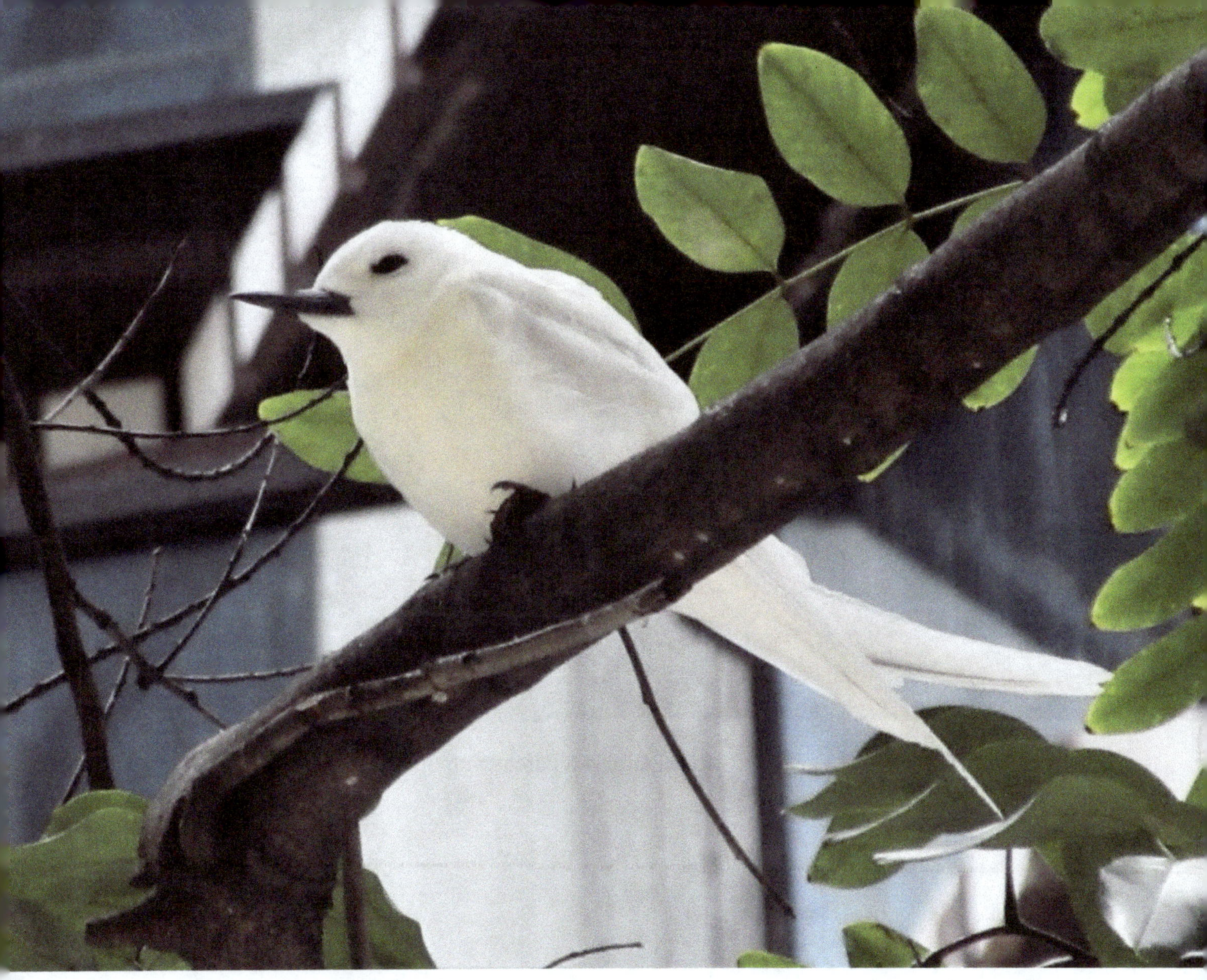

Day 74 after sighting

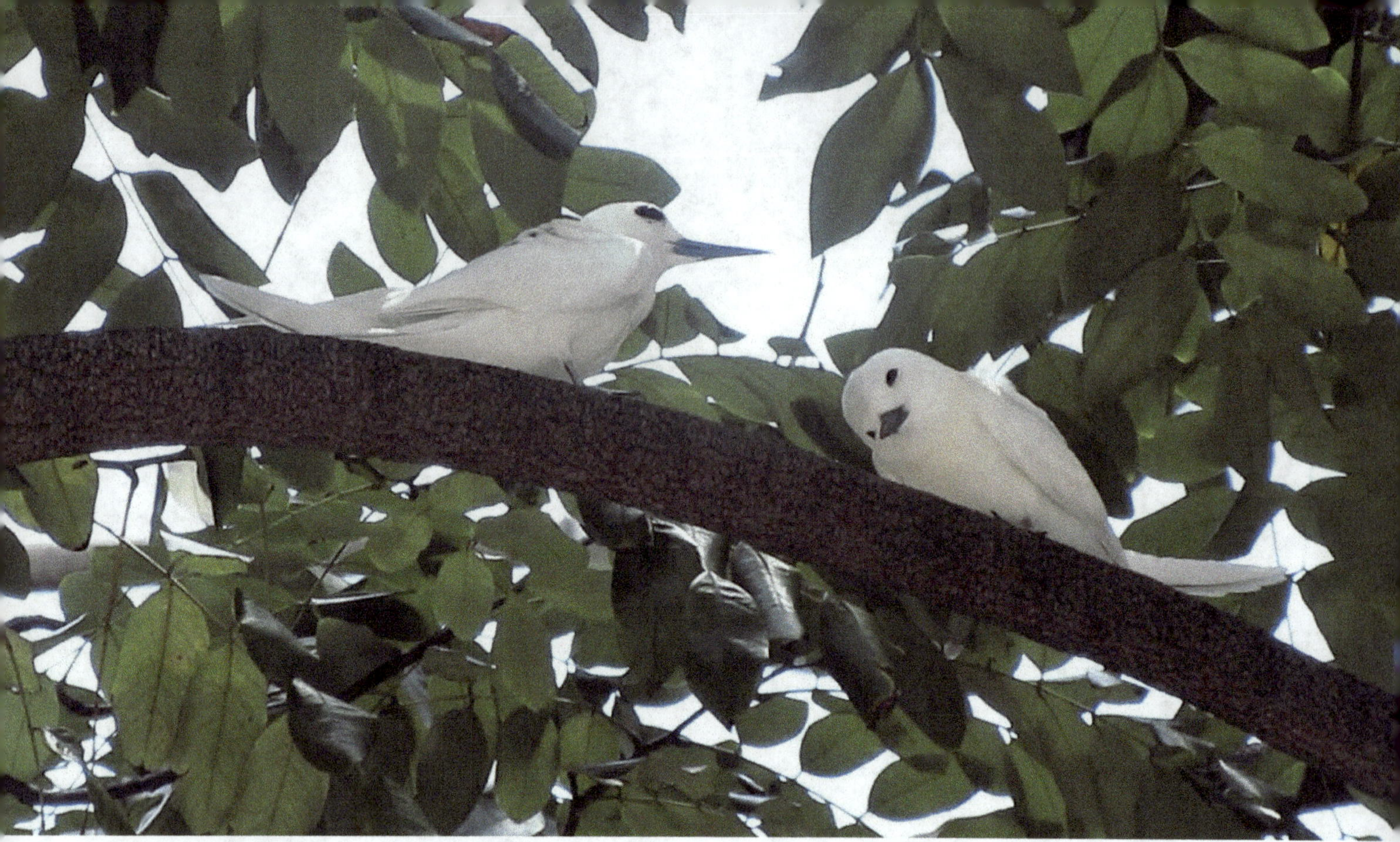

Day 75 after sighting: A parent with Sunny

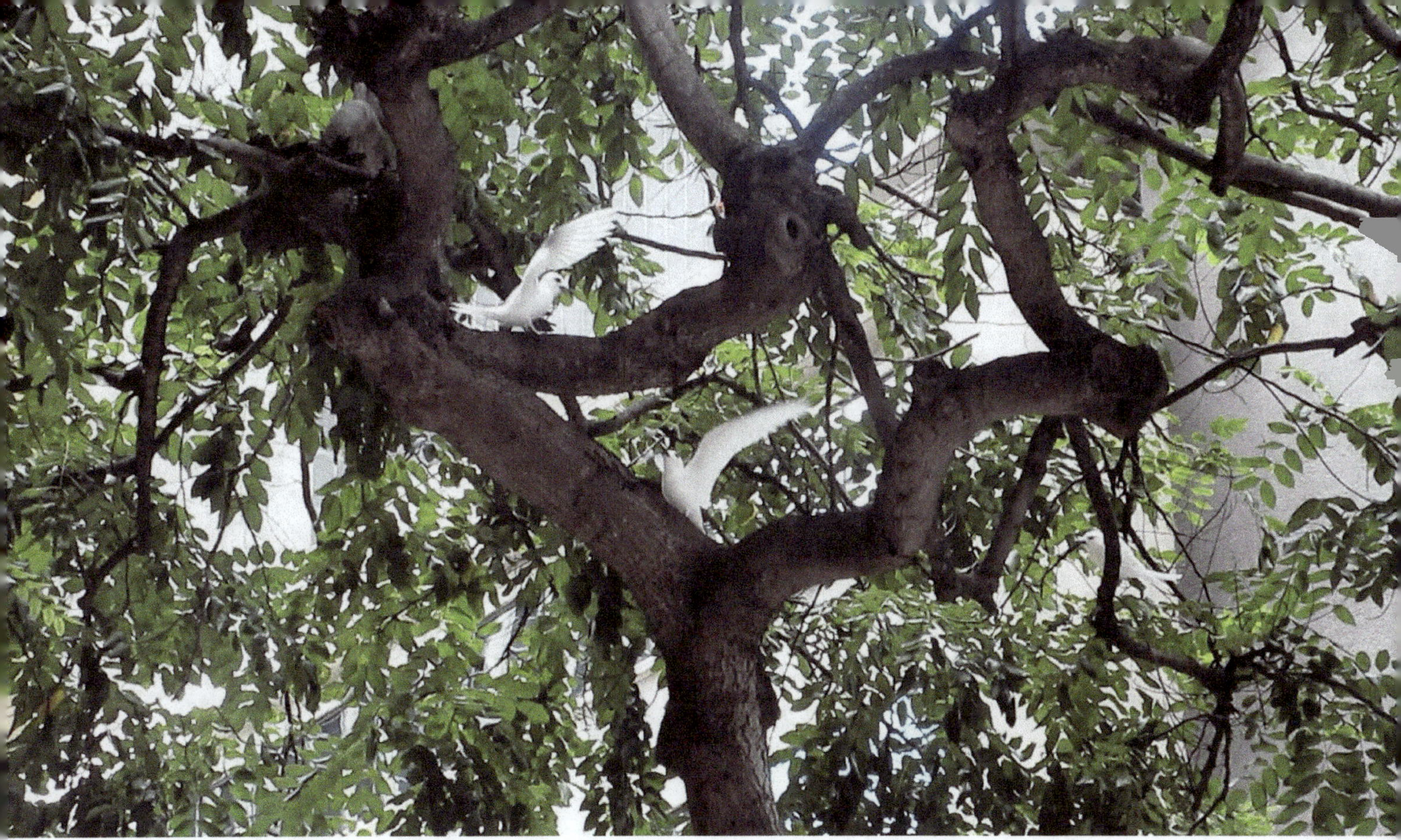

The parents and Sunny

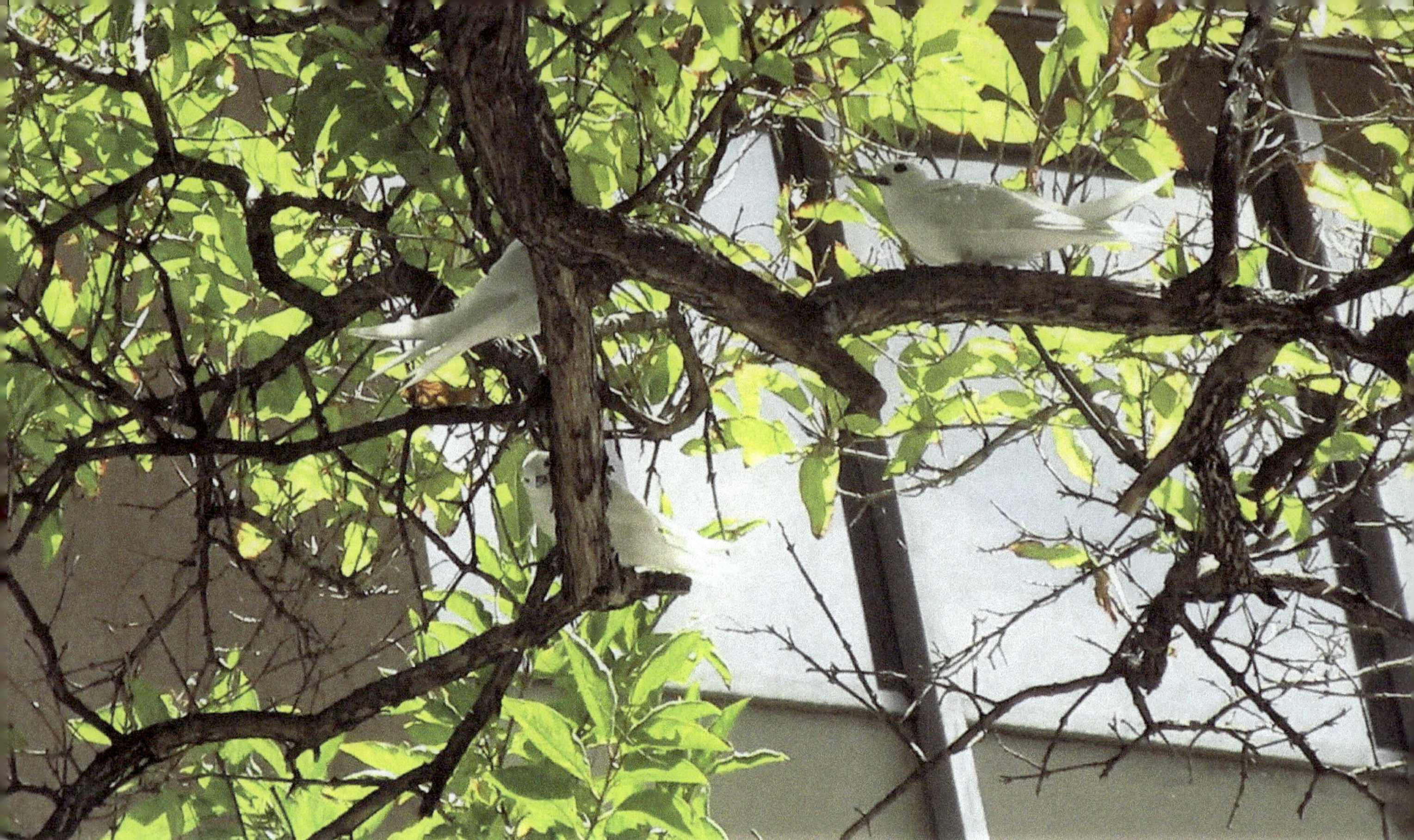

Day 79 after sighting: The parents with Sunny

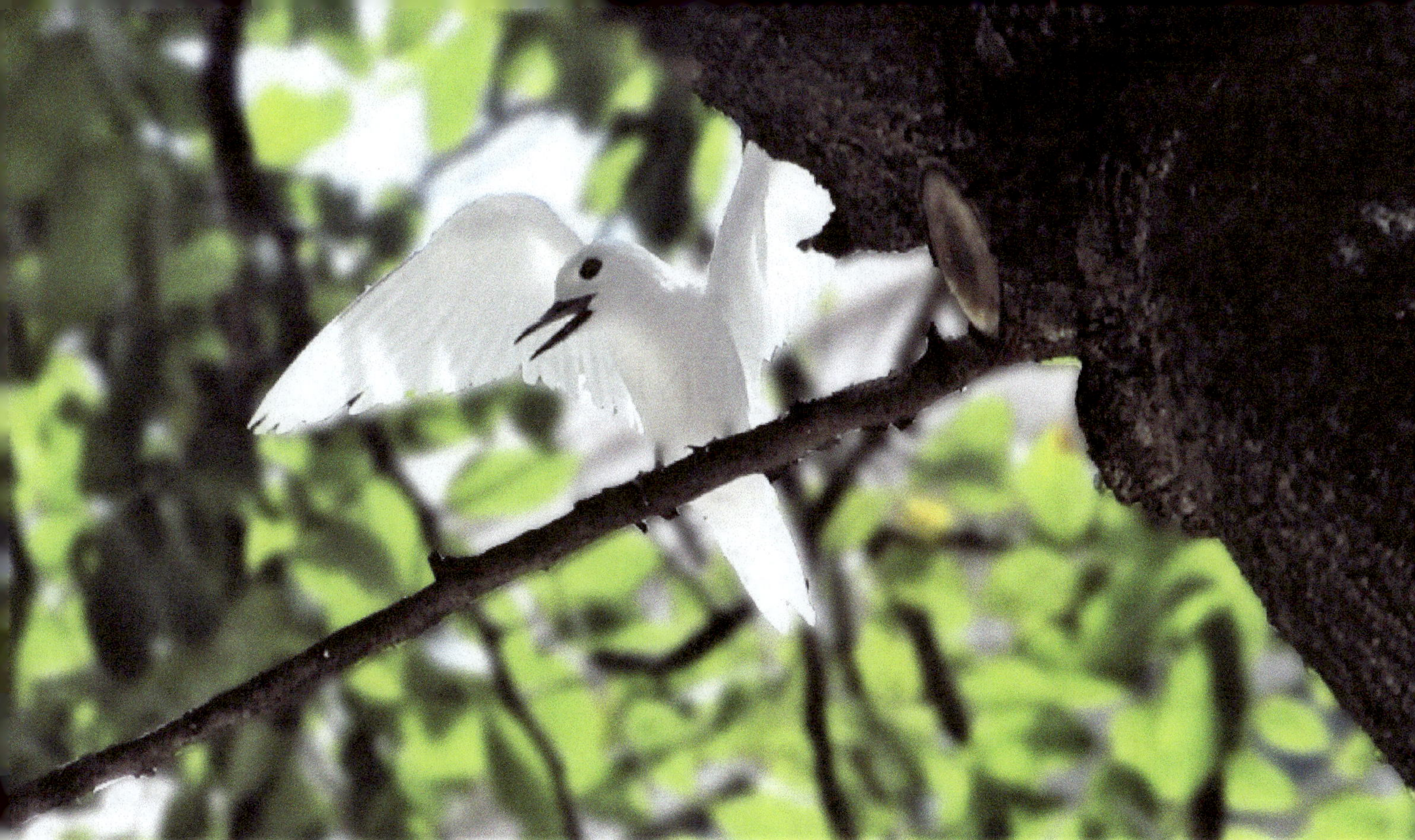

Day 85 after sighting: A last look at Sunny

APPENDIX

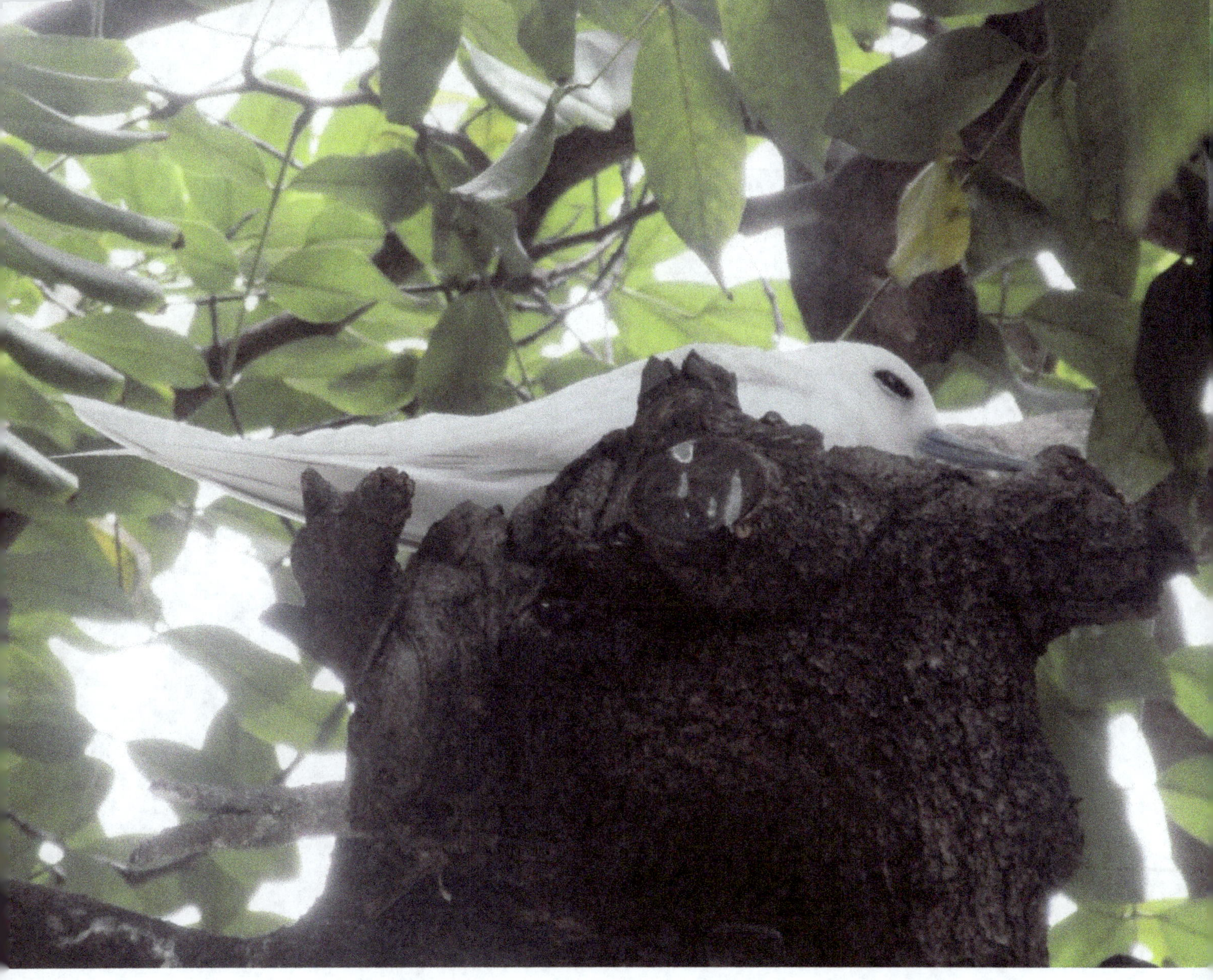

26 days later: An adult white tern is spotted in Sunny's former breeding branch each day until...

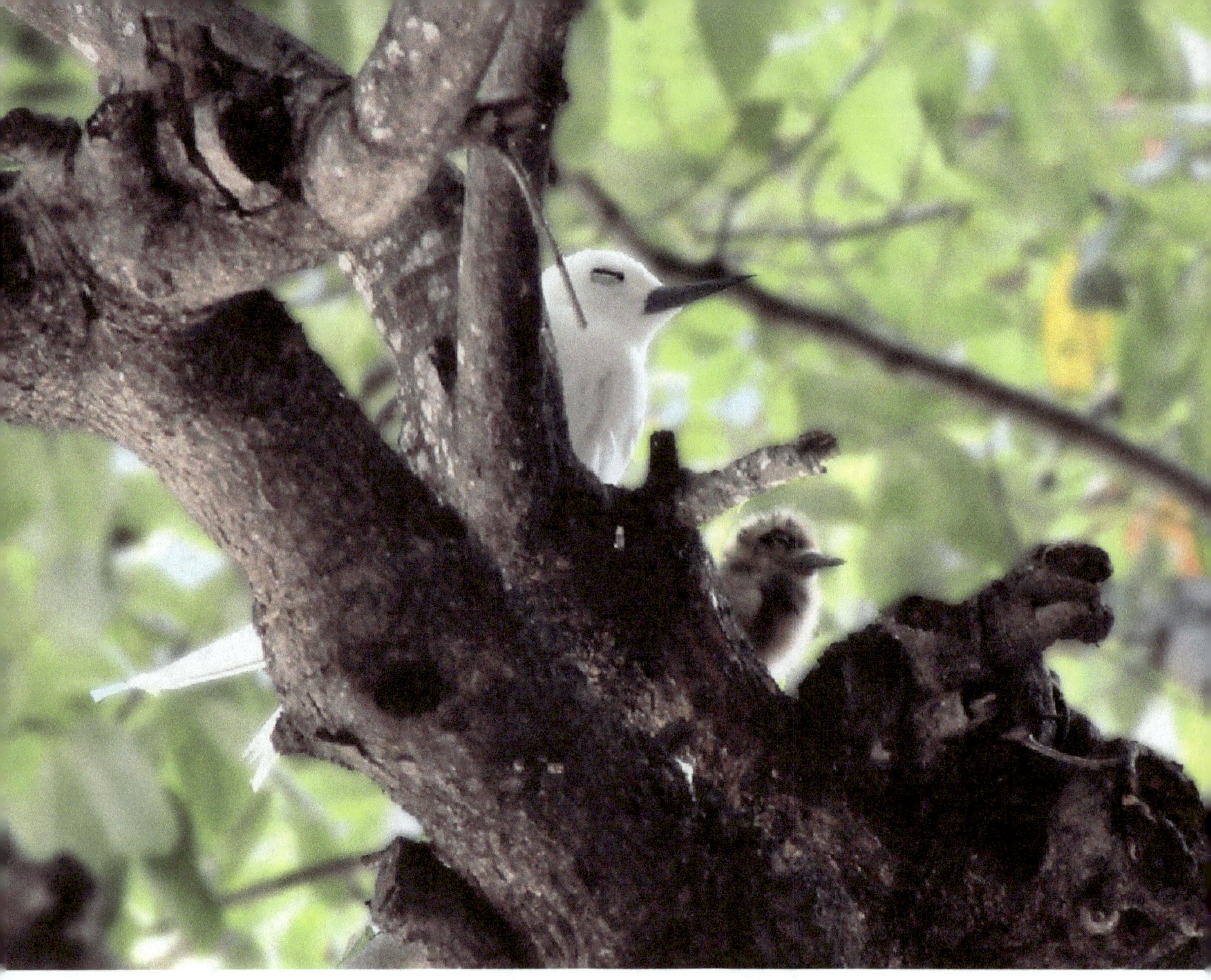

45 days later: Baby Nelly is spotted!

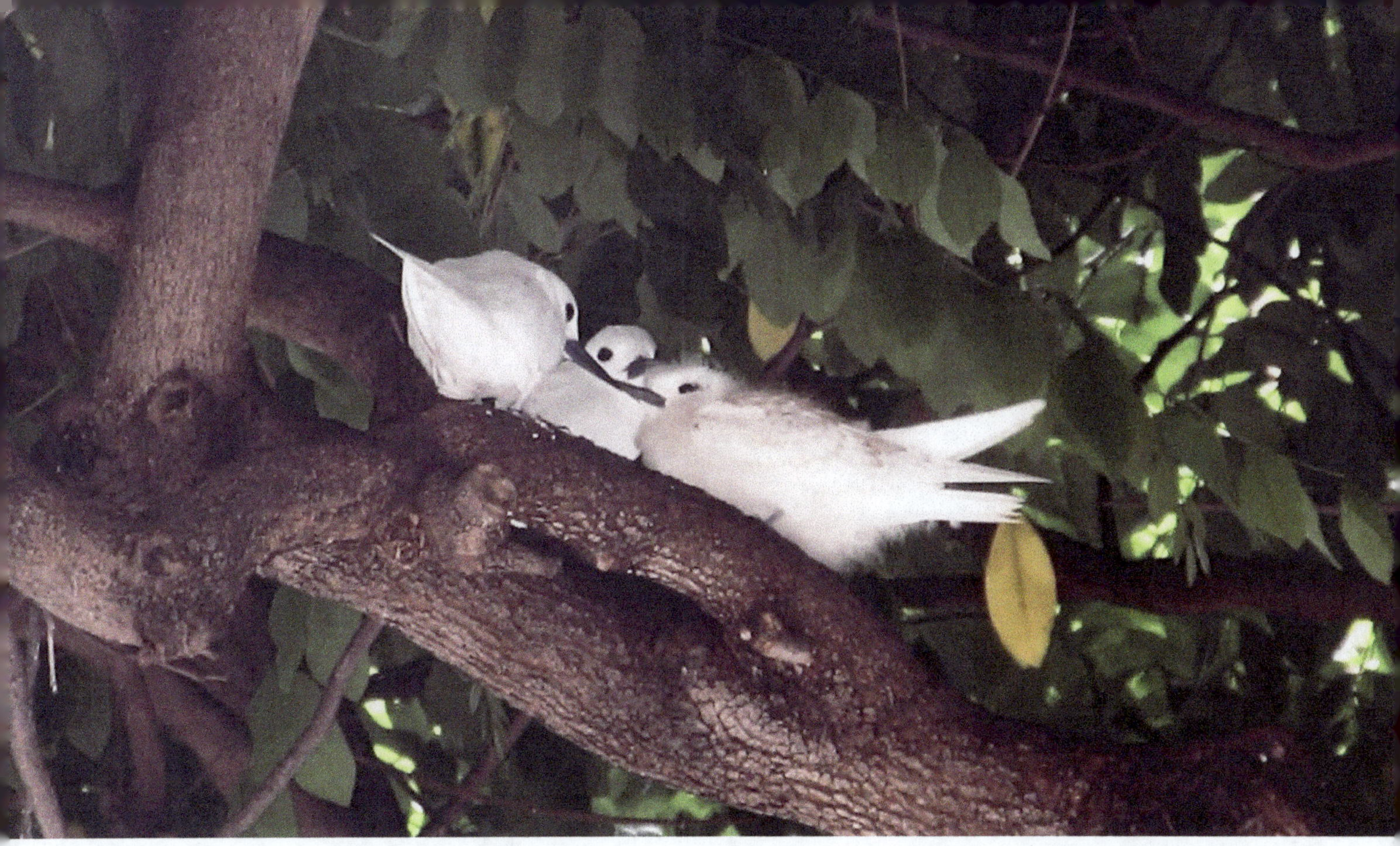

To view YouTube videos of the white terns, please scan the QR codes below with a smart phone's camera to open the links.

Shiro

Skye

Sunny

More Books by the Author

www.ingramcontent.com/pod-product-compliance
Lightning Source LLC
LaVergne TN
LVHW061248100826
845148LV00008B/1065